GW01007655

WHOSE JERUSALEM?

by the same author

THE TOKOLOSH

POLITICAL AFRICA

AFRICAN PROFILES

INTO EXILE

THE CRISIS OF INDIA

THE RACE WAR

AMERICA'S RECEDING FUTURE

THE STRUGGLE AGAINST HISTORY

edited

SANCTIONS AGAINST SOUTH AFRICA

SOUTH-WEST AFRICA: TRAVESTY OF TRUST

(with Ruth First)

RONALD SEGAL

WHOSE JERUSALEM?

The Conflicts of Israel

JONATHAN CAPE
THIRTY BEDFORD SQUARE LONDON

FIRST PUBLISHED 1973

JONATHAN CAPE LTD, 30 BEDFORD SQUARE, LONDON WC1

ISBN 0 224 00880 3

PRINTED IN GREAT BRITAIN
BY EBENEZER BAYLIS AND SON LTD
THE TRINITY PRESS, WORCESTER, AND LONDON
ON PAPER MADE BY JOHN DICKINSON LTD
BOUND BY G. AND J. KITCAT LTD, LONDON

CONTENTS

PREFACE

This is a book about Israel. But I have devoted little space to the history of Zionism or to the argument over whether Israel should ever have been established. The literature on the history of Zionism is vast, and Israel exists. My purpose has been to examine Israeli society as it is and the dynamics of its development.

Yet a book about Israel must be a book, too, about the Arabs. For, of course, the existence of the Arabs, within Israel and without, remains essential to the disposition of Israeli society. I have, therefore, looked at how each side sees itself and the other; and have tried to show that much of what each sees is only its own illusion. And I have hence thought it necessary to examine Arab societies as well: in explaining the context of Israel and in searching out the prerequisites of peace.

I deal in some detail with Egypt, and particularly with the significance of Nasserism: its achievements and failures, and the predicament that is its result. I then treat of the Lebanon and Jordan: countries with social systems that seem so different from each other but that are both in important measure products of the struggle between Arab and Jew. And intermittently and at last, I consider the experience and attitudes, the divisions and dilemma of the Palestinians in their own Diaspora.

Such accompanies a venture into the interior of Israel: where the Jews, so victorious in battle, more and more confront themselves in a crisis of identity. For here is increasingly evident the contradiction between the idealism of the pioneers and the prevalent imperatives of the state. Here, increasingly urgent, is the clash between the covenant with man and the Covenant with God. Here, the world to which the society belongs is increasingly challenged by the world of which the society needs to be a part. Here, alongside the avowal of a vigorous democracy, is the politics of an increasingly authoritarian management. Here, where all Jews were to be brothers together, are separately the rich and the poor, in an increasing turbulence of competitiveness and complaint. But here, too, in consequence, may be found the possibilities for a new vitality of vision that will make of the Return not a mere clinging to the present; still less, a retreat into the priorities of a remote past; but the probing of a future to liberate man from the fear of himself.

I have, happily, met those, on both sides of the conflict, who seek what is reasonable and right in the cause of the other and reject what they see as unreasonable and wrong in the assertion of their own. Theirs is the courage of hope. Yet they seem so often like prisoners in separate cells, talking only to themselves because they do not know how or what to communicate. I trust that, though it may serve for nothing else, this book will provide them with some small help to understanding each other.

I have tried throughout to be just. But I do not pretend to be objective. I have a profound prejudice: an engagement to the value of people rather than the value of states and of shrines. It is this engagement which the continuation of their conflict would so corruptingly deny to both Arab and Jew. And yet there will be no creative resolution of their conflict, for either, outside an inclusive commitment by both. The passions of contending nationalisms have had as their inevitable issue the present violence and despair. They are yesterday's tomorrow.

R.S.

WHOSE JERUSALEM?

I

Of David and Goliath: and similar tales

In an exploration of Israeli society, the continuing conflict with the Arabs provides an obvious point of departure. And this is not only because the conflict so crucially affects the society's development: for anyone not shut inside a commitment to one or other of the nationalisms involved, the rival rhetoric that is employed reveals, as it seeks to hide, much of the real Israel.

Certainly both sides in the conflict are armed with facile insights to interpret it. There are those for whom it is another Vietnam war, with the capitalist West using Israel to confront the revolutionary strivings of the Arab peoples; or for whom Israel is manifestly another white South Africa, sustained by the rich white world to secure and advance the subjugation of the coloured poor.

Needless to say, there are others who see the conflict in similarly simple, if different terms: as yet another attempt, by Hitler's Arab heirs, to destroy the Jewish people; as a vital stage in the Soviet strategy to dominate the world; as the refusal of various Arab despotisms, with an uncertain hold on power, to admit so unsettlingly close an example of a truly democratic state.

To the Israelis and the supporters of their cause, Israel is David in combat with Goliath;* a small country challenged by an enemy gigantic in numbers, but itself formidable in justice and courage and faith. To the Arabs and the supporters of their cause, Israel is the Goliath, gigantic with American arms and money, whom the David of the Arab nation will, informed by justice and courage and faith, eventually defeat.

* Thus, for instance, Shimon Peres, at present (1972) Israel's Minister of Transport and Communications, entitled his book on the arming of Israel *David's Sling* (London: Weidenfeld & Nicolson, 1970).

The insights, as the personifications, are spurious. But there is still substance enough in each to rescue it from flat dismissal.

In 1956, Israel was allied, in a military assault on Egypt, with a France which sought thereby to arrest Egyptian support for the nationalist rebellion in Algeria, and a Britain which hankered to re-establish control over the Suez Canal and the politics of Cairo. At the time, the United States condemned the invasion and forced a retreat.* But since then, with Gaullist France courting Arab support for its pretensions to an independent role in world affairs, and Britain consigned by economic problems to pursuing the new salvation of a European voice, the United States has more and more openly made the running as patron and protector.

Without American money, and the equipment that it purchased, Israel's victory in the war of 1967 would have been far less certain, and certainly far less swift and massive. And how, to be sure, public opinion throughout the capitalist West (including France, where the government denounced Israel as the aggressor) rose to that victory. Still today, despite its pretences at pressure on Israel to withdraw, the United States allows and encourages the Israelis, by continuing and even increasing the flow of assistance, to keep their 1967 conquests.

But it is, after all, only part of an overall pattern. The United States and its allies are involved in the support of every reactionary Arab regime, from the Saudi to the Moroccan; and in ambiguous relations with such regimes as are no more than rhetorically radical. They back Israel, more or less openly, through their governments or private corporations, because Israel is itself a manifestation of advanced industrial capitalism; and Israeli strength keeps the Arabs nation distracted and weak.

Of course, the West and Israel may ask for peace. But it would be a peace with Israel's territory and strategic situation significantly enhanced; and a peace directed at using Israel's economic and technological advancement to turn the Arab world into a vast market for Israeli and Western products.

* Arabs variously cite as the reason for this: American duplicity; a bout of enlightened self-interest; rivalry within the Western imperial ranks for the control of Arab oil; and the threat of confrontation with the Soviet Union.

It is the Palestinian people, dispossessed of their land in Israel and refugees throughout the Arab world, or living without the rights of citizenship in the occupied territories, who can constitute a sort of Vietnamese National Liberation Front, engaged in a guerrilla war of attrition with help from the radical Arab states.

A second insight of the Arab case is the similarity between Israel and white South Africa. After all, the pioneers of white settlement in South Africa were refugees, too; from Catholic power and intolerance in Europe. And the subsequent history of the Afrikaners was long informed by the resistance to British imperial ambitions. The cause of the Jewish state has enjoyed support from the same sort of liberal opinion in the West that rose to the defence of the Boer republics at the turn of the century.

The unique identity of the Afrikaner nation is now undeniable. And the cry of the Afrikaners – that they have nowhere else to go; that no reasonable refuge offers itself; that they are engaged in their conflict with Africans for no less than their very survival as a people, after centuries of separate existence – is not without its resemblance to the profile of Israeli nationalism. (Which is one reason why, for all the recent past of organized and even institutionalized anti-Semitism among them, the Afrikaners regard Israelis today with a kind of kinship.)

And just how different has been the treatment of Arabs under their control by the Israelis from the treatment of Africans by white South Africa? Under the wrappings, many of the goods are the same. Land has been expropriated under various pretexts from Arabs who did not flee, and at times of relative peace; with compensation long delayed and, when finally paid, far below real value.* And this plundering has been extended even to Druze land; though the Druzes have never been considered a significant security risk and are, indeed, permitted to serve in the Israeli armed forces.

Whatever the security excuse, the Israeli Defence Laws have operated to treat Arab citizens quite differently from Jewish ones, with restrictions on movement, curfews, detention or banishment, and the confiscation or destruction of property. And though

* The author met several Israelis, not otherwise noticeably radical, who were severely critical of the relevant law for the Acquisition of Land (Operations and Compensation), 1953.

military rule within Israel proper has receded since the Six Day War, the occupied territories are administered on the basis of economic but not political integration. Some forty to fifty thousand workers from these territories have already been sucked into the Israeli economy, in an effective relationship not so remote from that between white South Africa and the Bantustans.* Indeed, many Israelis see in what would be a virtual Bantustan a solution to the problem of the West Bank: whose overt political autonomy would be in pawn to an inescapable economic subservience.

Certainly, as the Israeli authorities have been quick to declare, such workers earn more in Israel than they would in the territories themselves, let alone almost anywhere else in the Arab world. But this argument is, after all, rather like the conventional apology of apartheid: that Africans in general earn much more in South Africa than they do elsewhere on the continent, and that the borders must be controlled to prevent illegal immigrants from coming to enjoy the notorious discriminations of racial policy. Yet even given the accuracy of the South African government contention, what matters, of course, is not the difference between black earnings in South Africa and black earnings elsewhere, but the difference between the earnings of blacks and the earnings of whites within the same country. Similarly, what matters in an assessment of Israeli society is that in general Arab labour from the occupied territories earns substantially less than does Jewish labour: not because, as in South Africa, the state explicitly requires it, but because there is, in institutionalized Jewish labour organization, a form of pressure on employers not possessed by migrant Arab labour.

And the parallel with white South Africa is taken further. Israel is essentially a Jewish state, and Jewishness has been made an essentially biological phenomenon. By the Law of Return, 1950, Israeli citizenship is all but automatically conferred on any Jew who arrives and asks for it. And a decision was recently taken to confer Israeli citizenship on Jews still living abroad who choose to claim it. On the other hand, to become a Jew, it is not enough to

* In January 1972, migrant workers from the occupied territories constituted 8% of the skilled labour being newly supplied to industry, and no less than *three-quarters* of that being supplied to the building sector. Their share in Israel's total labour increment jumped from 22% in 1969 to almost 30% in 1970 and 1971. (Report in the *Jerusalem Post*, 4 April 1972.)

fulfil certain residential and other civil requirements customary in other countries. It is not enough even to be born in the Jewish state. A Jew is someone born of a Jewish mother.

Religious conversion provides the significant exception. But such conversion is not made easy, and implies a religious commitment. In effect, therefore, Jews are what they are because they were born such, regardless of their religious beliefs; and Gentiles, whether affiliated to some other faith or to no faith at all, may be or become Israeli citizens, but never Jews. In a state so essentially Jewish, such Gentiles are nationals outside the dominant nation: citizens, whatever the guarantees of their equal civil rights, inevitably of the second class.

By far the bulk of the Gentile population affected by the existence of this Jewish state is Arab; and popular Jewish attitudes to the Arabs are accordingly crucial. In April 1971, the findings were published of a *Time*–Louis Harris poll, conducted in association with Public Opinion Research of Israel Ltd.* A 'carefully selected sample' of Israeli Jews – 1,177 in number – were questioned on their views of different issues.

Some 25% of them, a high enough proportion in all conscience, admitted that prejudice existed against the Arabs. But actual attitudes presented a still darker picture. Some 23% said that they would be bothered if an Arab sat beside them in a restaurant; 26%, if they had to work closely with one; 49%, if an Arab family moved next door; 54%, if their children had an Arab teacher; 74%, if their children became close friends with Arabs; and 84%, if a friend or relative were to marry an Arab. Asked whether they agreed with specific statements, the results were:

STATEMENT	YES	NO
Arabs are lazier than Israelis	53%	36%
Arabs are less intelligent than Israelis	74%	19%
Most Arabs have a blind hatred towards Israel	68%	26%
Arabs are more cruel than Israelis	75%	17%
Arabs are not so brave as Israelis	80%	12%
Arabs are more dishonest than Israelis	66%	20%
Arabs are inferior to Israelis (my italics)	67%	23%

* *Time*, 12 April 1971, pp. 27–8.

Significantly, the 'most biased Israelis are recently arrived Sephardic Jews from Africa and Asia, many of whom lived in Arab countries. The least biased are native-born Sabras, followed by the Europe-bred Ashkenazi Jews.' But then such Sephardic Jews are in general poorer than the Sabras or Ashkenazi Jews, and closer to Arab culture. Their higher measure of prejudice betrays in part an anxiety to establish their Jewish credentials by a rejection of everything Arab; and in part a desire to compensate themselves for a sense of communal inferiority within the Jewish nation, by a sense of Jewish national superiority.* Surveys of colour prejudice among South African whites show a similar pattern.

And if these are popular attitudes, the outlook of the leadership is not such as seriously to discourage them. This has long reflected an identification with Western culture as self-evidently superior to any other, and a corresponding disparagement of the culture in the immediate environment. Jewish immigrants of Oriental background were considered material not for a dynamic process of integration, from which a new and more creative culture might emerge, but for absorption by the culture already in command.

David Ben Gurion, who did so much before the establishment of Israel and subsequently as prime minister to influence leadership attitudes, repeatedly made clear his anxiety that the Oriental immigrants would debase Israel into a 'Levantine' state. 'We do not want Israelis to become Arabs. We are in duty bound to fight against the spirit of the Levant, which corrupts individuals and societies, and preserve the authentic Jewish values as they crystallized in the Diaspora.'†

The real Diaspora included, of course, the Levant. But, in this context, Ben Gurion clearly limited the crystallization process to the European sector; and 'authentic Jewish values' to the compass of Western – mainly Eastern European – Jewry.

* A broad distinction may be drawn between those who come from countries of the culture associated with the West, and those who come from the various cultures, collectively more or less disparaged, of Africa, Asia and the Arab neighbourhood. (Jews from South Africa are, of course, 'Western'; as are those from the communities in Latin America.) And the distinction has been made the simpler because the Western Jews belong in general to the Ashkenazi Judaic sub-culture; and the 'Oriental' Jews to the Sephardic one.

† Quoted in *Le Monde,* 9 March 1966.

One of Israel's leading writers, Haim Hazaz, has been more explicit.

> And who *are* we? One people? Decidedly not! We are communities, communities ... We must try and bring European culture to the Oriental communities. We cannot afford to become an Oriental people. I feel great resentment at such a development. We had to travel a road of 2,000 years to become a European Jewish cultural division, and now it is impossible to turn the wheel backwards and accept the culture of Yemen, of Morocco, or of Iraq.*

Now it is not at all self-evident that 'European culture' is the vanguard of human achievement. And the assumption by the Israeli leadership that it is, suggests to the Arabs a particular form of imperialism which is no less to be resented or feared for being projected as benevolent.

It may even be that there are some values in Arab culture which it would benefit Israel, and Western societies in general, to adopt. It may be that Israel should shed certain European cultural values, such as competitive consumption and the cult of the gross national product, that take the destructive impact on the natural and human environment so little into account. It may well be that much in contemporary Arab culture which Israelis find so distasteful or distressing, from the techniques of political terror to the expression of racial or religious intolerance, owes something to Western cultural example.

But then, like the white South Africans who regard Western civilization as self-evidently superior to all indigenous African culture, the Israelis, with very few exceptions, know next to nothing of the culture they so easily disparage. The Arabs within Israel or under Israel's control are considered as fit to learn only, rather than also to teach, when they are not considered merely as a problem. And those Israelis, many of them in positions of influence now, who visited as soldiers parts of the Arab world during the

* Part of an interview with the Israeli evening newspaper, *Ma'ariv*, Rosh Hashanah special issue, 1967; quoted in Nissim Rejwan, 'The Two Israels: A Study of Europeocentrism', *Judaism*, A Quarterly Journal of Jewish Life and Thought, Vol. 16, No. 1., Winter Issue, 1967. Nissim Rejwan is himself a Jewish immigrant from Iraq.

Second World War, talk and write as though nothing had substantially changed in Arab society since then. However different the reasons, the Jews in Israel, along with most of those abroad who support their cause, are as effectively sealed off from Arab culture today as are white South Africans in general from the African.

If there is some substance to such insights of the Arab side, there is some substance, too, in the insights of the Israeli.

Certainly, those who see Arab enmity as still one more stage in the long persecution of the Jewish people offer abundant evidence that Arab attitudes to Israel are informed by an unmistakably 'racial' hatred. They point to statements made by Palestinian representatives like Ahmed Shukairy about driving the Jews into the sea; the sporadic popular dissemination of notorious anti-Jewish propaganda, like 'The Protocols of Zion'; the anti-Jewish rhetoric and conduct of existing Arab regimes. Colonel Qaddafi, the master of Libya, whose policies effervesce with a religious fanaticism, makes no apparent distinction between Jews and Israelis as 'the children of death'. The government of Saudi Arabia forbids the entry not only of Israelis, but of all Jews, whatever their citizenship or opinions. The government of Iraq hangs in public some of its own Jewish citizens, on charges of spying that few informed Arabs there or anywhere else take at all seriously. Israeli soldiers, capturing the Golan Heights in the Six Day War, came upon school textbooks with caricatures of Jews scarcely distinguishable from those in the popular press of the Third Reich.

But the genocidal threat looms, for many Jews, in the total hostility to Israel itself. For the state year by year encompasses a higher proportion of world Jewry (5·7% in 1948; 14·6% in 1957; 17·7% in 1968). Talk of destroying or 'liquidating' Israel, therefore, all too easily excites comparison with 'the Holocaust' and its 'liquidation' of six million Jews, more than a third of world Jewry, in 1940–45. For how is Israel to be liquidated without the liquidation of its citizen defenders? When Abba Eban, Foreign Minister of Israel, cites in his speeches the fevered statements of Arab governments and newspapers about wiping Israel off the map or tightening the noose around Israel's neck, he has an audience that needs little nudging to see the intended casualty as not a particular state, but as yet more millions of Jews.

And the inference is confirmed by a vocabulary of retribution. 'We are facing you in the battle and burning with desire for it to start, in order to obtain revenge,' cried Nasser on the eve of the Six Day War.* Or, as Walter Laqueur has written:

> The Syrian government was (and is) almost Maoist in its inspiration: it constantly emphasizes the class struggle, the proletarian nations, the vanguard of the working class. But when it really got excited, its broadcasts assumed a different tone: 'By God, if it is decreed that we have to wade through seven seas of blood and that the whole nation has to sink in blood to get revenge for its honour and dignity, then we will wade through the seas of blood and we will risk everything ...' No more atheism, class struggle or dialectical materialism; instead, God, blood, nation, revenge, honour, dignity.†

Israel and the Jew become confused in the passionate assertions of the Arab cause. 'The student of Arab opinion and Arab thought', writes Professor J. L. Talmon of the Hebrew University, 'is often horrified to watch the growth of the anti-Israel obsession to the point of it having become the cornerstone of a kind of systematic Manichean metaphysic, with the Jew as devil incarnate.'‡

Paradoxically, however, many of those very Jews, in Israel and abroad, who hear in Arab hostility the old sounds of the pogrom and death camps, claim that peace in the Middle East would be far more probable if the peoples of the area were left alone to confront their differences. What they mean, of course, is not that Israel should turn its back upon the West, let alone upon the Jewish communities there, from whom so much in immigration and economic help is still hoped; but that it is Soviet intervention in the area which constitutes the main obstacle to a settlement. Israel, even without American backing, would be able now to ensure its survival, and so make the Arab states accommodate themselves to reality, were it not for the power of the Soviet Union, which

* In a statement on Cairo Radio, 4 June 1967; quoted by Eban in a speech at the United Nations, 19 June 1967.

† From Walter Laqueur, 'Is Peace in the Middle East Possible?' *New York Times Sunday Magazine*, 27 August 1967.

‡ From an article in the *Observer*, 10 September 1967.

supplies them with the means and the confidence to try yet again for victory on the battlefield.

And why should the Soviet Union be so concerned over the fate of the Arabs? Ideological affiliations could scarcely be a factor. The Soviet leadership has never allowed the persecution of Egyptian communists to interfere with its support for the Egyptian regime; just as it has backed an Arab cause whose various professing representatives encompass monarchies and military dictatorships of passionate hostility to Marxist ideas.

As with other countries, so with the Soviet Union, the interests of the state are paramount in the development of foreign policy. It is the expansion of Soviet power, through economic relationships, diplomatic agreements, military bases and facilities, and not moral concern for the Arabs, that conditions Soviet conduct in the Middle East.

Having made itself virtually indispensable to the present economy and military posture of Syria, Iraq and, above all, Egypt, by far the most important Arab state, the Soviet Union has penetrated deep into one of the major preserves of Western power. Its naval and air forces have crucial facilities close to a vital source of energy for the Western economies; and any reopening of the Suez Canal would now make it at least as much a Soviet as a Western waterway. What in the end, for the Soviet Union, therefore, is the struggle between Israel and the Arabs, but an opportunity to diminish American influence and promote Soviet ascendancy?

Indeed, if the Soviet leadership reveals a moral concern with the fate of any people in the area, it is, negatively, with the fate of the Jews. For despite the initial Soviet support that made the sanctioning of a Jewish state by the United Nations possible, Israel is now regarded as a dangerous entity. It is not merely that Israel is so closely tied to the United States: the very existence of an Israel glamorous with military victory and the American way of life has significantly promoted the internal problems of the Soviet state. The rising demand of Soviet Jews for the right to emigrate to Israel casts serious doubt on both the allurement of life under Soviet socialism and the avowed equality of treatment meted out to all Soviet citizens; while Jewish dissent inevitably fuels general civil dissent, with the pressure of example.

Nor, unhappily, is evidence lacking for the existence of an anti-Semitic strain in Soviet politics. Just as the repudiation of Stalinism by the 20th Party Congress scarcely involved a total retreat from Stalinist techniques, so the virus of Stalinist attitudes to Jews has survived, if somewhat less potently, to infect the view that many in the Soviet leadership take of the Jewish state and its Arab enemies. In considering the Six Day War and its consequences, Professor Bernard Lewis has written:

> The point is sometimes made that Jewish or pro-Jewish sentiments can lead to unbalanced and unrealistic policies. This is of course true. It is equally true, though less obvious, that anti-Jewish sentiments can have the same effect. The hysterical violence and traditional anti-Semitic symbolism of Soviet attacks on Israel show that the offence of the Israelis in Soviet eyes, were [*sic*] greatly aggravated by the fact that they were Jews. These Soviet reactions also suggest that one of the motives of a pro-Arab policy may have been a desire to hurt the Jews, and that this emotional impulsion may have warped the judgement of policy-makers and led them to a degree of indulgence to Arab wishes which was ultimately harmful to Soviet and even Arab interests.*

There is evidence, too, for the contention that Israel's political system scarcely suffers in any comparison with its Arab counterparts. It is true that the Lebanon has democratic institutions. But these are largely a façade, with the political balance between Muslim and Christian kept by privy deals among the leading families, and the army a constant threat of intervention. Furthermore, the façade does not conceal explosive contrasts between rich and poor. Indeed, within a few miles of the banks and the boutiques, the luxury hotels and apartments of Beirut, live peasants in a feudal relationship to their landlords; while the anger of the urban unemployed or poorly paid fills the streets with sporadic tumult.

And if the Lebanon presents a somewhat sorry spectacle, what of the other Arab states? Saudi Arabia is a medieval relic; Jordan's

* From an article in *Foreign Affairs*, January 1968; quoted in *The Israel–Arab Reader* ed. Walter Laqueur (Harmondsworth: Penguin Books, 1970), p. 409.

monarchy is sustained by a tribal militarism; and the throne in Morocco rests on an alliance between the strong-arm methods of the army and secret police, and the profiteering of a corrupt business community. The Libyan engagement may be too transported for pertinent comment. But what of the other professing progressives: Algeria, Syria, Iraq, the Sudan and, above all, Egypt?

In Algeria, the revolutionary promise of the long and costly war against the French has fallen to the military coup and the prerogatives of 'guidance': it is the soldiers and the civil servants of the state machine who have inherited the earth of the wretched. Syria merely stumbles from one army coup to another, while the living standards of its citizens stagnate or decay, and the rhetoric of the ruling Ba'ath (Resurgence) movement conforms less and less to reality. Iraq, with its public executions not only of Jewish citizens but of leading figures in the ruling Ba'ath movement, is a source of embarrassment and dismay to the Arab dream of a socialist commonwealth. The Sudan is a military dictatorship in power by coup and counter-coup: with the leaders of its trades union movement, the most developed in the Arab world, hounded, imprisoned and killed by the authorities.

And what of Egypt, the Arab centrepiece, with all its talk of socialism? The Nasser revolution expropriated the old rich, many of them foreigners, and put members or supporters of the regime in their place. Former Free Officers, or their brothers and uncles, now control substantial enterprises, private and public, with standards of consumption to match their new dignity; while, for the mass of the Egyptian peasantry, history has hardly moved. Nasser filled his jails, seldom after much of a judicial process, with dissenters who thought and spoke of socialism too seriously.

Certainly he exposed in his death, as in his life, the sham of Egyptian democracy. For who decided that Sadat should succeed as president? The selection was made by a tiny group of ministers, and perhaps by the need to keep a balance of power among the most influential. And then, what could be less surprising than that Sadat, with his hold on the totalitarian state established, should proceed to eliminate his rivals, in a trial for conspiracy?

The Arab regimes are variously authoritarian; and their popular basements are those of acquiescence, not choice. In this context, a study by a former chief of Israel's Strategic Research Department,

Y. Harkabi, on the reasons for the Arab defeat in the Six Day War, while predictably selective, contains an important truth.*

For Harkabi, the crucial factor must be sought in the weakness of the social links which join Arab to Arab. Because of this defect in the social fabric, each Arab soldier, in the critical moments of combat, finds himself fighting not as part of a cohesive force, but as an isolated individual. In consequence, each tends primarily to look after himself, and the unit disintegrates.

Israeli interrogators found that Egyptian commanders did not even know the names of the men in their companies; while Egyptian officers in general displayed in captivity an estrangement from each other and even sometimes a marked mutual hatred. Harkabi distinguishes between 'state building', where social integration flows from the individual towards the centre, the regime, the state; and 'nation building', where such integration flows from one individual to another. In the second, there exists a sense of belonging, freely developed; and under the influence of this, the individual readily subordinates his private interests to the collective good. In the first, such a sense is imposed and does not reach beyond a ritual display of unity.

> Among the Egyptian people there is a consensus of admiration for Nasser, but this does not create real cohesiveness ... This enthusiasm may well be a kind of escape through public ecstasy from the sadness and loneliness of the individual in a society lacking in cohesion and rife with internal hostility ... 'Arab socialism' does not engender consciousness of the need to work for the common good. The absence of political consciousness and the difficulties in establishing 'the Arab Socialist Union' result, in good measure, from the feeling that everyone has to fight his own battles in life, from the atomism of society and the weakness of its bonds.

The contrast that Harkabi draws between the conduct of Egyptians and Israelis on the battlefield is confirmed by most outside observers. Israeli officers do not abandon their men under fire. Indeed, they are celebrated for leading from the front; and the

* 'Basic Factors in the Arab Collapse during the Six Day War', in *Orbis*, a quarterly journal of world affairs published by the University of Pennsylvania Foreign Policy Research Institute, Vol. XI, No. 3, Fall 1967.

casualties among them in the Six Day War were relatively much higher than among the ranks. 'The awareness that the very existence of the nation and the individual and his family hinged on the outcome of the conflict – this consciousness of a common destiny – has had a unifying effect and has been at the root of that common readiness of Israeli military units to press forward despite danger.'

Such is sufficient to confront the parallel with the Vietnamese conflict, drawn by so many advocates of the Arab cause. The American forces in Vietnam, despite a technological superiority over their opponents far greater still than that of the Israeli over the Arab, have failed in part because the war itself has been for them a source of social disintegration rather than cohesion. The incidence of distrust and even conflict between officers and men, of disobedience and desertion, has been in obvious contrast to the solidarity of their antagonists. And the fighting quality of the Saigon forces has been scarcely better, and often, with the undercover supporters of the National Front among them, a great deal worse.

The truth is that the Vietnamese challenge has been one by a coherent and concentrated mass nationalism. And in the Middle East, such nationalism has been far more an Israeli than an Arab attribute.

The crux of the Vietnamese parallel, of course, stands or falls with the Palestinians themselves. And here, as some of the younger Palestinians are quick to acknowledge, the Vietnamese model is inextricably a nationalist and a revolutionary one. The Vietnamese struggle against foreign dominion and divisiveness has been crucially a struggle, too, against a form of social organization which that foreign dominion and divisiveness have sought to promote.

It is, indeed, precisely because the Palestinians are as yet more fragmented than united by ideas of social transformation that the Vietnamese model is relevant, but for purposes of contrast rather than comparison.*

Even the movement of armed resistance is itself fragmented, into competitive organizations of a revolutionary Marxist com-

* The issue of Arab and Palestinian nationalism is treated in greater detail in Chapters 2 and 3.

mitment; competitive organizations of a more or less conservative character, in the politics of the Arab world; and the largest single organization, Al Fatah, which contains revolutionary, conservative and compromise elements at loggerheads with one another. And beyond is the vast bulk of the Palestinian population, dispersed across several territories; and far from united even in sympathy with the cause of armed resistance, let alone behind a particular resistance organization.

Among the many hundreds of thousands on the occupied West Bank, a traditional land-owning class, with its prosperity much promoted by the acquisition of Israeli agricultural techniques and the new Israeli market for its products, watches and waits: hostile to armed resistance; prevented by its nationalism from working towards incorporation into the state of Israel; but scarcely allured by the prospect of incorporation again into the state of Jordan, which used to exploit West Bank resources for the economic development of the East Bank, and whose regime has, since, built its power on a narrow Bedouin base. Yet what would an autonomous West Bank allow, but an effective subservience to Israel?

Watching and waiting alongside, in leadership, is the merchant class, whose fortunes have in general been much advanced by the Israeli occupation, and whose members are all too aware of the depressed conditions on the East Bank produced by civil clashes, the drying up of tourism, and the deteriorating relations between Jordan and its Arab neighbours. And the hesitancy of these classes is sustained by a peasantry of small-scale proprietors, also more prosperous than before; and a landless work force whose employment and income have significantly risen with Israeli rule.

To be sure, ideas of militant resistance have some home: especially among lawyers, doctors and others of the professional class, for whom Israeli rule is an outrage without economic compensation and even sometimes with related economic loss; among the intellectuals and students, whose idealism remains ascendant. But without a sufficient local constituency of support and with the possibilities of far more profitable employment elsewhere, they tend to emigrate and enter the exile pattern of Palestinian politics.

Only in the Gaza Strip, where the Popular Front for the Liberation of Palestine (P.F.L.P.) has commanded some significant support, has there been a serious display of resistance to Israeli rule.

But this has been a terrorism narrowly contained, so that it may have embarrassed but scarcely endangered the occupation.

On the East Bank, where so much of the Palestinian population lives, the insistent issue is not Israel but the Hashemite regime itself. 'I wish', said an Egyptian intellectual of the Left who had spent several terms of detention in Nasser's jails, and who is close to the leadership of the more radical Palestinian resistance organizations, 'that we wouldn't talk so much about turning Jordan into another Hanoi. It is already another Saigon.' Yet on how to confront the Hashemite regime, or even on whether to confront the regime at all, there is little agreement.

For the hundreds of thousands in the refugee camps of Jordan there is a ready audience for any rhetoric that flourishes some prospect of escape from their degradation. But the camps are effectively contained, by their very emplacement, from posing any military threat; and those in them who are not prepared merely to invite being butchered, find their way usually into the resistance organizations and into exile. And then, which resistance organization is the refugee to join? The radical ones, which speak at least in terms of a consistent revolutionary alternative, however distant and costly the approach, encounter a population still largely traditionalist in outlook. 'They begin, our radicals,' said a Syrian Marxist in Lebanese exile, 'by announcing to the refugees that there is no God. But the refugees believe in God. They have been brought up to believe in him. And what other comfort have they had?'

For the rest, the Palestinian diaspora stretches from highly paid employment and successful enterprise in the Gulf States and even America, to the squalid and closely contained refugee camps of Syria and the Lebanon. Some of the most vivid intelligences and noble commitments among the youth anywhere today are to be found among Palestinians at universities across the world. They are ready to sacrifice promising careers, and indeed their very lives, to liberate from Israeli rule what they regard as irrevocably their land. Yet how are they to work for this end?

The Vietnamese parallel is strategically untenable. The terrain of the Middle East is not the terrain of South-East Asia, and guerrilla warfare in the first has not the cover from air strikes by the enemy that guerrilla warfare in the second enjoys. The battle for

Saigon persists because Hanoi exists. But where is the Hanoi of the Middle East? And Hanoi has in part been secured from all that American power might otherwise have succeeded in doing because Peking exists. But where is the Peking of the Middle East? Above all, perhaps, the Vietnamese revolutionaries have been tempered to an effective military force by years of unification behind a set of specific leaders and ideas. There is no such unification – indeed, no sign of such unification emerging – among the Palestinians.

The Vietnamese parallel is spurious; and being spurious, it depreciates the real predicament of the Palestinian. For whatever the suffering that the engagement to revolutionary nationalism in Vietnam has entailed, it has achieved sufficient success to encourage confidence in the outcome. Behind the Palestinians stretches only the repeated defeat of their hopes; and before them, no course to credibly close success. For the foreseeable future, their agony is open-ended; and to claim it to be otherwise is nonsense no less cruel and corrupting than is the Israeli abuse of Palestinian guerrillas as 'gangsters'.

The parallel seeks to fit both the Middle Eastern and the Vietnamese conflicts into a design of universal application and irresistible force. But the facts have proved refractory. And the consequence, as the Palestinian radicals are discovering, is disillusionment, indifference and despair. Sympathy for their cause among radicals in the West is not what it was. The Palestinians look increasingly less like the Vietnamese, as their momentum of resistance declines; and the Israelis look less like the Americans as their occupation thrives. The process may be a productive one if it begins to disengage the Palestinians themselves from the theatre of horror in which they are both actors and audience, while the script is supplied by someone else.

The parallel between Israel and white South Africa is no less untenable. Historically, the vast majority of Jewish pioneers did not consider the indigenous population fair game for conquest, butchery or enslavement; as did the Afrikaners. Indeed, after the failures of the first wave of immigration (1882–1903), with its largely colonialist disposition, the dominant principle of settlement was the refusal to exploit Arab labour, even on a wage basis; in the belief that a Jewish homeland had to be based on self-reliant and co-operative enterprise. The difference between an Afrikaner penetration, infused with a Calvinist ethic of rugged individualism, and a Jewish one infused with a socialist commitment, is manifestly crucial.

British rule in South Africa played with a limited suffrage for Africans, not least as some counterweight to Afrikaner power. But for the overwhelming mass of Afrikaners and a substantial sector of the English-speaking settlers, white supremacy was no less than a fact of nature. The steps by which all non-whites were subjugated for their land and their labour, and excluded from any share in power, seem in retrospect to have been only too predictable; despite the widespread willingness among the Africans and especially the Coloured to accept white leadership in a gradual movement towards the grant of equal citizenship.

The Palestinian experience was notably distinct. There was a disposition among the mass of Jewish settlers to live as an equal if separate community alongside the Arabs, and even a significant opinion in favour of a bi-national state. That the leadership of the Arab community in the main resisted any such prospect and, above all, the immediate pressure for Jewish immigration, was not surprising. But clearly it was this resistance which itself importantly promoted the establishment of the Jewish state; as, subsequently, the rejection of that state by its neighbours led to its territorial expansion.

If Israel is not then either David or Goliath, what of its Arab enemy? The charge that the Arab world is infused by a racial fury against the Jewish people and seeks some belated version of Hitler's final solution, is absurd to anyone who has travelled and searched in the area. This does not mean that the evidence so diligently assembled by Israeli specialists like Harkabi is to be dismissed. But such specialists too often see and report no more than the circle of their magnifying glass allows them.

To start with, it must be recognized that nothing remotely comparable to the Jewish experience in the Christian West across the centuries is to be found in the history of the Arab world until the recent past of Western ascendancy there. Jews in North Africa and the Near East openly welcomed the Arab armies of eruptive Islam, as a release from the oppression of their Christian rulers.

They became, along with Christians and Zoroastrians, 'protected persons' or *dhimmis*; and though they possessed in theory fewer rights, and fewer obligations, than did Muslims, this in practice proved little of a bar to social advancement. They could travel and reside where they chose; were not forbidden to own and cultivate land; and were to be found in virtually all economic occupations. Indeed, they participated widely in the development of finance, trade and industry 'in sharp contrast to ... medieval Europe where they were progressively and systematically excluded from one sector of the economy after the other, so that by late medieval times only the most degrading and menial occupations were open to them'.*

Their participation in government, as advisers to caliphs or within the civil service, was no less notable. And though on occasions their prominence caused jealousy and resentment, and accordingly measures to reduce their numbers in office, this virtually never affected the wider Jewish community. In so far 'as Jews suffered from such measures, they did so together with other *dhimmi* officials. There is no record of a single attempt in the whole of Islamic history to exclude Jews as such from public office.'† Thus, on the solitary occasion when Jews were persecuted, during the caliphate of al-Hakim in Egypt, this was a persecution aimed at the whole large *dhimmi* community, and not specifically at the Jews.

Only under Western rule, with the Crusader invasion of Palestine and subsequently the North African conquests by Christian Spain in the sixteenth century, did the Jews of the area find themselves singled out as the victims of deliberate oppression and even massacre. And it was again, in modern times, with the arrival of Western dominance, that classical anti-Semitism of the Western type emerged. In part this was a manifestation of moral mimicry among an Arab elite that asserted its claims by adopting as its own the attitudes and manners of its imperial masters. In part it was a product of colonial policies, by which the Jewish community was allured to the imperial cause through being accorded a sort of

* Merlin Swartz, 'The Position of Jews in Arab Lands following the Rise of Islam', in *Reflections on the Middle East Crisis* ed. Herbert Mason (Paris and The Hague: Mouton & Co., 1970), p. 25.

† Ibid., p. 26.

intermediate, entrepreneurial place between the metropolitan rulers and the indigenous mass. And in part, of course, it was a reaction to the Zionist movement itself.

There were outrageous incidents.* And there were outrageous leaders like Haj Amin El Husseini, the Mufti of Jerusalem, who crowned his career by retreating to Berlin during the Second World War. Yet in the very assessing of the Mufti's poisonous influence, one authority on the period of the Mandate has made clear how foreign to the Arab tradition this particular influence was.

> Though a man of great slyness and skill in argument he did not make the common mistake of sophisticated leaders by giving his followers a complex programme. He gave them one of the utmost simplicity: Down with the infidel! In Palestine, as in most Moslem countries, there was no great anti-Jewish feeling, and an Arab could be anti-Zionist without indulging further enmity to Jews. Under the Mufti's influence this was all changed. The enemy was the Jewish people. To be a Jew was in itself an offence. Arab nationalism adopted anti-Semitism on the coarsest European model.†

Yet the model was so soon so horribly to be discredited in the West itself, as to discredit in the Arab world also, those there who had been its disciples. And, indeed, as the discrediting of the ideas discredited the leaders who had propagated them, so the discrediting of the leaders in turn discredited the ideas. For anti-Semitism was not an essential manifestation of Arab nationalism, but a feature of Arab nationalism in a particular form under a particular leadership. It was a form and a leadership concerned not with changing the internal structure of Arab society, but with displacing its foreign by an indigenous dominance, of landlords, entrepreneurs, religious and secular notables. It failed signally to displace such foreign dominance, and above all to arrest the Zionist endeavour. The war of 1947–8, which ended with an Israel so far reinforced, hastened the advance of a nationalism which emphasized social revolution, and of a new leadership to conduct it.

* The author was in Morocco during the nationalist movement against French rule in the early 'fifties, when several Jews were butchered in the supposed cause of liberation.

† Christopher Sykes, *Cross Roads to Israel* (London: Collins, 1965), p. 155.

Whatever the character of that new leadership, its successes and its failures, anti-Semitism has scarcely been a significant feature of it. In Egypt itself, Nasserism crushed such social forces as the Wafd party and the Muslim Brotherhood, which had promoted anti-Semitism to distract attention from their own political bankruptcy, or to concentrate it on the cause of Islamic revivalism. Moreover, the shift from the old leadership was informed by a growth in the influence of revolutionary thought. Individual left-wing movements and leaders might be chastised, outlawed, overwhelmed. But much of their vocabulary and some of their ideas became the moral equipment of the new regime. And among this equipment classic anti-Semitism had no place.

The same process, if somewhat more protractedly, has occurred within the Palestinian Arab struggle. There, it was rather the Six Day War of 1967 that decisively discredited the leadership of those like Ahmed Shukairy, for whom racist rhetoric had been a refuge from national impotence and the hazards of attempting to develop a social policy. Indeed, the old leadership is now blamed for having, by this very rhetoric, contributed to the Palestinian defeats, since any evidence of anti-Semitism among the Palestinian Arabs was so effectively exploited by Israeli propaganda in the world outside. And, of course, revolutionary thought, with its repudiation of racist ideas, has found no more remarkable an acceptance anywhere in the last few years than among the young of the Palestinian resistance movement.

Certainly, for the vast majority of Arab intellectuals, the cult of anti-Semitism now seems what it really was, an aberration of Arab history. They are, with reason, outraged by charges that anything like Hitler's 'final solution' would be contemplated in the Arab context. And the more that they know of Jewry's long tribulation in the West, the more outraged they are. They argue, and there are Israelis who would argue likewise, that the Nazi death-camps were the culmination of a Western Christian process which included the massacres of Jews during the Crusades, the expulsion of Jews from Spain, the pogroms of the Russian empire, the Dreyfus case in France. To project the culmination, without the whole prerequisite process, on to the Arab world, is for them the product of sheer ignorance and a malignant propaganda.

And they argue, too, again with reason, that the only credible scenario that could be written for a Jewish holocaust would involve an Arab holocaust as well. For even in the unlikely event that the nuclear powers of the West, and in particular the United States, would stand aside, they suppose that Israel already disposes of weapons that could exact a terrible price. And short of such apocalyptic possibilities, what have the Jews of Israel genuinely to fear from yet another war? A few thousand casualties would scarcely be the 'final solution', and the chances would favour yet another costly Arab defeat.

And there, they admit, lies the paradox. For the weaker the Arab posture, the stronger does its rhetoric tend, in compensation, to become. This may be regrettable, and they regret it, but it constitutes something very different from a dedication to genocide. The phrases used against Israel, of liquidation and the gallows, are phrases of a kind commonly employed by a nation's leaders against an enemy in war. It is only because of a Jewish past irrelevant in this context that such phrases take on, for the Jews themselves and for a guilt-ridden Western public, a peculiarly sinister meaning.

To be sure, there is a lunatic fringe in the Arab world, as elsewhere. And its exponents are usually to be found far from the field of battle, under regimes which are justifiably uncertain of their command. To judge the Arab world from Saudi Arabia is to judge the Arab world not by the present but by the least reputable passage of its past. And to judge even Libya alone by Colonel Qaddafi would be a mistake. True, there have been deplorable things done in Syria and Iraq. But they have been done by one warring faction of the Ba'ath to another, even more than to Jews. Indeed, those hanged in public as Israeli spies have not always been Jewish, let alone spies. And whose cause has all this helped?

I remember one Arab intellectual, now in exile in Beirut, who had been high in the leadership of the Ba'ath and attempted to conciliate its warring sections in both Syria and Iraq. His recital – shrewd, lucid, mordant, ironic – of the rise and self-mutilation of the movement, was hilarious and horrifying at once.

'How we rubbed our hands when the Israelis went too far and attacked Beirut Airport. Little Lebanon, neutral Lebanon, Christian or, anyway, half-Christian Lebanon; peaceful Lebanon with all that wholesome devotion to business. The West was very upset.

And then in Baghdad they went and publicly hanged some Jews. "What are you doing?" we said. "You must be mad." And, of course, poor Lebanon disappeared from the headlines and we had those disgusting pictures instead.

'But they were also hanging their own colleagues in public. I flew to Baghdad on behalf of the central committee to talk to them. "How can you do this?" I said. "It's barbarous." And they said, "Yes, it was a mistake." And on the way back to the airport, in the streets, there were crowds, and I stopped the car. There were public hangings again.'

In Cairo, I visited the homes of left-wing intellectuals who were married to women of Jewish birth, and who led risky lives under Nasser because of their views and not because of their wives; I talked over the past in one of its relics, the Gezirah Club, with one of the original Free Officers; I discussed the career of Nasser with those who run *Al Ahram*, the most powerful newspaper in Egypt: and it was difficult for me to take seriously the reports that I had heard abroad of anti-Semitism in the Arab world. But then the Arab world is exactly that: a whole world of its own, with people and places, ideas and events of utter discordance across its extent. If a strain of classic anti-Semitism exists in certain sectors of Argentinian society, who in Israel expands the significance to everyone in Cuba and Chile?

What seems clear is that a hostility to Jews as Jews does exist in the Arab world: but that it is erratic; regarded in general as both intellectually disreputable and politically counter-productive; and accordingly marginal in its influence and impact. Furthermore, this is itself confronted by a more or less furtive admiration for the power and efficiency of the Zionist movement, and the success of Israel on the battlefield. There is, for instance, within the Egyptian elite, a sort of masochism in sporting the symbols of the defeat that the Arab cause has suffered. Though the British firm of Marks & Spencer, controlled by a Jewish family of energetic Zionist sympathies, is prominent on the Arab boycott list, the wearing of Marks & Spencer clothes, often with the label left attached for careful display, has become almost a claim to social refinement. In some of the Lebanese press, Israeli leaders, especially Golda Meir and Moshe Dayan, are caricatured with what looks, to an outside observer at least, like a reluctant affection. And the senior military in Jordan often seem to have abandoned a mental colonization by the British for one by the Israelis.* Israel does appear to have, for many in the Arab world, a glamour that scarcely squares with what so many Israelis believe to be ubiquitous Arab attitudes.

The danger of this belief, indeed, is that it may promote precisely the attitude it assails. It may succeed in convincing many Arabs that they are what their enemy and the world at large claim them to be. It is in itself a major source of Israeli fear and inflexibility; obstructing the search for some dynamic settlement of the strife. And if there continues to be no approaching likelihood of such a settlement, many Arabs may turn, in frustration and despair, to the hysteria of racial and religious fanaticism. This may well not immediately damage what the Israelis see as their cause: since it would probably make the Arab world a more vulnerable victim of moral and political haemorrhaging and military incompetence. Yet in any but the most short-sighted view, Israel would pay, in its own way no less, as a consequence. Certainly, the evidence available of developing Jewish attitudes to Arabs suggests a two-way traffic in the possibilities of unreason.

But the Israelis, like the Arabs, so often throw their stones in apparent blindness to how much of their own houses are glass. And nowhere perhaps is this more manifest than in the complaint by each of the other's subservience to an imperial power. For if much of the Arab world, and in particular Egypt, has come to depend on Soviet assistance, what of the relationship between Israel and the United States? It is no belittlement of the efficiency, cohesion and courage of Israel's citizen army in war to maintain that the state would be far more vulnerable than it is, without the assistance in advanced technical equipment and in massive financial flows, both private and public, from the United States. In fact, on the very argument of many Israelis that the Soviet Union aims at dominating the whole area, it is the nuclear capability of the United States and not the armed might of Israel that would credibly deter the Russians from moving directly to achieve their aim. Yet the mass of Israelis would not allow that their state is, therefore, an

* The Middle East is replete with paradox. I was told in Amman that King Hussein watches Israeli television nightly almost without fail. My informant was so authoritative that I thought the story worth repeating in Israel. 'How odd,' came back the all but invariable response. 'We turn on Jordan television, as an escape from ours.'

American satellite. And its successful resistance to American pressure for concessions in the interests of a settlement, would support them.

But why do these same Israelis then deduce that the dependence of Egypt or any other Arab state on the Soviet Union, for sophisticated military equipment and economic subsidy, must imply just such mere satellite status? I was in Israel during the late spring of 1971, when the Soviet–Egyptian treaty was signed. The government and press treated the event as extending the Brezhnev doctrine to the Middle East, so that any uncongenial developments in Egypt could henceforward be crushed by direct Soviet intervention. And whether or not all those in the Israeli government and press who proclaimed this believed it, nearly all individual Israelis with whom I spoke echoed the cry. I argued that what was manageable by the Soviet Union in Eastern Europe was not equally manageable in the Middle East, since the facts of geography made a difference; that the mere conclusion of a treaty might reaffirm or disguise, but did not change, the reality of relationships; and that had the Soviet Union been able, by this reality, to ensure as she chose, we might well have seen someone other than Sadat as Nasser's heir. But all this met with confident dismissal.

It is a dismissal plainly incompatible with events in the Arab world. The most Machiavellian interpretation could not convincingly accommodate to Soviet commands the killing of communist leaders in the Sudan. (The conflict between China and the Soviet Union would itself argue strongly against any suggestion of Soviet connivance. The Sudanese communists were in general loyal to the Moscow line; and it is the Numeiry regime which is now seeking a close relationship with China.) Yet what did Egypt, in her supposed subservience to the Soviet Union, do to affect this course of events? There is no doubt that she could in the circumstances of the time have done much. She might well, for instance, have thrown her moral weight, and even a shrewd element of her military, behind the initial success of Major Hachim el Atta's coup, to secure it. And at the very least she might so have acted when Numeiry came to power again as to prevent all or much of the vengeance that ensued. But there is simply no basis for believing that the Sadat regime intervened on behalf of the Soviet Union; even to influence the Libyan government against sending back to death at home the two Sudanese officers kidnapped from a British plane.*

Nor would the alliance of Egypt and Syria with Libya in some constitutional arrangement seem to serve Soviet interests, as these are seen in Israel. Colonel Qaddafi yields place to no one in the Arab world as an enemy of 'communism'. And to the measure that Libyan oil wealth would flow, presumably along with ideological passion, to Egypt and Syria, the attractions of the Soviet relationship would diminish. Indeed, the Sudan retired from the early confederal moves because of Sudanese communist hostility. And the supposed plot against Sadat, for which so many of Egypt's former leaders, including those generally considered closest to the Kremlin, were tried and convicted, seems to have had much of its impulse in opposition to the confederal moves.

But then, of course, it is the very character of the Sadat regime, and its sources of power, that most clearly contradicts the charge of Soviet overlordship. The men who rule Egypt today support the Soviet connection as one of convenience; to be modified, as opportunity suggests, in the Egyptian interest.† There is no illusion that Soviet assistance is disinterested; and anything but a desire to walk the way of a people's democracy under Soviet control.

The truth is that both Egypt and Israel, each in her own way, constitute major examples of the limitations on super-power influence. The patron, whether the United States or the Soviet

* Colonel Babikir el Nour, who was to head the government had the coup's success continued, and Major Farouk Hamadallah.

† Since this was written, it has been confirmed by the decision of the Sadat regime, in July 1972, drastically to reduce the Soviet military presence in Egypt. Though Soviet instructors would, according to *Al Ahram*, stay on to train Egyptian troops, some 20,000 other Soviet military personnel, many of them responsible for operating missile defence emplacements, would be required to leave the country forthwith.

The official Egyptian report was predictably couched in terms of a victorious nationalism. It cited three distinct measures.

'1. A decision to terminate as of July 17 the mission of the Soviet military advisers and experts who came at our request, and to replace them with our sons in the Egyptian armed forces in all the tasks they used to carry out.

'2. The military installations and equipment set up within Egyptian territory during the period following the aggression of June 1967, will be the sole property of the Arab Republic of Egypt and under the administration of our armed forces.

'3. A call within the framework of the Treaty of Cooperation and Friendship with the Soviet Union for an Egyptian–Soviet meeting at a level to be agreed upon for consultations regarding the coming stage.' Cairo, 18 July 1972.

Union, can bribe, press, threaten. But its only real ultimate sanction is to abandon the client altogether. And as long as the consequences of abandonment are not in the patron's own overall interest, this option is, as the client knows all too well, a hollow one.

Indeed, it is increasingly obvious that the patrons themselves want a settlement of the Arab–Israeli conflict as soon as possible; lest another outbreak of fighting should force either of them into a choice between provoking the other too far or beating a humiliating retreat. With movements of militant disaffection in the subjugated world scarcely discouraged by events in South-East Asia; with the dollar in difficulties; with a multitude of social ills ever more urgently demanding treatment at home; and with the balance of power in the world made far more unstable by the rise of China, Japan and the European Economic Community as formidable forces; such a settlement would be welcome enough to the United States. But the Soviet Union is, if anything, yet more eager. For within the Middle East it is the American client which holds the upper hand, and the Soviet patron which is, therefore, more likely to find itself facing the choice between risking a direct super-power confrontation and allowing its own clients to suffer a further defeat. With the Sino–Soviet ideological differences very far from resolved, and with the first convincing steps taken by the United States towards some accommodation with China, a flare-up in the Middle East would seem to offer small source of profit. Moreover, the sheer economic cost of Soviet involvement must look less and less congenial: with the rising demand inside the Soviet Union for higher living standards meeting serious industrial and especially agricultural difficulties; with an uneasy Eastern European empire, searching for rapid economic development to counter domestic discontent; with the claims on Soviet money and equipment from the Asian front. Besides, a Middle Eastern settlement would be unlikely to damage major Soviet interests. The opening of the Suez Canal, for instance, would serve such interests now far more than would its continued closure. And Soviet influence in the Arab world, especially Egypt, would remain because of the need for Soviet technical and economic aid. I met no Egyptian who believed that the United States would be willing, even were the Egyptians so, to meet the cost of substantially supplanting the Soviet Union.

In short, the vision of the Soviet Union as the major obstacle to any settlement of the Arab–Israeli conflict, as an imperialism waxing fat on instability and war in the Middle East, simply does not fit the facts. It does not take account of an imperial need to consolidate rather than expand, and to shift priorities as events in the world require. Israelis, with their own Manicheism, seem to be living in the age of bipolarization which the United States, the Soviet Union and many Arabs recognize as having passed.

Nor is this Manicheism justified in political contrasts between Israel and the Arab world. Israeli society itself is no pure David of democracy; and Arab society, no absolute Goliath of totalitarianism. The form of social institutions is not necessarily their force. How vital, how vigorous has Israeli democracy been, when the varying strengths of political groupings have stayed much the same since the establishment of the state? Yet in that period the total population has increased to more than three, and the Jewish population closer to four, times what it was; while the nature of mass immigration has produced a Jewish majority of Oriental background, or a culture significantly different from the one which engendered just these political groupings. And in that time, too, the economy of the state has profoundly changed, with the development of capital-intensive agriculture; of a dynamic industrial sector that has transformed the skills and living standards of the labour force; of consumption patterns that encompass conspicuous luxury and a conspicuous deprivation.

How vital, how vigorous is a democracy in which public opinion polls invariably reveal an overwhelming support for the government, and a respect for seemingly the mere possession of leadership? Shortly before her election as prime minister, Golda Meir featured in one of the regular polls on political popularity with around 1%. Three weeks after taking office, and with scarcely sufficient time to have demonstrated her capabilities, she was chosen by two out of every three of the respondents.

It is true that the civil order is unchallenged by the military one. But since the two are so intermingled, it does not follow that the military one is subservient. Indeed, a convincing case can be made out for the contrary. A senior official of the Israeli Treasury described his problems without complaint. 'The army tells us what it needs; and we have to find the money, that's all. How can we argue? We must be sure that we can survive as a state. That comes before anything else.' Consuming some 25% of the gross national product, and some 40% of total state expenditure, the military must exercise an enormous impact on social policy. Yet how are their demands to be adequately assessed and controlled by the civilian leadership, let alone by the electorate at large? Even were the Ministry of Defence under the command of a civilian expert, it would be difficult enough. With the command enjoyed by a general, whose military career has earned him so much personal popularity and prestige, the cause of the armed forces can virtually write its own ticket. And who represents this cause but a military leadership with no basis in democratic election?

Nor does the military arm stretch only across the economy. The censorship of news and opinion is pursued in all matters affecting security; and where the operations of security involve so much of civic activity, the effect on democratic functioning must be disquietingly large. That the effect has, in fact, been contained as far as it has, is a tribute less to what the military and much of the civilian leadership all too apparently would like, than to the critical traditions of the dominant Jewish culture, the liberal loyalties of certain newspapers, and the ingenuity of individual journalists. It is pertinent that Tel Aviv and Jerusalem are, like Budapest and Cairo, cities celebrated for the political joke.

And all this ignores the Arab citizens, whose formally equal civil rights can be seriously qualified or denied in the interests of security. It may well be true that given the nature of their role, military authorities in Israel are less arbitrary, less oppressive, than their counterparts elsewhere in similar circumstances have been. But this would not make them unarbitrary or unoppressive. As with the call of the armed forces on public expenditure, those who conduct the security services are also those who are believed to know best how security should be conducted, and are therefore effectively free from civilian checks. And whether or not in the end the average Arab citizen of Israel enjoys in practice more substantial civil rights than does the average citizen of an Arab state, is not as relevant to the value of Israeli democracy as whether or not he enjoys in practice substantially less than do his Jewish fellow citizens. The ridicule to which Israelis hold up the democratic pretensions of Arab society would be rather more damaging to the Arab cause were their own pretensions free of the ridiculous.

The nature of social management in Israel is far more complex, of course, than either such pretensions, or indeed the criticisms of them here, convey. But then this is true, too, for Arab society. I was in Egypt during those weeks of March 1971 when Heikal opened in the pages of *Al Ahram* a public controversy on the realities of power in the Middle East, and the need to 'neutralize' the United States by an Egyptian display of readiness to reach a settlement.

It was not a controversy confined to the upper reaches of power. Clerks in government departments, teachers, shopkeepers, shorthand-typists wanted to know what my reaction was and eagerly gave me theirs. They were, overwhelmingly, behind Heikal in his judgments; and it soon became evident that this was largely because they recognized the deeper social argument beneath the one on the specific conflict with Israel. The debate over realism was a debate also over the direction that Egyptian society should take now, in the aftermath of Nasser's death. How much longer were higher standards of consumption to be postponed, for the sake of a war that Egypt was likely to fight only to lose yet again? Why should Egypt always have to meet the major cost of pursuing Arab unity, while other Arab states did nothing, or took from Egypt with one hand and shook the other in her face? Why should Egypt be locked into dependence on the Soviet Union, when other countries were able to enjoy assistance from the Soviet Union and the United States alike? Which of those offering themselves as Nasser's heirs were most likely to seek a reasonable settlement in the Middle East, and steer Egypt between chaos and dictatorship?

Such a debate scarcely constituted a profound and pervasive exercise in democracy. But it was far, too, from the closed bureaucratic processes of the Soviet system; from the military despotisms of a Greece or a Brazil; even from the Caesarism of a Nasserist Egypt. And in retrospect there seems little doubt that the course of the debate promoted, as was intended, the necessary backing for the 'liberalizations' of the Sadat regime and their related peace overtures.

Yet it would be as wrong to see in all this a political expression without genesis or precedent in the Nasserist past, as to suppose it a popular involvement in the control of power. Nasser himself did not take kindly to criticism. But there was criticism none the less. Short stories, literary reviews, even political analysis of circumspect self-limitation, reflected the existence of an exploring intelligentsia. Several of the young intellectuals, especially on the radical Left, spent much of the Nasser era in jail. But they emerged neither cowed nor rigid: only resolved, rather, to re-examine their old ideas in the context of new events and discard the unsound. Paradoxically, though Egypt remains today, as does the Lebanon in a different way, far less open a society than Israel, I found in Cairo, as in Beirut, a far less dogmatic, derivative, superficial criticism of current political orthodoxies than I did in Jerusalem or Tel Aviv.

On the other hand, this Arab intelligentsia is much smaller and more isolated a sector of the total population than is its Israeli counterpart. And even the sector in Egypt that conducted the debate after Nasser's death was one crucially from the literate, urban middle classes, within a population still overwhelmingly illiterate, rural and peasant. But then, even in so literate, highly urbanized and industrialized a society as Israel, how popular is effective involvement in the processes of decision?

The Manichean vision of a democratic Israel and a totalitarian Arab world is an absurd and dangerous deceit. There exist, instead, in the Middle East peoples of differing historical experience and social composition, with correspondingly different attitudes to each other and to themselves. Seeking to explain and establish their respective claims as totally valid, they turn these attitudes into myths. And among these myths, perhaps the most mutilating is that myths themselves are the exclusive equipment of the other side.

2

The Arab context: Egypt

I was buying pencils in a small shop near the Hilton, and he was buying film for his camera. Smiling, he nudged his way into conversation. 'You are English. It is not the same accent as the American. You are a tourist.' 'No, a writer.' 'A writer. How interesting. I am a teacher. Of physical education. I am going to meet my friend. He is also a teacher, like me. Will you come with us to Groppi's? Please? I would like to talk about Europe. I know Europe.' 'I would like to talk about Egypt.' 'Yes,' he said with less enthusiasm, 'we can talk about Egypt also.'

His friend Ahmed was, at twenty-six, two years older than he; but had never been out of Egypt, and deferred to Mohamed's superior experience. For Mohamed went abroad each year, during the long school holidays, to work as a waiter in Austria and supplement his earnings by some slick pavement commerce. He would take with him Egyptian commodities, a small carved occasional table or two, a few marquetry boxes; sell them in the streets of Vienna, at the sort of premium that the exotic demands; buy European clothing, cosmetics, pens; and on his return to Cairo, sell them at the sort of premium that almost anything from Europe will carry.

He himself, and Ahmed, showed only a profound contempt for Egyptian manufactures. 'You must not buy that,' one of them would say, as I went with them through the huge Cairo bazaar. 'It is Egyptian. It will fall apart after a few days. You will see. It is all show. Not made well, like they make things in Europe; to last.'

On the revolution of Nasserism, they were both cynical, with Mohamed the voluble spokesman and Ahmed beaming his agreement. 'Socialism in Egypt? What socialism? You have seen the fast cars, and the buildings in Zamalek.* And we get £17 a month

* A posh quarter of Cairo, where many of the Egyptian elite and foreigners live.

after taxes. Anyway, who wants socialism? The Egyptians don't like the Russians. When the Americans used to come here, they bought a lot and never argued about the price. The Russians buy very little and always argue.' Ahmed interrupted. 'I want to get married. But my girl friend only earns £17 too, and she is also a graduate. And it will cost us £500 to buy a place to live in. And what will the wedding cost?' He lapsed into silent dismay.

I asked them about Nasser, and the war. Mohamed was indignant. 'Why did we need the war? It was all a mistake. Look what it cost us. But that man, he spent money like water. Syria, Yemen, the Congo. Half a million pounds a day in Yemen, and so many men. He wanted to stretch himself; to be leader of the Arab world. Egypt was not big enough.'

They were caricatures, Mohamed and Ahmed. But they were caricatures that caught, grotesquely, the character of a class; and a class whose outlook informs much of the Arab world. There were still, when I was there in the spring of 1971, photographs of Nasser all over Cairo. Without exception, those I encountered showed Nasser in Western dress; with a carefully folded white handkerchief peeping from the top pocket of his jacket. And Sadat is reported to be even more devoted to expensive British styling. Both men came, as did most of the Free Officers who made the revolution of 1952, from what is still best described as the petty bourgeoisie.*

It is easier to define this class by what it is not than by what it is. It is not the landless peasants, hiring out their labour; or even those with a mere splinter of land. It is not the industrial labour force; or the poor of casual or no employment. And, at the other extreme, it is not the large proprietors, of land, factories, shops, buildings for rent; the top bureaucrats, senior army officers, and the successful in the professions: though many of these may have come from a petty bourgeois background and continue to hold corresponding ideas. It is, in part by this process of subtraction, the richer peasants; the middle ranks of the army; the mass of tradesmen, owners of small workshops or restaurants, self-employed artisans; the multitude of minor bureaucrats in the public sector of industry and in government; the teachers, and the vast

* While there remains no satisfactory English equivalent for 'bourgeoisie', 'petty' does well enough for the original French 'petit' – little or minor.

majority of doctors, engineers, technicians in public employment; the clerks and secretaries and shop assistants and waiters, taxi-drivers and hairdressers.

It is, thus, a class containing considerable differences of income, of education, of urban development. But in general its members are above the level of poverty on which the bulk of the population subsists, as they are below the level of wealth on which the tiny elite parades; are more or less literate, in a society overwhelmingly illiterate; and either live in the urban areas or visit them sufficiently. Above all, it is a class of particular status. At its lower end, for instance, its members may have less of an income than the mass of industrial workers enjoy; but they regard themselves as having risen beyond the degradation of industrial work. At its upper end, its members may have substantial property; but not of the kind that yields or represents substantial economic or political power.

Now it is from the perspective of this class that the impulse and career, the achievements and limitations, of the Nasser era may best be seen. And nowhere was the impact of this era more remarkable than on the land. By the eve of the Free Officer coup, the pattern of ownership had become socially explosive. Only 5·7% of proprietors owned 64·6%, or nearly two-thirds, of the country's cultivated land; with a mere 0·5% owning 34·2%, or over a third. At the other extreme, 72% of all proprietors, with no more than 13% of the cultivated land among them, owned less than one *feddan* each:* though two *feddans* constituted the least from which a peasant family could sustain itself. The average holding of a large-scale proprietor was 3,765 *feddans*; of a small-scale one, 1·5.† And some 1·5 million families, or some 8 million Egyptians, owned no land at all but survived by share-cropping or selling their labour directly.

The dominant class of richest proprietors enjoyed a social ascendancy in the countryside, especially of Upper Egypt, that might reasonably have been described as feudal. But it was essentially a class of well-developed rural capitalism; sufficiently

* One *feddan* = 4,201 sq. metres, or just over one acre. Figures from Peter Mansfield, *Nasser's Egypt* (Harmondsworth: Penguin Books, 1969), pp. 199–200.

† Anouar Abdel-Malek, *Egypt: Military Society* (New York: Random House, 1968), p. 16.

related to foreign and indigenous finance to constitute the dominant political class of the country. Its minor element consisted of those who managed their own land themselves, producing either cotton or foodstuffs for the market at home or abroad. Its major element was a *rentier* one, whose members leased their property, usually through a succession of intermediaries. Indeed, the consequent soaring in the cost of land for rent, by 472% between 1938/9 and 1950/51, did much to sharpen the rural crisis. And the rented proportion of total land leapt from 1·7% in 1939 to 60·7% in 1949 and 75% by 1952.*

The various rural reforms initiated by the Nasser regime struck more and more heavily against this class. The huge holdings of the royal family were confiscated; and foreign estates, expropriated with compensation. A limit, eventually reduced to 100 *feddans*, with compensation for expropriated land, was placed on individual family holdings: the limit to include waste, fallow, and any leased land. And the area so available for redistribution was to go by preference to former tenants, owning less than 5 *feddans* themselves, and to permanent agricultural labourers: the size of the holdings so granted to be between 2 and 3 *feddans* each. In all, about 1 million expropriated *feddans*, or 17% of the total cultivated area, were expected to benefit some 250,000 families, or 8% of the peasantry.

By 1965, the number of proprietors holding 50 *feddans* or more had increased from 6,000 to 29,000; and owners of 20 *feddans* and more, from 22,000 to 61,000. The combined category, representing less than 3% of all proprietors, controlled, as owners or tenants, over 45% of the total cultivated land.† In part this was because many holders evaded the statutory limit by distributing land to other branches of the family, thus increasing the formal number of owners without a corresponding real redistribution of rural wealth. And in part this was because the rural leadership, through supposedly representative institutions and in particular the co-operatives, was seized by the richer proprietors. Two examples should suffice.

* Ibid., p. 59.

† Figures from *Al Talia*, February 1968, p. 90; quoted by Michel Kamel in his essay 'The Political and Ideological Role of the Petty Bourgeoisie in the Arab World'. An English transcript of this essay has kindly been provided by the author, since the original, published in Beirut, is in Arabic.

According to the National Charter of May 1962, no less than half the seats in all elected bodies (essentially the Arab Socialist Union) were to be held by peasants and workers. But the definition of peasant was subsequently held to encompass all those owning up to 25 *feddans*; and the Arab Socialist Union came effectively to be dominated by the small minority of larger proprietors. Similarly, the law on agricultural co-operatives, which at first stipulated that 80% of the administrative councils were to be reserved for peasants owning less than 5 *feddans* each, was modified under pressure from the larger proprietors. The land ceiling was raised to 15 *feddans*; and illiterates were deprived of the right to election, though the vast majority of the rural proprietors were such.

This new class of proprietors that inherited the domination of rural Egypt from the landlords of the Farouk era was not slow to exploit its advantages. The reduction in rents under land reform laws applied to all property, regardless of size; so that richer tenants did disproportionately well, and enterprising proprietors were able to augment their holdings on the cheap. The vast increase in centralized public investment provided ample opportunity for those in control of the co-operatives to ensure that large loans were channelled their way. The flow of funds from the Egyptian General Institution for Agricultural and Co-operative Credit reached some £E 87 million in 1966/7; when interest-free loans totalling £E 60 million were already in the hands of the mere 2·5% of proprietors with individual holdings of over 25 *feddans*.*

Some of this credit was used, with government encouragement, for more intensive and profitable agriculture. Thus, the area cultivated for vegetables increased nearly threefold between 1952 and 1968, to 696,000 *feddans*; and the area of orchards, some two and a half times, to 207,000 *feddans*. Yet such cultivation, where not part of the few state farming schemes, was mainly undertaken by the richer proprietors, with less need for subsistence crops; holdings large enough to risk experiment; and, through their connections with authority, greater access to credit, technical advice, transport and marketing facilities.

Such agriculture has proved immensely profitable in many

* Figures from *Al Talia*, No. 9, 1966; quoted by Kamel.

instances. Yet, under pressure from this class, the agricultural sector has remained the only one that pays no tax on profit, even though small-scale tradesmen and artisans do.

What, then, have been the principal effects of the Nasserist rural reforms? The old landlord, big bourgeois class has been virtually swept away. Some of its former members continue to cultivate holdings much reduced, under rather different conditions; while others have invested the proceeds of compensation or timely sale in industry, property for rent, or lives of idle complaint. The room at the top of the rural economy has been taken by a new middle bourgeoisie, using and indeed developing land for the profit to be made out of cultivation, rather than for rent. And of this bourgeoisie, the remnants of the old landlord class represent a small and politically unimportant minority.

The major component, and beneficiary, of the reforms has been that section of the petty bourgeoisie which held or subsequently acquired from 10 to 15 *feddans* upwards. Such proprietors have looked upon as their own a regime which provided them with the means to dominate rural politics; receive facilities for diversifying and mechanizing agriculture; and ensure that reform did not proceed to a more radical redistribution of land.

Behind them are the larger numbers of those still petty bourgeois in function and outlook. Owning from 4 or 5 to 10 *feddans*, they are well above the struggle for mere subsistence, and may even employ two or three wage labourers each.* They may regard with a mixture of envy and resentment the new dominant bourgeoisie above them; but they fear far more the pressure from those with yet smaller holdings, and from the totally landless, for a redistribution of property.

For them, thus, the regime has been one worthy of allegiance. It has provided them, through the sale of expropriated land,

* Classification by just how many *feddans* a proprietor has is arbitrary and must be controversial. It matters immensely, for instance, where the land is and what crop is cultivated. My estimates, reached after discussion with those far more knowledgeable than I, are the roughest guides. The Annual Census Book of 1966 showed an increase in the number of owners with less than 5 *feddans*, between 1952 and 1965, from 2,642,000 to 3,033,000; and an increase in their share of the total area, from 35·4% to 57·1%. But given the character of rural reform in practice, it is likely that most of the increase in area served the upper ranges of ownership. The number of proprietors with 5 to 10 *feddans* was 80,000 in 1965.

resettlement on new land rescued from desert by irrigation schemes, and credit or marketing facilities, with the opportunity to acquire or maintain a significant measure of ownership. And it has, despite the distressing agitation of radicals, resisted eroding the priorities of proprietorship by any serious engagement to collective farming. Indeed, by its flow of resources to the countryside, and its ready response to the need for higher returns to encourage private investment in agriculture, it has made land at once more profitable and valuable.

But then what of those, by far the majority of the rural population, possessing no land at all, or no more than the substance of a miserable survival? The break-up of the vast estates at first made their condition worse, with the loss in demand for their labour. Measures to provide a minimum wage were introduced; but these were generally not enforced, with the glut of available labourers and the pattern of effective power developing in the countryside. If the crisis was contained, there were three main reasons. Some land was redistributed, to encourage belief in the prospect of recruitment one day to the ranks of petty bourgeois proprietorship. Some of the rural poor found employment on public works, notably the massive schemes of irrigation; others moved permanently to the towns, for the supply or promise of jobs opened by industrial development; and still others were accommodated in the vast expansion of the army. But above all, perhaps, although the high rate of population growth has confronted every effort to reduce the problem of poverty, there has been, simply, no leadership of rural revolt. Such leadership was, in the cities and countryside of Egypt under Farouk, essentially petty bourgeois: drawn from the class of proprietors with from 5 to 20 *feddans*. And, as has been seen, this leadership became the rural backbone of the new regime. In short, the mass of Egypt's rural millions have found themselves with a new set of local leaders, less alien for being closer in time and place than its predecessors; and promoting not revolt but allegiance.

The impact on urban Egypt has been more complex. The officers, dominated by Nasser, who seized power in 1952, had no common and coherent policy for the economic development of Egypt. But such a policy gradually emerged, under the pressure of events, with two main elements: emphasis on industrial growth through the direct operations of the state; and a reduction in the discrepancies of income.

The fuelling of the policy came from three principal sources. By a shrewd interplay of inducements to East and West, the Nasser regime achieved an enormous influx of foreign aid. In a few years, from the end of 1957 to somewhere in 1964, Egypt received a total, excluding military credits, of some £E 1,320 million: with £E 482·9 million coming from the 'socialist' states (£E 332·5 million from the Soviet Union alone); £E 782·5 million from the 'capitalist' states (£E 535·6 million from the United States alone); and the rest from international agencies.* The second source lay in the expropriation of foreign-held Egyptian assets and in the nationalization or sequestration of major assets in private Egyptian hands. Though compensation of some sort or another was often paid, this none the less placed much-enhanced resources at the government's disposal. For instance, total compensation to the Suez Canal Company was agreed at £E 28·3 million: while toll revenue rose from £E 24·3 million in 1957 to £E 53·7 million in 1962. And related to the second main element of policy, taxation soaked up a considerable quantity of private wealth. By the 'socialist' decrees of 1961, a limit of £E 5,000 a year in personal income was imposed; and though the decrees were too often evaded, not least by senior bureaucrats, through a system of fringe benefits, some resources did accrue to the state, and some redistribution of income did take place.

Finally, for all the corruption and waste that accompanied it, centralized planning promoted a more efficient use of national resources, as did foreign technical help. And, by the standards of the past at least, a high rate of reinvestment nourished industrial growth and employment opportunities. The number of industrial workers rose from 401,000 in 1952 to 724,000 in 1963. And even taking the real depreciation of the Egyptian pound into account, the rise in value of industrial production over the same period, from £E 313·8 million to £E 952·6 million, represented a significant rise in productivity as well.

* This estimate was made by Mansfield; see *Nasser's Egypt,* pp. 184–5. And Miles Copeland, in *The Game of Nations* (London: Weidenfeld & Nicolson, 1970), reported his U.S. State Department and British Foreign Office friends as considering the estimate 'substantially accurate' (p. 144).

This fast-growing work force has been no desperate constituency of revolt. In state-owned factories, unskilled workers have been able to earn £E 30–35, and skilled workers as much as £E 70 a month, for a 42-hour week. And in addition, they have enjoyed such benefits as free medical treatment and low-cost housing. Anyone who travels widely through Cairo today must mark the superiority of most housing for industrial workers in state enterprises to the run of that for casual commercial labour or the lumpen bureaucracy. Indeed, much of the industrial labour force is, and knows itself to be, a relative elite, with corresponding loyalty to the regime. A low-ranking bureaucrat in the Ministry of Information may earn £E 20 a month, or substantially less than do many unskilled industrial workers.

But it is the growth in the petty bourgeoise sector that has been most remarkable. With a total population of some 33 million at the end of 1966, Egypt had almost 800,000 in the state bureaucracy.* (And since each such state employee would conservatively account on average for the income of three other persons as members of his family, this represented some 10% of the population directly dependent on bureaucratic employment.) Michel Kamel, in his study of the petty bourgeoisie, defines as such those employed from the 6th to the 11th grade; and accordingly estimates their share of posts, on official figures, as 91% of all employees in the 12 grades, and 98% of all those in governate or provincial service.

Public employment has been the major factor in relieving the pressures from the increase in numbers of students. For the increase has been spectacular indeed. Including those pursuing technical courses, students numbered some 180,000 in 1959/60 and some 410,000 in 1968/9. And in the same period, the number of university students rose from some 88,000 (38,000 in 1951) to some 141,000; with the number of graduates annually, from 10,000 to 20,000.

Most of these last find jobs in the state apparatus, as minor bureaucrats. They earn little, around £E 17–20 a month; their earnings are slow to rise; and the prospects of advancement to senior posts are predictably remote. But they do not need to be reminded that they earn much more, much more securely, than do

* Exactly 785,856, according to government figures for 1966/7.

the mass of their countrymen; and they consider themselves as far above the highest paid industrial worker in social status as they may be below him in income.

Similarly compensated by status for relatively low earnings are those who go into other branches of public employment: technical personnel in the state economic enterprises; teachers; doctors or engineers in government service; who may also expect to earn between £E 20 and £E 25 a month for several years. And some find employment in the army.

The bulk of the armed forces, which probably exceed 650,000 men by now,* is drawn, of course, from the rural landless and urban unemployed, who look for little more than to be fed. But the army offers, as well, with or without some satisfaction of moral need,† a career that, by manifest precedent, may bring power and wealth. Many of petty bourgeois background have turned to it; and others, in rising from the ranks, have in the process assumed a petty bourgeois character.

Then, beyond ownership of sufficient land or public employment of sufficient status, there are the various bourgeois sectors of industry and commerce. In 1957, Nasser outlined the limits of state intervention. 'In dealing with feudalism, our aim was to transform tenants into owners. Thus we shall have a socialist, democratic, co-operative society. When the State intervenes in industry, it does not mean at all that it is the only capitalist. We believe that national capitalism is essential to strengthen and expand our economy and to achieve our country's economic independence.'‡

As in the rural, so in the urban areas, it was the big bourgeoisie, of trade, industry and banking, against which the reformism of the Nasser regime was principally turned. By the end of 1963, all the banks, heavy industry, insurance, and the major enterprises in mining, transport and trade, had been taken into the public sector. But in light industry and commerce, a middle bourgeoisie survived, in collaboration with the state: to thrive by accommodating

* A figure given by Nasser in July 1970.

† Some 30,000 university graduates, with tens of thousands more from secondary institutes, were reported to have joined the army after the Six Day War.

‡ Speech to the Co-operatives Conference at Cairo University, 5 December 1957.

on management boards those who stepped sideways from posts in the regime, or relatives and clients of those still in office.

More important, however, has been the development of what has been termed a 'state bourgeoisie'. In part this is composed of those holding key posts in military, political and cultural administration: the senior army officers; controllers of ministries and the civil service; eminences in the arts, and in the mass media. And here, the leadership has come crucially from the armed forces. Between 1952 and 1964, some 1,500 officers moved out of uniform and into the upper ranks of civilian power. And half the Council of Ministers installed in September 1966 consisted of army officers.

But the basis of the new class is the public sector of the economy, and here the personnel of management is more technocratic. Among 301 directors of public agencies appointed in 1962, there were 57 engineers and scientists; 57 others holding doctorate degrees; and among the remainder, a majority of graduates in law or business administration. In the main, these came from a middle or petty bourgeois background. Along with the far more numerous directors of individual companies under the control of the public agencies, themselves men of similar training and background, they enjoy considerable incomes: a maximum official salary of £E 5,000 a year, but with substantial further income in fringe benefits. And their counterparts in military, political and cultural administration see to it that they themselves get no less.

It is this middle bourgeoisie, of the state and private sectors, that insists on high standards of consumption and accounts for the luxury commodities, from new cars to tapestried chairs, on display in Cairo. And in doing so, it promotes similar tastes and aspirations, albeit limited by much more slender resources, among the petty bourgeoisie.

This petty bourgeoisie is far more than the ranks of rural proprietorship and state bureaucracy already described. The public sector has encouraged, with its prosperity, the small-scale enterprises of industry and trade in the private one. Between 1960 and 1964, the period of the sweeping measures against the big bourgeoisie, the number of individual economic enterprises increased from some 469,000 to some 494,000. Of these last, only 9,000 were in the public sector; and 469,200, or some 95%, involved only ten or fewer persons each. In all, such small-scale units employed 49%

of all registered workers. Trade dominated this area; with the services second; and the transformation industries last.*

Figures for the profits made during 1967 in the private sector of the transformation industries by establishments with less than ten workers are available and significant. Covering a range of products from textiles and chemicals to furniture and foods, the establishments had a production value totalling some £E 142 million. The value of requirements was estimated at some £E 86 million, of which wages accounted for almost £E 7 million: and the additional value was thus some £E 56 million.†

As with land ownership, the borderline between the middle and the petty bourgeoisie is imprecise. In the transformation industries, it would depend on the type of product; the machinery employed; the number of workers involved; the profit margin that could accordingly be extracted. Much of the private sector here is in the hands of the flourishing middle bourgeoisie. But much, too, supports the far more numerous petty bourgeoisie; whose members are self-employed, or employ each a very few workers.

Certainly the private industrial sector as a whole was profitable enough to promote investment. The development rate went up from 2% in 1965 to 3% in 1966, 4% in 1967%, and 7·9% in 1968, as the state nourished it with facilities to play its role as a producer and exporter.‡

The bulk of the petty bourgeoisie is, however, in the services and, above all, in trade. Indeed, though there are an estimated 750,000 traders, the number of those considered rich enough to pay tax is only 283,000.

One study of urban Egyptian society, published in 1961, provides some guide to approximate economic composition (see table overleaf). The anonymous author identified the 'popular masses' as those with no work listed, servants and the lumpenproletariat, together composing 51% of the total urban population; the 'proletariat' as a separate class, differing in its political and social attitudes; and the 'petty bourgeoisie', or 'lower middle class', as

* Figures from the *National Bank Review*, 1968.

† Figures from the Central Department of Public Mobilisation and Statistics, March 1968.

‡ Nabil El Sabbagh, 'The Third Five Year Plan and the Private Industrial Sector', *Economic Ahram*, 1 November 1969.

subordinate office workers, the regular self-employed, and the middle managerial ranks, together composing 31%.

Index	*Category*	*Population*	%	*Total income p.a. (£E m.)*	*Per capita income p.a. in £E*
0	No work listed	2,988,000	37	—	—
1	Servants	934,000	12	20	21·4
2	Lumpenproletariat	186,000	2	5	26·8
3	Regular wage-earners	400,000	5	16	40·0
4	Proletariat	790,000	10	48	60·8
5	Subordinate office-workers	1,117,000	14	118	105·6
6	Regular self-employed	736,000	9	94	127·7
7	Middle managerial, etc.	614,000	8	83	133·5
8	Middle class and aristocracy	240,000	3	203	845·8
	Total	8,005,000	100	587	73·4 (ave.)

SOURCE: *Tiers-Monde,* 11, No. 6 (1961), pp. 186–7.

The general picture is unlikely to have changed very far. But some qualifications are necessary. The 'proletariat', especially in the public sector, has without doubt increased relatively; and contains within itself considerable discrepancies in income, between skilled and unskilled labour, and between the public and private sectors. The 'middle class and aristocracy' has altered its composition, if almost certainly not its overall share in the total income, with the measures against the old big bourgeoisie and the rapid development of the state bourgeoisie instead. Yet nothing suggests that the proportion occupied by the 'popular masses' is not still numerically dominant and politically sunken; or that the essential constituency of the regime has ceased to be the substantial 'petty bourgeoisie'.

The degree to which the regime itself recognized and reflected this, was made clear enough in the principles upon which representatives to the National Congress of Popular Forces were chosen, in 1961/2.* Taken with the measures to exclude from political rights the 'enemies of the socialist revolution', on the Left as well as the Right, the briefest analysis suggests an all but exclusive involvement of the middle and petty bourgeoisies. The masses of agricultural labour and micro-proprietorship were effectively unorganized and hence unrepresented. The enrolled total of little more than 1 million peasants indicates how closely under the command of relative riches the agricultural co-operatives were. Of the worker delegates, only 40% were to come from the industrial sector, through trades unions dominated by officials subservient

* See Appendix I.

to the regime. It is scarcely surprising that the Congress itself, and the Arab Socialist Union which came out of it, should have been seen as no more than the regime and its instruments of control in fancy dress. Indeed, if seen at all ...

The telephone switchboard of the Nile Hilton in Cairo is attended by Egyptian women of widely varying ages, but a common fluency in English and bright manner. I was trying to telephone Khaled Mohieddine, one of the original Free Officers and an eminent figure of the orthodox Left, who had moved in and out of one office or another as the mood of the regime shifted, and who was now ensconced in the Arab Socialist Union. Having found it impossible to reach him at the home number I had been given, I resorted to the hotel switchboard. 'I think', I said, 'he now works at the Arab Socialist Union. Would you ask for him there?' There was a marked pause; and then: 'The Arab Socialist Union? What is that, please? A company?'

I suppose that I could have been talking to the only Egyptian who had never heard of the Arab Socialist Union; or at least, never heard of it in a translatable form. But the gales of laughter with which my Egyptian friends greeted my recital of the conversation suggested that the telephonist was either exquisitely representative, or had a highly developed sense of political realism.

The character of reform in Egypt has been considered in some detail because Egypt was the first of the Arab states to undertake so substantial a redistribution of power and wealth in modern times; and because Egypt, by population, geography, industrial muscle, cultural dominance, and the charismatic leadership of Nasser, has unquestionably been the paramount Arab influence.

Indeed, Egypt has been the prototype of other avowed 'revolutionary' states in the Arab world. All these reflect the Egyptian structure of change: a regime with a crucial military element (usually coming to power by a coup d'état); and though ready enough with pretensions to socialism of some kind, ruling from above through artificial instruments of popular 'consultation'. The thrust of reform is directed against the foreign economic presence and the indigenous big bourgeoisie, for the development of a middle, largely 'state' bourgeoisie; with the essential support of a far more considerable petty bourgeoisie, whose pressures for employment are contained by the rapid expansion of the bureaucracy and the armed forces. Some planned industrialization in the public sector promotes a proletariat of relative privilege and hence political acquiescence. And the countryside is controlled by a new class of peasant proprietors, middle to petty bourgeois, that exploits to its own advantage the public resources for agricultural investment. There remain the numerous poor of the countryside, landless or with mere subsistence holdings; and the numerous poor of the cities, permanently unemployed, casually employed, or in employment yielding only a precarious survival.

Thus, despite the commitment to revolution developed during the war of independence against France, the subsequent Algerian experience, with all its differences, has ultimately reflected the Egyptian model. Settler-owned land has been inherited by the workers on 'self-managed' estates, to support a new rural Muslim class of privilege; while the traditional peasantry is caught between stagnant production and rising population.

	Numbers (thousands)	*Average earnings (tens of dinars)*	*Total incomes (tens of millions of dinars)*
Economy:			
Workers	300	300	90
White-collar workers	100	350	35
Master-craftsmen, small traders, etc.	180	300	55
Executive staff	25	600	15
Public Service:			
Civil	180	600	110
Military	120	600	70

The distribution of urban income in 1963/4 indicates the pattern, as shown in the table above.

> Some 450,000 new jobs were created outside agriculture: 180,000 workers, white-collar workers, small entrepreneurs, and executives in the urban economy (especially in the autonomous, self-managed sector); 150,000 civil servants; and 120,000 soldiers. These new layers of the population, together with the 100,000 or so colonist-employed workers who formed the nucleus of the self-managed agricultural cooperatives, have up till now been the ones to benefit most from independence and from the departure of the *colons*—

much more than the peasants engaged in traditional agriculture or the less skilled or less well-placed urban working class. Indeed, they are practically the only ones to have benefited from the European exodus.*

The Algerian regime talks of 'Islamic socialism'. And the more flamboyant Libyan one is similarly disposed. The Egyptian regime of Nasser was, along with successive regimes in Syria and Iraq, devoted to the virtues of 'Arab socialism'. Yet it is scarcely possible to examine the social structures and political institutions of such states without being puzzled by the use of the word socialism at all.

A probe of the practical interpretations given to such phrases by the regimes themselves discloses above all a passionate nationalism. In his address to the National Congress of Popular Forces,† Nasser cited, as the first of the six principles that had inspired the start of the 'revolutionary march' in 1952, 'the destruction of imperialism and its traitorous Egyptian lackeys'. And this commitment to the expulsion of Western ascendancy fuelled events throughout the Arab world.

Yet nationalism was not, of course, merely a matter of 'honour' and 'dignity', though the flourishing of such concepts was, and still is, frequent. An end to foreign ascendancy was expected to bring much else: prosperity for indigenous industrialists and merchants from the expulsion of expatriate interests; more land for the lesser proprietors and some land at last for the landless, with the break-up of the large estates; more and better-paid jobs with the growth in government and the planned progress of the economy; an end to the disgraceful contrast of luxury and destitution; a popular control of political processes. These expectations were not self-evidently compatible with one another; but were generally held together by a heady flow of rhetoric. Ten years after the 1952 coup, Nasser would thus enunciate the other five original principles of its impulse: 'the destruction of feudalism; the destruction of monopoly and of the domination of capital over government; the inauguration of social justice; the creation of a strong national army; and the construction of a sound democratic system.'

* Samir Amin, *The Maghreb in the Modern World* (Harmondsworth: Penguin Books, 1970), pp. 136–9.

† In Cairo, on 21 May 1962.

The struggle against foreign ascendancy could be protracted, as in Egypt, and ferocious, as in Algeria. But sooner or later, it had to be proclaimed at an end, if those who had come to power instead were to secure themselves there. The time had arrived to fulfil the expectations; and the incompatibility of these could no longer be escaped. If the state seized major indigenous elements of the industrial and trading sectors, the more effectively to increase employment and incomes by adjusting the direction of investment and raising its rate, the regime had to confront the hostility of those who lost so much property and power in consequence. The regime could not together deliver higher incomes and full employment, land for the landless and larger holdings with credit and equipment for the existing peasant proprietors. It had to choose whose expectations to fulfil; and in choosing the petty bourgeoisie it had to confront the hostility of those who were, or spoke for, the disappointed. Between the Right and the Left, therefore, it had to propound a middle ideology,* which offered reform without revolution.

The character of that middle ideology was consistent with the character of the new regimes: which came to power through armed action, under the command of officers with a petty-bourgeois background. It does not follow, of course, that all these officers were mere ideological images of their class: one of the leading Free Officers in Egypt was Major Khaled Mohieddine, already a committed Marxist revolutionary. But it would have been astonishing indeed, if most of such officers did not reflect in their ideas and aspirations the particular sub-culture from which they came. Furthermore the mainstream of the nationalist movement itself had had its source in their own social background: among small- to medium-scale peasant proprietors; minor traders, government employees, white collar workers, students, intellectuals. Students and intellectuals were especially influential in a society where so much illiteracy existed, and education was so highly prized. And this group was itself in the main from the petty bourgeoisie.

In the petty bourgeois sector as a whole, and not least within its

* Needless to say, the ideology here treated was one which developed, with variations in different states, and in response to inevitable vicissitudes, over several years.

more educated constituent, there was a strong attachment to the institution of private property. Foreign interests and the indigenously owned vast estates might be, should be, expropriated: but any proposals to interfere with the essential rights of property were favoured by no more than a tiny fringe of convinced Marxists, and met antagonism even from those at the bottom of the petty bourgeois scale. Indeed, it would be fair to say that in the absence of a mass revolutionary movement with an understanding of how the traditional institutions of property might be transformed, many of the rural landless and urban unemployed looked to a redistribution of private property rather than to the promise of public ownership.

Related to these prevalent views on property and production was a concern with the glories of the Arab past and the values of Islam. Confronted by the triumph of Western Christian materialist culture, petty-bourgeois nationalism all too readily sought refuge from humiliation in asserting the splendours of Arab history and the claims of Islam to moral regard. Arab unity was thus projected as a credible way of not only humiliating the triumphant West in turn, but restoring the Arab nation to a splendid place in history. And an Islamic fanaticism, with a strong infusion of fascism, had powerful support within the petty bourgeoisie, including its intellectual ranks. Indeed, the Muslim Brotherhood was to emerge as Nasser's most formidable enemy in Egypt. For though Nasser himself, like many of his colleagues, was a devoted Muslim, his devotion seemed excessively concerned with finding texts in the Koran to support his own 'socialist' policies.

Finally, and there is no contradiction here, the Arab petty bourgeoisie, and especially its educated element, had been mentally colonized by the processes of Western mastery. The tastes, the manners, the values of their rulers had been assimilated in varying measure by the very nationalists who cried most passionately for liberation. Nationalism was, for many, a way of getting what their imperial masters had, so as to become more like what their imperial masters seemed to be. There was, in this attitude, a profound respect: and with it, a profound desire for approval. After all, defeat and subjugation are the less mortifying to the degree that the conquerors are worthy of regard. Even apart from its other preoccupations, the predominant petty bourgeois mind accepted at face value the distaste in which socialism was held by the principals of Western culture. And the Soviet interpretation of socialism, which was the form that the regime essentially encountered, was scarcely such as to surmount this resistance.

The new regimes accordingly propagated a middle ideology that promised suitable reforms while carefully laying down the limits. This entailed state intervention in the economy; the elimination of any competitor, from a class of great wealth; beyond that, the sanctity of private property, with the rejection of state-owned collective farms as a major element in agriculture, or of a state monopoly in industry and trade; a formal dedication to the cause of Arab unity; and the continued state establishment of Islam.

In April 1963, a manifesto on the principles that would govern the projected new Federal State of the United Arab Republic was published, over the signatures of Nasser and the presidents of Iraq and Syria. It began:

> In the name of the Merciful Compassionate God,
> In the name of the Almighty God ...

and went on to declare:

> The delegations in all their discussions were inspired by faith that Arab unity was an inevitable aim deriving its principles from the oneness of language bearing culture and thought, common history-making sentiment and conscience, common national struggle deciding and defining destiny, common spiritual values stemming from Divine messages and common social and economic understanding based on liberty and socialism.

To be sure, the project collapsed. But it did so not because of any avowed ideological revulsion from the 'inevitable aim' of Arab unity or the importance of 'common spiritual values stemming from Divine messages'.

Two further elements informed the middle ideology. The radical regimes needed development aid for their economies, not to mention a supply of weapons, or of credits to purchase them, for 'the creation of a strong national army'. The doctrine of 'positive neutralism' in foreign policy seemed appropriate enough to such an ideology; and offered the prospect of profitable relations with the Western states and the Soviet bloc alike. Too close an association with one side would correspondingly reduce the sources of assistance from the other and promote a propensity to interfere. It was a doctrine that early showed its worth; and if events have subsequently made the going rather rough, it allowed, and still does, a great deal of hopeful travelling.

Last has been the interpretation of democracy. For, of course, only the most deplorable regimes in the Arab world would deny any commitment to the principle. But how should regimes reaching power by military coups risk freedom of political discussion and activity, which might lead to reversal at the polls? On the right lay the danger from the old parties, whose discredit might soon be displaced by an orchestrated impatience at the inadequacy or misdirection of change; with the new frustrations of a material advancement necessarily contained, and with the reinvigorated old claims of religious leadership. On the Left lay the danger of a communist-organized mass movement, which could use the suffrage, and the disillusionment of the sunken multitudes, as a hoist to power.

Under various names, and with various contrivances, the answer was 'guided' democracy: under a leadership that, albeit effectively self-appointed, claimed to represent not any particular class or opinion, but the nation. An early submission by Michel Aflaq, the founder of the Ba'ath Party, prefigured this attitude. 'We represent the entire nation which is still in slumber, ignorant of its reality, unaware of its identity, forgetting its needs. We have preceded it; thereby we represent it.'*

The failure of the 1963 federation was largely due to the refusal by the Ba'ath leaders in Syria or Iraq to countenance even the limited election processes provided in the draft constitution. Their excuse was the threat from the Right; but it was the popularity of Nasserism itself that they feared. And Nasserism itself, not only in Egypt but in Syria, during the period from 1958 to 1961 when it ruled there, revealed its peculiar definition of democracy. The Syrian Left was as antagonized by the attentions of the Egyptian-directed political police, as was the Syrian Right by the socialist measures imposed from above. Petty bourgeois discontent in the army produced the coup of September; and there was no organized

* 'For Regeneration'; quoted by Kamel.

popular force to resist. In the end, democracy, like socialism, was what each regime proclaimed it to be: only the need for sufficient popular support or sufficient military allegiance affected the content of the proclamation.

> 'The question is,' said Alice, 'whether you *can* make words mean so many different things.'
>
> 'The question is,' said Humpty Dumpty, 'which is to be master – that's all.'

This does not mean that such mastery was the sole impulse behind the seizure and exercise of power. The regimes represented the attitudes and aspirations – often, in the social context of the time, generous ones – of the men who led them. But as these men opened change, so they closed it. Just as they did not see beyond their own particular attitudes and aspirations; so they did not, or would not, see beyond themselves as the proper instruments.

And in consequence they have raised at least as many social issues as they have resolved. Indeed, the new issues are more formidable than the old: since in resolving the old, the regimes have exhausted so many of the possibilities that previously promised rescue. How, then, has the middle ideology been able to survive for so long? The answer lies largely in the transformation of nationalism itself. In place of the old dynamic, the struggle against direct Western dominion, is the new and far more complex one: the struggle against Israel, and among differing attitudes to the cause of Arab unity.

The Jewish state was a factor in the old nationalism, too, of course: first, because Zionism itself was seen as no more than a ploy of Western imperialism; and then, because the failure of the Arab armies to defeat the new state in 1948 was blamed on the existing regimes, which were associated with imperial control. In fact, paradoxically, it was these regimes that had sought to use nationalism to ensure their own survival, by confronting Israel. Some of the military who would later be prominent in the Egyptian Free Officers Movement were opposed to such confrontation partly for this reason; and it was the humiliation of nationalism in the ensuing war that contributed so much to the ousting of the regimes held responsible.

But Israel did not go away as a result. And its presence was a rebuke to the new regimes, which seemed no more capable than the old ones they had displaced of defeating the Jewish state. Their dilemma has been chronic. An accommodation with Israel would deprive nationalism of a major tributary to its popular flow, and would direct more searching attention to the substance of social change at home. Yet if continued conflict with Israel, however merely rhetorical, discourages the popular mood from wandering in dangerous directions, it simultaneously encourages expectancy of some success in the conflict, and threatens inactivity, let alone failure, with a nationalist retribution. Then again, a settlement with Israel would make less evident the need for such large military establishments as the Arab states presently sustain and to which the regimes by their nature are devoted. Yet conflict with Israel requires a measure of military expenditure that makes economic development to meet gathering social needs impossible.

The dilemma has been especially pressing for Egypt: not only because Egypt borders on Israel, and thus has had the immediate problem of how its forces should behave across cease-fire lines (other states are similarly placed); but because, by its size, its situation at the centre, and its cultural primacy, Egypt so easily sees itself as the natural leader of the Arab world. It was a leadership that the Nasser regime could have chosen to deny, at least for the while, as so costly, in moral and material resources, as to pre-empt the successful restructuring of Egyptian society. But the character of the regime and, above all, of Nasser the man, made of just such leadership a preoccupation instead.

In the process, nationalism became concerned not only with Arab unity, an ideal of recurrent vigour, but with the pretension of Egypt to lead in the progress to that ideal. In some states, notably Syria and Iraq, supporters and antagonists of this pretension, and the policies with which it was associated, struggled for control, on the sands of the middle ideology, while festering social issues went unattended. The very irrelevance of the struggle to the real needs for change promoted a fervent factionalism that set civilian and military elements of the Ba'ath, and different groupings within each element, contending for power. In other states, like Jordan and the Lebanon, regimes with no credible claim to a middle ideology and serious social reform, projected themselves as the guardians of national independence against an Egyptian appetite for empire.

There was, unhappily, too much substance in the accusation that the Egyptian regime seemed more concerned with leadership of the Arab world than with the revolutionary values that such leadership was supposed to represent. The Egyptian officials in Syria during the years of union did behave far too often like so many proconsuls. And Egyptian failings were to be yet more forcibly revealed in Yemen. There, in September 1962, an army revolt against the Imam seized the main towns and declared a republic. The Imam, however, escaped to pursue resistance, and the leader of the revolt called on Nasser to help. Egyptian forces were immediately dispatched. They were to stay three years; increase to encompass a third of the whole Egyptian army; and present an imperial spectacle of planes bombing tribal settlements. Indeed, townsmen who had greeted them as saviours on their arrival, turned in resentment to assail their conduct as that of an occupation force. Caesarian regimes such as Nasser's, it was once again demonstrated, did not, could not, make revolutionary armies, for either the domestic market or export.

These were the circumstances that contributed to the disastrous war of June 1967 with Israel. A Syrian regime of passionate revolutionary pretensions but with so tenuous a revolutionary content that the arming of the populace could scarcely have been contemplated for a moment, sought to cover this discrepancy with a vigorous display of its devotion to the Palestinian cause. Attempts to divert the headwaters of the Jordan, attacks by Palestinian commandos from Syrian territory, and minor incidents along the border involving regular Syrian forces, were accompanied by propaganda of ecstatic ferocity. That the Syrians did not want war, the Israelis were sufficiently assured. But at a time when Israel was in the grip of economic recession, with mounting unemployment and a Jewish emigration beginning to overtake the influx of new settlers, the Eshkol government was vulnerable to charges of weakness in dealing with the Arab enemy. Israeli reprisals, and the threat of more to come, sent representatives of the Syrian regime scurrying to Cairo, where a joint defence agreement was signed in November 1966.

But the next Israeli chastisement was directed at Jordan, after an act of sabotage on an Israeli road near Hebron. The Israeli army attacked the village of Samu' with a show of force that seemed to have gone beyond government purposes. 'Our action was originally intended to be more limited in its scope and effects than it proved in practice,' Foreign Minister Eban stated on French radio.* Palestinian demonstrations on the West Bank, demanding arms and accusing the Hussein regime of cowardice, were not easily suppressed; and Hussein sought to protect himself by attacks on Nasser—for hiding behind the U.N. forces on the Egyptian frontier and for allowing military supplies to reach Israel through the Straits of Tiran.

The Arab tragedy that followed had its source in the character of the regimes involved and, not least, in that of the protagonist. No one, to be sure, can know the balance of calculation in Nasser's mind as events gathered to the Israeli attack. But those in Egypt and abroad with close experience of his personality and judgments, seem convinced that he never wanted the war or thought that it would occur: but that his commitment to his prestige in the Arab world led him to take risks for a political victory; and that the intelligence he received encouraged him to suppose so small a difference between Israeli and Egyptian military capacities as to make the risks of war sufficiently worth running.†

That the intelligence was faulty is evident. But evident, too, is that it could hardly have been anything else. Men of such great personal power are surrounded by those who are or soon become minions, seeking only to please by conveying what is welcome and withholding what is not. And since such minions tend to compensate by surrounding themselves with those whom they may treat as minions in turn, a network of gratifying misinformation reaches through the armed services from the ranks to the ruler of the state. There are those who claim that Nasser was shrewd enough to know this and make allowances. But if this was so, the allowances that he could bring himself to make were far from adequate.

After further incidents on the border between Syria and Israel, partly provoked by Israeli cultivation of the demilitarized zone, the cry that it was time to teach the Syrians a lesson was increasingly

* Quoted by Maxime Rodinson in *Israel and the Arabs* (Harmondsworth: Penguin Books, 1968), p. 182.

† Private interviews with the author.

raised by leading Israeli activists like Dayan and Peres, who were outside the government looking in and who had a dominant constituency of support in the army. In April 1967 Israeli planes shot down several Syrian MiGs and probed as far as the suburbs of Damascus. Further Israeli threats against Syria followed an act of sabotage near the Jordanian border. On 12 May, General Rabin went so far as to declare that no government in the Middle East could feel safe until the revolutionary regime in Damascus had been overthrown; and reports from Soviet and Egyptian intelligence confirmed for Nasser the Syrian fears of an imminent Israeli attack. Under mounting criticism for his passivity from his Arab rivals, and with an Egyptian general at the head of a nominally 'unified Arab command', Nasser resolved to act. Egyptian forces moved in strength towards Sinai; and on 16 May, the Chief of the Egyptian General Staff asked the commander of the U.N. forces to evacuate observation frontier posts on Egyptian territory.

The request was referred to the U.N. Secretary-General, U Thant, who replied that Egypt could not order any movement of U.N. forces; but could only withdraw the authorization of 1956 by which such forces were stationed on Egyptian territory.* The issue thus became the U.N. presence not just on the Sinai border but at Sharm-el-Sheikh, the military post dominating the Straits of Tiran and so the passage from the Israeli port of Eilat to the Red Sea. Conquered by the Israelis in 1956, this post had been evacuated under pressure from the United States, for occupation by U.N. forces, whose presence permitted the bulk of Israel's oil supplies to use the passage. Driven by U Thant's reply to choose all or nothing, and derided by the Jordanians for his empty gestures, Nasser demanded the withdrawal of U.N. forces from all Egyptian territory and ordered the Egyptian reoccupation of Sharm-el-Sheikh. Then, on 23 May, came the announcement that the Gulf of Aqaba would now be barred to Israeli shipping. Israel had repeatedly warned that denial of free passage through the Gulf would excite a military response. Yet Nasser would not stop short of this one last step that seemed to promise a resounding political victory: depriving Israel of the principal gain made in the Suez war, and restoring Nasser himself to a dominance of Arab

* Israel had refused the presence of U.N. forces on her side of the frontier and continued to do so now, in answer to a suggestion from U Thant.

nationalism not experienced since the nationalization of the Suez Canal.

A tidal wave of elation, with the prestige of Nasser at its crest, swept across the Arab world. It was the triumph of the middle ideology: its shortcomings forgotten, its militarist content excused, its conservative alternatives submerged, in the roar of nationalist excitement. Israel, seemingly locked in ineffectual diplomatic manœuvres, had had its weakness successfully probed. Now the day of retribution was at hand. The Arab press and radio reflected the ecstasy of a Palestinian leadership contemplating the annihilation of the enemy. Mosque and church summoned God to the battlefield. And the Eyptian army command, seeking solace for the inglorious Yemeni years, prodded Nasser to press his advantage.

Partly carried away by the very passion he had provoked, Nasser grew less cautious in his speech. On 28 May, at a press conference, he declared that the Palestinians would be justified in attacking Israel to recover the rights of which they had been robbed. 'If the war of liberation becomes a total war in the Middle East, we are ready for the struggle.' But meanwhile Egyptian diplomacy, under pressure from a Soviet Union now alarmed by the prospects of war, was giving busy assurances of peaceful intent and offering the possibilities of negotiation on the whole Palestinian issue. From his new position of strength, Nasser perhaps hoped for major Israeli concessions over the refugees and the 1948 borders that would allow an acceptable settlement, with the Egyptian leadership accorded the due of its endeavours.

But in Israel, responding to the Arab mood, public opinion moved in support of the militants. The Eshkol government was committed to exhausting the diplomatic possibilities first, but was now being openly attacked by army chiefs. 'It is becoming increasingly evident', General Rabin declared, 'that the only force which can be relied upon in this country is the army.'* Across the West, demonstrations of support for tiny Israel, menaced by extinction, gathered strength. Then, on 30 May, doubtless alarmed by his deepening isolation in the Arab world, and not immune to the infectious vision of impending Arab triumph, King Hussein flew to Cairo and signed a joint defence pact with Egypt. The ring

* Quoted by Eliahu Ben Elissar and Zeev Schiff in *La Guerre israélo-arabe, 5–10 juin 1967* (Paris: Juilliard, 1967), p. 97.

around Israel now seemed closed. Two days later, an Israel Government of National Unity was formed, with Eshkol delivering the portfolio of Defence, which he himself had held, to Dayan. On 5 June, Israel struck.

The full failure of the new Arab nationalism was revealed in the Six Day War. The advantages of surprise, a strategy brilliantly executed and a superior command of advanced technology do not alone account for the extent of the Israeli victory. The Syrians and Jordanians could fight badly or well only as the sort of professional armies that they were, not as nations in arms. And the Israelis who advanced along the Golan Heights reported, with something more than self-righteousness, the vast differences they found between the living quarters of officers and those of the ranks. If many of the ordinary Syrian soldiers seem to have behaved like rabble in retreat, they had scarcely been conditioned to behave otherwise. But it was the Egyptian forces which most appallingly disintegrated, with officers abandoning their troops and seizing equipment for precipitate flight. It may well be untrue that Egyptian forces fired on their own soldiers retreating across the Suez Canal to prevent their carrying back reports of the disaster in Sinai to Cairo. What matters still is that such stories were current in Cairo more than three years later. The nationalism of the middle ideology had so far failed to produce a 'socialist' and 'democratic' collective involvement that the most hideous betrayal of men by one another, if not actually practised, could at least be easily believed.

In such a situation, the survival of Nasser in power was scarcely astonishing. Certainly the regime helped along the street demonstrations which clamoured for him to withdraw his resignation from the presidency. But in the absence of any edifying alternative, a popular rallying behind the person of Nasser, in some measure perhaps as the tragic hero who symbolized the Arab tragedy itself, was all too predictable. Besides, Nasser's acceptance of responsibility was hedged with the excuses of imperial intervention; the pledge of united Arab resolve for eventual victory; and reminders of the triumphs achieved by the revolution. It was not the middle ideology that had failed, but its appreciation of how strong and cunning had been the powers of darkness confronting it.* Still

* See Appendix 2.

needed was a trial of senior army officers to fix the more precise blame for failure; and this followed shortly.

That Nasser's death should have produced the sort of struggle for leadership that it did, might as reasonably have been anticipated as that his body would be enshrined in a Cairo mosque. There was no immediate appeal to public opinion. The succession went to Vice-President Anwar Sadat whose background and career had been so close to Nasser's own. Nasser's father had been a post office employee; Sadat's, a petty civilian clerk with the army. Both Nasser and Sadat had been educated in Cairo and gone to the military academy at Abbasiyah, where they had been classmates and become friends. Both subsequently were members of the Free Officers Movement. But it was Nasser who led, and Sadat who followed. Indeed, on the night of 23 July 1952, when the coup was mounted, Sadat was at a Cairo cinema with his wife, and on receiving a message from Nasser, made immediately for the radio station to proclaim the seizure of power.

Henceforward he held various offices of more or less high distinction but not of substantial responsibility. He was made editor of the newspaper *Al Goumhouriyah*; secretary-general of the Islamic Congress; president of the National Assembly. He was a functionary whose personal allegiance to Nasser was beyond question; and his appointment as vice-president of Egypt recognized this. But his duties were not such as to give him a source of significant power.

And that may well be why he achieved the succession so smoothly. There were four apparently far more formidable rivals who had less cause to take Sadat seriously than each other. Zakaria Muhieddin had been appointed immediate successor by Nasser in his resignation broadcast of June 1967; and though his light had dimmed since then, he represented the hope of an opening to the West and to liberalizing economic policies, with an appropriate constituency of public support, and with Heikal pressing his claims in *Al Ahram*. Ali Sabry, commonly regarded as closest to Moscow, was the clear favourite of the functionaries in the Arab Socialist Union and of many in the technocratic class. Sharawi Gomaa, as Minister of the Interior, controlled the police. And Sami Sharaf, Minister for Presidential Affairs, was close to General Mahmoud Fawzi, commander-in-chief of the army, and had a reputedly powerful base in the units stationed around Cairo.

Within less than a year, Sabry, Gomaa and Sharaf were standing trial; and Sadat was, for the while, undisputed master of Egypt. The divisions in the regime surfaced in the spring of 1971, with the Heikal articles in *Al Ahram* on the need to adopt a policy of realism. At issue, of course, as those who discussed Heikal's soundings with such passion knew or suspected, was far more than a new posture towards Israel: entailed was an adjustment of the middle ideology, and of the politics associated with it.

Mohamed and Ahmed, the two young teachers, represented, however extravagantly, a strong and articulate petty-bourgeois opinion: which wanted peace; an end to costly foreign engagements, and an Egypt that cultivated its own garden instead; a Western involvement to balance the Soviet one; a far more substantial flow of consumer goods; and less evidently authoritarian a political process. It was in large part a demand for some of the delights associated with Western liberalism.

Al Ahram spoke for and nourished the opinion. Its literary editor, Louis Awad, himself a Copt, voiced the resurgence of an Egyptian particularity. 'If you search in the six reading books taught from Grade 1 to Grade 6 in Egyptian schools, you do not come across the name Egypt even once. You only discover stupid poems that begin, "I am an Arab. My father is Arab. My brother is Arab. Long live the Arabs".'*

I had lunch, during that spring, with another member of the staff of *Al Ahram*, an academic whose brother had been a leading member of the Muslim Brotherhood. 'You see,' he said, 'we are a small country, as the world goes. We must learn to act like one. We must stop pretending to be the new force of Islam. We only make enemies; we recall to black Africa an Arab past of slave-trading and conquest. We must see our Arab relationships in proportion. We poured our resources into the Yemen and Syria. And for what? We cannot afford to take on ourselves the leadership of Africa. Where are the means? There is so much that has to be done here. And in our foreign policy, we must stop mixing politics and business. Each has its own rules. We can have influence by sending out our teachers and technicians. We will be valued as we are useful.'

* Quoted in *Time*, 17 May 1971.

Good heavens, I thought, his model is Israel.

And he went on, 'We will have a peace settlement, if only the Israelis are reasonable. But America must move soon, and knows it. Soviet involvement in our economy has so far been loose. But take the huge new programme for rural electricity. It must draw us much more tightly together.'

Heikal himself was at the centre of the controversy, though it was difficult to believe that he was writing without at least the acquiescence of Sadat. He recounted with bitterness the immediate aftermath of Nasser's death, when 'I was down'. It must have been a dangerous time indeed, for a man who had been Nasser's confidant; and whose continued command of *Al Ahram* must have excited such jealousy and resentment, for the independent power of which it disposed, if not also for the outlook that it might promote.

Heikal's own character called for the emerging articulate mood in Egypt. 'I never wanted to be a minister. I refused again and again. I was away when Nasser appointed me, and I fought against it when I got back. It was put to me that I was needed, and I had to give in. But only for a while.'

There could be no doubt of his delight at having rid himself of the job. 'All I want is to be here, running *Al Ahram*. You have met members of the staff. We have Marxists, and anti-Marxists; those who think that Egypt's golden age was under the Mamelukes, and those who look back to the Pharaohs. I remember once when Nasser came to talk with some of our writers and critics. And after hearing them, he asked in surprise, "But does no one believe in Arab unity?" And the answer was no. And so it was for politics as a whole. The party was sterile. It was *Al Ahram* that reflected the conflict of ideas.'

He had learned to be suspicious of the fist in the glove of collective leadership. 'I was on a boat with Krushchev and Nasser together, for several days. I tell you that there is no such thing as collective leadership in the Soviet system. And there must be something wrong with the socialist state where leadership is so single.'

Nasser made Heikal important: by giving him his trust; by using him as a test for his ideas and a scout for his policies. I suspect that after Nasser's death, Heikal wanted above all to be seen as important in his own right; to be seen as having a mind of his own and exercising his own influence. But further, I suspect, he wants never again to find himself, as he did at the heels of Nasser's death, so vulnerable to enemies; so close to oblivion.

Much of his character is revealed in his intense sense of loyalty. There are those on *Al Ahram* who profoundly dissent from his views, but who readily tell how he tried to protect them from Nasser's displeasure, interceding for their release from detention and meanwhile keeping them on the staff of the paper and paying their salaries. If there was in this something of the patron who looked on his clients as projections of his own personality, there was, too, an attachment to the value of human relationships, to the decencies of trust.

And doubtless there is much to be made of his own petty-bourgeois affiliations, with his parade of success uncertainly over-dressed. His office at *Al Ahram* would not embarrass the board of a major multi-national corporation; and his gentleman's farm, with a line in imported flowers, is in the English county tradition.

What is clear is that Heikal aimed at a liberalization of the political climate in Egypt after Nasser, which would secure and enhance the role of *Al Ahram* as a source of social influence, rather than as a mere mouthpiece of bureaucratic decision. 'The army will not stand for this,' shouted an Egyptian diplomat at a dinner party in Cairo, where argument raged over Heikal's article on the massacre of Egyptian forces that would follow any attempt by them to cross the Canal. 'It is deliberate demoralization. He should be put on trial for treason.' But the army did 'stand for' it. And Sadat must have been correspondingly reassured in the policies he was unfolding.

The open split in the regime came with Sadat's support for a confederal association of Egypt with Syria and Libya. The plan was promoted with little of the pan-Arab fervour that had informed previous ventures. And it was seen by many Egyptians as a further move in the 'opening to the West': promising some control of Syrian adventurism, and involvement with a Libyan regime whose hostility to Arab communists and to the influence of the Soviet Union in the Middle East was beyond doubt. At a meeting of the Arab Socialist Union's central committee on 27 April 1971, Ali Sabry reportedly attacked the proposed association and demanded where Sadat had got the authority to proceed with it. Less than a week later, Sabry was dismissed from his post as Vice-President of Egypt.

It seems that, whatever the extent of the plot which Sadat later claimed to have been mounted against him, the opposition to his leadership was poorly co-ordinated. Perhaps the more powerful of his rivals still distrusted each other too much; perhaps they still could not bring themselves to take him seriously enough. On 12 May, according to Sadat himself, he was informed that Sharawi Gomaa had ordered security police to surround the radio station and prevent him from entering. He dismissed Gomaa from office at once, and on the following day was presented with the joint resignation of five ministers, including General Fawzi, Minister of War, and Sami Sharaf. Minutes afterwards, Cairo radio announced the resignations to the accompaniment of martial music. But if this was supposed to have toppled Sadat, the attempt fell flat on its face. There were no street demonstrations; and the army did not move. Sadat placed his main opponents under arrest; began a purge of their associates from all posts of influence; and declared an era of personal freedom, with an end to the well-established methods of the security police in intimidating opinion. Late in August, over one hundred people went on trial, with Sabry, Gomaa and Sharaf among them.

In Israel, it is commonly maintained that Egypt is controlled by the army. But where was the army during these events? The explanation seems to be that it was so divided as to have neutralized itself. A sufficiently strong element did not want another war, with the likelihood of another defeat for which the army would suffer the blame as well as the casualties; and welcomed the new policies for which Sadat was believed to stand. Like its civilian counterpart, the petty bourgeoisie in uniform looked for something other than Nasserism without Nasser. And unless the army was effectively united against him, Sadat was safe behind the presidential guard. Indeed, if any armed force may be held to have played a significant part in the victory of Sadat, it was this palace guard, whose presence and probable loyalty may well have dissuaded Sadat's rivals from attempting to mount a more direct attack upon him.

But the survival of Sadat's new policies, and of Sadat himself, can scarcely long be secured by the palace guard and the differences within the army at large. Some settlement with Israel that would restore all conquered Egyptian territory, at once or by convincingly rapid stages, must be the measure by which all related policies, such as the opening to the West, the association with Libya, and domestic liberalization, are judged. The achievement of terms that would not so abandon Syrian and Palestinian claims as to make Egypt unanswerably subject to the charge of betrayal, would also be necessary, of course. But in the present mood of Egyptian nationalism, it is the return of lost Egyptian territory that is the first preoccupation.

This 'national problem' is serious enough for Sadat. But in modern Egyptian history, the 'national problem' has generally been allied to the 'social' one, with each reinforcing the other. In the early 'eighties of the last century, the movement of Colonel Ahmed Arabi, regarded today as the father of Egyptian nationalism, was aimed at prising Egypt loose from the Dual Control of Britain and France, whose financial supervision on behalf of European creditors constituted the real power behind the Khedive. But much of the movement's force was social: involving the peasants, discontented at crushing poverty; and the educated middle classes of the towns, in revolt against a Khedival rule that was at once oppressive, corrupt and weak. Arabi succeeded only in provoking British armed intervention and the imperial guardianship of Egypt for decades. Yet his example became a reminder and an impulse.

British rule was not without its benefits in the development of agriculture, industry and administration. But the emphasis on cotton production turned Egypt into a country almost totally dependent on a single export crop; foreign investment so dominated the modern sector of the economy that by 1914 over 90% of the capital in joint-stock companies was owned by foreigners; and the growth of capitalism in countryside and town promoted the riches of the few and the poverty of the many. The resultant divisions were sharpened by the economic boom of the First World War and its aftermath, with prices tripling from 1914 to 1920, and a food shortage reaching famine proportions. The nationalist upsurge in 1919, led by Saad Zaghloul, involved peasants who cut communications, seized land, and even proclaimed local republics; workers, whose trades unions took on a political role; the petty bourgeoisie of small traders, minor officials, teachers and students, with many from the professions; and even a substantial sector of the urban rich and the large-scale landowners, who saw the prospect of dominating the country's wealth with the expulsion of British rule.

In 1922, Britain conceded the end of the Protectorate. But the force of independence was effectively denied by the four Reserved Points: the security of British imperial communications; the defence of Egypt against foreign aggression; the protection of foreign interests and of minorities; and continued control of the Sudan. The constitution that followed in 1923 gave considerable powers to the king, who would employ them in the interests of a British presence that was the ultimate protection of his throne.

The extent to which this presence could still be deployed in command of Egypt was dramatically revealed in 1942. King Farouk, in a spasm of self-assertion, seemed about to appoint a prime minister suspected by the British of sympathies with the Axis. British forces surrounded the palace, and the king capitulated. It was a humiliation that did much to promote a militant Egyptian nationalism, which the seething social problems reinforced. A decade later came the Nasser coup.

The 'national problem' now is the Israeli occupation of Egyptian territory. And the 'social problem' is all too evident. There are the multitudes who gained little or nothing from the Nasserist era: the landless labourers and the peasants with tiny plots in the countryside; the poorly paid, casually employed or totally jobless in the swelling cities. There are the many whose era it seemed for a while to be: the mass of the petty bourgeoisie who now seek some real advance in their living standards and easily resent the elite of government and the economy. There is a massive constituency for revolt against a regime which can solve neither the 'national' nor the 'social' challenges confronting it.

3

The Arab context: Lebanon; Jordan; the Palestinians

The sumptuous house, with a reception room that could comfortably have accommodated a moderate bazaar, was in a busy Beirut street, among the banks and boutiques that signified a fashionable shopping district. A white-jacketed butler opened the front door and ushered me straight into the library, where the wooden eagle on the desk and I appraised each other until my host arrived. A small dapper man, he commanded one of the major Christian parties in the Lebanon.

'We are', he explained, when the polite preliminaries were over, 'the Switzerland of the Middle East. Look at the other Arab states. They have revolutions, for democracy, for liberty. But the soldiers give the orders. And there, in the new constitutions, is Islam, always Islam. We have the one real democracy in the Arab world. We have the only secular state. And that is why we are the refuge: for Christians, Druzes, all sorts of Muslim heretics. If Islam should ever take over here, what do you think would happen? You have seen, in Beirut, the hippies, with their long hair? It is like Paris.' Switzerland, it seemed, was not enough.

'It pays everyone,' he continued, over tea. 'For the whole Arab world, this is where the rich have houses and bank accounts, and come for the shops and the bars and the cabarets. What is the result? Everywhere else in the Arab world, it is the Greeks, the Italians, the Christian Arabs, but only a very few Muslims who are rich. Here many, many Muslims have money. And even the less well-off have their television sets, their small cars. That is why we must stay as we are, a centre of trade and tourism. For what else have we got? Apples!' And he stared bleakly at me, as though I were the orchards of the Lebanon.

'I wish', said a young Marxist intellectual in Cairo some weeks later, 'that they'd stop calling Lebanon the Switzerland of the Middle East. It is the Middle East Hong Kong.' And what he implied by this comparison is plain enough. The celebrated Lebanese skyline conceals considerable squalor. Indeed, private luxury is attended by such neglect of public services as to impress the visitor's stomach no less than his eye with Lebanese shortcomings. Sufficient social acquiescence seems ultimately ensured less by what the local multitude enjoys than by what it knows or is persuaded that the multitudes elsewhere in the region suffer. The vaunted national prosperity is itself in large measure a result of regional conflicts and tensions. And the money that flows into the country for investment demands a very high return to compensate for the risks involved. Above all, the society may not be, as is Hong Kong, colonial in form; but in force it is significantly so. The Western affiliation, despite its support from Christian anxiety and entrepreneurial interest, remains perilously imposed on a component of the Arab world.

Yet the Lebanon is no Hong Kong, either. It does not continually suck in population for employment in its thriving industries. It has too little thriving industry for the job-needs of its own natives, many of whom have left in consequence to settle abroad. In fact, there are far more Lebanese living outside the Lebanon today than inside it. An Israeli parallel would suggest itself: except that Israel is still gaining in population from the Jewish Diaspora, while the Lebanese Diaspora is still gaining from the homeland.

The truth is that the Lebanon is, simply, the Lebanon of the Middle East. It is unique. Without anything approaching, proportionately, the Swiss or American industrial bases, it has a service sector that generates some 68% of the national income, compared to some 55% for the service sector in Switzerland or the United States.*

It is, primarily, a shop. More than a third of the total manufactured goods that it imports go to the outside Arab market, either as re-exports or as commodities sold at home to visitors. And it is accordingly the claim of Arab radicals that the Lebanon is merely the commercial agent of the advanced industrial West in

* 'Capital Services and the Revolutionary Party', *Socialist Lebanon*, No. 11, May 1968.

exploitation of the backward Arab hinterland. Indeed, even such Lebanese industry as exists is seen as intrinsically part of this colonial process. Producing in important measure for export, the major indigenous firms are either in partnership with foreign capital, employing foreign technicians and purchasing goods from the foreign source of investment; or manufacturing, under patent, the commodities of foreign corporations. 'Look at the figures yourself,' one Lebanese political journalist angrily advised me. 'We have a surplus in our trade with every Arab state, and a deficit with every Western one.'

But the Lebanon is also a major station in the transit trade, for raw materials, principally oil, moving from the Arab hinterland to the West, and for industrial goods moving from the West to the Arab hinterland. It is a major refuge for Arab capital, seeking a relatively safe and profitable home in real estate or bank deposits. Its proximity and common language, its abundance of uncommon entertainments and merchandise, and its carefully cultivated Western allure, make it a tourist centre for many in the middle as well as the upper reaches of income across the Arab world.

And last, its relatively liberal treatment of dissident men and ideas, makes it a refuge, too, for movements and publications, with a corresponding material as well as moral revenue. ('The regime is very clever,' complained a prominent Syrian exile with reluctant admiration. 'It lets the refugee leaders say more or less what they like, and watches results in the Lebanon. When a movement seems to be getting out of hand, the police still leave the leaders alone, but fall on the local following. And so we stay heads without bodies.') Certainly the best bookshops in Beirut are the best in the whole Middle East: with the sort of selection in the literature of the main European languages available otherwise only in Israel; with locally published Arabic books, pamphlets, magazines, pressing viewpoints so vigorously available nowhere else; and even with American or European publications of a distinct Israeli sympathy.

Being so largely parasitic, Lebanese prosperity is precarious. During the Suez war of 1956, income from services fell by 14% from the previous year's total; and in the domestic crisis of 1958, with civil war simmering between the exponents of Nasserism and the too openly West-aligned government of President Camille Chamoun, this income fell by well over a quarter of its 1957 value.

Furthermore, in an economy so dependent on the influx of capital for deposit, movement in the international money markets may have an immediate and drastic impact. When the bank rate in the United States or a major European country rises far enough, a flood of foreign money leaves the Lebanon, to produce a financial famine through the entire economy.

Yet overall, the development of the service sector has so far been such as to promote an adequate domestic acquiescence. The Lebanon has a *per capita* income more than twice that in Egypt, Syria, Jordan or Iraq.* To be sure, this encompasses enormous contrasts in living standards between rich and poor. Wages represent a mere 10% of the commercial sector's value, alongside 5% for rent and 85% for profits. But what state intervention has done in the Arab countries of the middle ideology, private capitalism has done in the Lebanon: it has produced a large petty-bourgeois constituency of support. The Lebanon has proportionately rather fewer minor bureaucrats, army officers, technicians in state economic enterprises: but it has proportionately rather more owners of small shops, restaurants, cafés, hotels; lawyers, doctors, chemists, engineers, in middle-income private practice; self-employed artisans; office clerks and shop assistants, hairdressers and taxi-drivers, waiters and touts. Together with the ranks of agricultural proprietors living above the level of subsistence and below that of the large landed estates, and with the more skilled and highly paid industrial workers, these have been the willing subjects of the major entrepreneurs in the direction of the economy.

Such an economic system is curious enough. Far more curious still is that it should have been nourished by a political system that might reasonably be considered incompatible. For the service sector, so advanced in its character and functioning, so closely connected to the international money markets and trading patterns of industrial capitalism, has developed in company with what may best be described as a political feudalism, founded on religious divisions.

The primary religious split is that between the Christians, who

* The gross national product, *per capita*, for the year 1969, in $ U.S. was: for the Lebanon, 580; for Iraq, 310; for Jordan, 280; for Syria, 260; and for Egypt, 160 (*World Bank Atlas, 1971*, published by the International Bank for Reconstruction and Development).

constitute roughly half of the total population, and the Muslims. The Christians are thus scarcely a small minority; but they have been encouraged to consider themselves as such within the wider environment of the Arab world, and as accordingly confronted by the menace of being submerged. The Muslims, on the other hand, enjoy the assurance of the wider environment, but have been encouraged to see themselves as vulnerable within Lebanon itself, to the Christian ascendancy. Furthermore, there are divisions within each of these primary groups. Other Christian sects are easily disturbed by the numerical preponderance of the Maronites; as are the Druzes and other minor Muslim communities by the numerical preponderance of the orthodox.

The divisions have been both cultivated and contained by being institutionalized. Thus, the legislature is so composed as to ensure a high measure of proportionate representation by particular community; and the proportions are largely reflected in the executive. The presidency of the republic, effectively the most powerful office, goes to a Maronite Christian; while the prime minister is a Sunni Muslim, and the president of the Chamber of Deputies is a Shi'ite one. Ministerial and civil service posts are distributed with like regard to the relative weight of each major, and minor, community.

And the communities are individually so organized as to perpetuate the system. They enjoy a substantial measure of judicial autonomy (so that, for instance, a Maronite marrying under Maronite law cannot get a divorce except by Maronite law, and hence only in the rarest of circumstances). They command the education of their young: since the vast majority of Lebanese schools are theirs. They may and often do employ their economic, as well as their political, influence to advance the loyal and chastise the troublesome among their members.

It is a system custom-made for feudal politics. Leading land-owning families in their respective districts combine their economic power and social prestige with the claim to embody and protect the dominant local religious affiliation. And, indeed, the eminences of the various major political parties in the country come in general from just such families. Even the chief social democrat, a kindly man with an addiction to Indian mysticism and the vision of a Lebanese movement triumphant 'like the British Labour Party, or

Mapai',* has his power base not in the populace of Beirut, but in a rural religious community where his family has long been prominent. And his Beirut apartment is crowded with village constituents, come to seek redress for their grievances or favours for their allegiance.

This feudal relationship has correctly been described as contractual rather than representative. The political baron is guaranteed his parliamentary seat and thus, often, a springboard to further office, in return for the benefits that he may accordingly confer: employment or promotion in the civil service or in the private sector of the economy; commercial contracts and licences; administrative or judicial indulgences; public works in his constituency; and, not least, the safeguard of communal interests.

The system has been surprisingly little affected by the massive internal migration to Beirut, in part because of the strong communal tie; in part because the Lebanon is so small that communication between the countryside and the metropolis is frequent and easy; in part because the feudal distributive arrangements themselves link the metropolis so fast to the countryside; and in part, doubtless, because the population shift has in the main been too recent for a far-reaching erosion of popular psychological attitudes, so that many of those who work and live in Beirut continue to regard themselves as primarily attached to their native rural area. Indeed they often keep a building or tiny plot of land there, to help preserve the attachment and its social role.

It is a system that has served well enough the big bourgeoisie, to which the leading feudal families belong or are profitably connected. But 'to everything there is a season'. And the preachers of business have grown increasingly impatient with a political system whose traditional, laborious functioning does not meet their peculiar devotion to efficiency. 'It is too feudal,' complained a banker, whose brother commanded one of the three major Christian political parties in the country. 'The political leadership does not represent the dominant economic interests.' Such men have not, of course, pressed for anything like displacement of the system: since this might well bring the whole social structure crashing down on their own heads. They have sought, rather, the

* The main political party of organized labour in the development of Israel.

further movement of effective power from parliament to the executive: with the emphasis on technocratic promise.

Their first important victory came in 1958 with the civil crisis over Nasserism. The manœuvres of the Chamoun administration to protect the Western interest by blocking the entry of influential Muslim politicians to parliament, produced a mounting Muslim resentment, which exploded at the moves to get Chamoun himself a second consecutive presidential term, in defiance of the rules. The settlement of General Fuad Chehab, commander-in-chief of the Lebanese army, who then served as president of the republic from 1958 to 1964, increased the number of seats in parliament to accommodate those leaders outside who enjoyed significant support, but effectively transferred much more power to the executive. A Cabinet appointed to represent, and accordingly contain, the dominant conflicting trends ruled by means of 'extraordinary legislative decrees', which automatically became law if not debated by parliament within forty days, and which were seldom referred to parliament at all. And such bypassing of the legislature in the cause of efficiency has, since, been the established treatment for symptoms of social illness.

So far, the primary symptom has been an educational one. For it is the disaffected students, in high school and university, who seem the major source of civil unrest. In part, this is because the schools themselves are so inadequate, with poor facilities and teaching standards, and with curricula of an antiquated elitism. 'We are still Napoleonic,' the then Minister of Education, one of the young technocrats, complained to me in Beirut. 'Only 10% of those in school qualify for higher education, and less than 5% find places in technical and trade schools. And what are we to do with the pressure on the few professional outlets? We have one thousand law graduates a year. One thousand!' He looked astonished at his own information. 'These feudalists must come to terms with industrial capitalism, or poverty and frustration are simply going to force a way through them.'

The truth is that the present and likely future growth of the service sector cannot satisfy the sort and extent of aspirations that Lebanese society excites. A favourite cry within the big bourgeoisie, among the technocrats and from politicians with a social democratic commitment, is 'industrialize!'. But agreement gives way to argument over who should pay for the process. The flow of investment capital into the country can scarcely be used. It only comes for the high short-term return that has been available in the service sector, especially through land and building speculation, but not generally in industrial investment: much of it, indeed, is banked in the Lebanon for withdrawal 'on demand'. And so, something less than a fifth of the total loans made by the Lebanese banks has been going into industry and agriculture combined.

The Lebanese rich themselves might reasonably be expected to meet much of the cost, through high taxes whose proceeds the government could then employ to encourage industrial development. But not only are the personal tax rates for the rich derisory; it is estimated that the state succeeds in collecting no more than a quarter of the taxes imposed.* In 1971 the twelve technocrats who, with a veteran politician as prime minister, composed the government under an avowedly reformist president, came up with the first of several projected decrees to promote the industrialization of the country. Customs duties were raised on hundreds of 'luxury items'. But that the burden should not fall too provokingly upon the rich, luxuries were apparently defined so as to include toothpaste and lavatory paper, along with Scotch whisky and fur coats. Leading merchants combined with the consumer multitude in indignation at the decree, which was hastily withdrawn. It had been compounded, the president declared, of 'mistakes, mistakes, mistakes'.

The Lebanese economy is stuck. And nowhere is the gathering revolt more evident than among those within the swollen petty bourgeoisie who find their further progress barred. Their sense of confinement is moral as well as material. Having emerged from the mental cellar of mere subsistence, they search for some meaning, personal and collective, beyond the mere engagement to consumption which their society displays; and which proclaims their own relative failure, as it proclaims their relative success. Educated beyond their opportunities, and drawn to a consumption beyond their means, many see themselves hopelessly caught in a deepening dusk of neglect. They are ready recruits to the radical ideas propagated by refugee movements, especially those of the Palestinians, in their midst.

* *The Economist,* 16 October 1971.

Indeed, albeit without the same 'national problem' of occupied territory, the Lebanon is scarcely less involved in the issue of Israel than Egypt is. To begin with, the physical Palestinian presence is proportionately far greater than in any other Arab state of the region, after Jordan itself. The number is commonly estimated at between 200,000 and 300,000, in a total population of some 2 million. Many even of those who live in the special refugee camps have been absorbed into the labour force, if only on the feudal estates. Many others, especially the more skilled, educated, articulate, live in Beirut or other urban areas, where they function in virtually all aspects of the modern Lebanese economy, from manual labour to the peaks of business and the professions.

Predictably, there are those in the Lebanese leadership who easily see and proclaim a threat in this Palestinian presence. 'They blame us and the communists, interchangeably, for any social unrest,' said one, a daughter of George Antonius.* And a former president of the republic provided more direct evidence. 'As for the Palestinian refugees,' he announced shortly, in discussing the prospects of the Lebanon, 'we cannot keep them. They upset the natural balance of the population.'

For him, all too clearly, they did. At the head of a major Christian party, and with ambition still keen, he measured the mass of those refugees as so many more Muslims for the ranks of his rivals. And besides, what but a threat must those embittered, inflammable refugees have seemed to that private principality of his: with armed guards patrolling the abundant gardens; costly hunting guns lining the study walls like an oil millionaire's parade of Impressionist pictures; and courtiers walking across the carpets with slippers on their voices, bobbing 'oui, Monsieur le President',' non, Monsieur le President', 'bien sûr, Monsieur le President'.

Even those refugees who are much more prosperous now than they ever were in Palestine, and many of whom are quick to quarrel with the self-avowed revolutionaries among their fellows, are a threat to his Lebanon. They want their homeland back; and they will not let Lebanon be, to pursue its peculiar social commitment in its traditionally circumspect way.

* Author of *The Arab Awakening* (London: Hamish Hamilton, 1937), a seminal work in the literature of Arab nationalism.

'Yes, we get tired, very tired,' said one of these in Beirut. 'But we never get quite tired enough. Some of the Palestinians here did seem at last to start thinking of themselves as Lebanese. But it wasn't deep. I remember, when Nasser made his speech in May 1967, one such man brought out and showed me the keys to his house in Palestine. He had done so well here. But all the time he had kept the keys. And now he was getting ready to go back.'

From the offices of the resistance movements in Beirut, from the university campuses, from the trades unions, the young Palestinian Left fuels young Lebanese disaffection; while other Palestinians, less radical but scarcely less articulate, press the Lebanese government to act, or not to act, as the cause of the struggle against Israel demands. And to act or not to act is a continual choice, with inescapable consequences. The Palestinian resistance groups seek to operate across the border, in Israel itself. To let them or prevent them: either course invites reprisals. And since the reprisals of the Israeli government are at present more to be feared than the reprisals of Palestinian opinion with its Lebanese support, Palestinian opinion is defied. But being so defied, Palestinian opinion assails the structure of Lebanese power, which it holds responsible, and finds allies in Lebanese discontents.

And the issue of Israel is still more pervasively there. For directly and indirectly, the development of the Lebanese economy has been largely its product. The very establishment of Israel shifted to the Lebanon the considerable transit trade that had previously used Palestine. And the success of Israel in surmounting the commitment to destroy her, with the humiliation of the Arab regimes involved, soon afterwards detonated a social upheaval in the region that sent private capital scurrying for safety to Beirut.

Yet these are rapids that run dangerously close to the rocks of war, or of peace. 'We can't have war,' one politician blandly explained to me in Beirut. 'We're too weak to protect our borders. And the social balance here is so easily upset. But then there are problems for us in peace, a real peace. Who is going to send their ships here, when they can send them to Haifa? And all those sheikhs who come to Beirut now for the bright lights and the girls, won't they go to Tel Aviv instead?' He looked at me expectantly. 'Well, then,' I said, 'how do you plan to survive?' He smiled. 'Ah, there will be no peace, and there will be no war.'

Yet it is unlikely that this state of suspended animation in the Arab–Israeli conflict, even were it feasible for long, will profit the Lebanon in the future as it has in the past. Egypt, Syria, Iraq are no longer the sources of fugitive private capital that they were, since the various measures of 'socialist' expropriation there. On the contrary: Egypt after Nasser may well succeed in attracting private capital at present lodged in the Lebanon; with the increasingly congenial terms provided by Egyptian economic policy and industrial infrastructure. Investment funds from the oil states increasingly flow straight to the more sophisticated and secure management of European banking. For rapid expansion, the transit trade requires rather more than a continuing condition of limited turbulence in the region. And Arab tourism is finding Europe less distant or costly than it supposed.

How will Lebanese society respond? Intensive industrialization might provide at least an interim economic solution. But it would require, and in the process yet further excite, profound changes in the functioning and priorities of power. And it is difficult to see how the process itself would be initiated, or long sustained, in isolation from the course of the Arab–Israeli conflict.

There, to be sure, is the essential challenge. Will the Lebanon become a battlefield, across which Israel is drawn ever further into the quicksands of conquest? Will the Lebanon join some Arab common market, to develop a new Arab nationalism on the basis of a co-ordinated economic endeavour? Will the Lebanon, even, move towards a general settlement involving a confederation with some independent Palestinian state and Israel herself: on terms that would perhaps promote the economic importance of Beirut as a port, and the political importance of the Lebanese religious balance? Such possibilities may seem extravagant. But they are, surely, at the very least no less so than that the society should continue as it is. Indeed, the question must be not whether profound social changes are soon likely in the Lebanon; nor whether such changes must burst the banks of the particular entrepreneurial nationalism that the Lebanon has made its own: but in what wider regional and ideological movement such changes, by their character, will find their place.

'It is mainly the Palestinian refugees here who are the poor and discontented,' announced the small dapper Lebanese politician with the wooden eagle on his library desk. 'And there must be a Palestinian state for them – in Jordan, on the East Bank, on the West Bank, but somewhere – with money to make it prosperous and stable. To talk of Palestine as a definite place is nonsense. The Lebanon has well over a hundred years of its own history behind it. What was Palestine but a part of Syria?'

And yet, paradoxically, it is Lebanese nationalism that now seems moribund: the pursuit and excuse of a system that has had its season; while Palestinian nationalism is an impulse to social change not only among the Palestinians themselves, but throughout the Arab world.

There can today be no reasonable doubt about who rules in Jordan, and how. It is the king, through the army. And this fact reflects the victory for the while over an insurgent Palestinian nationalism, not of a Jordanian nationalism, but of a Bedouin tribalism, served by its service to the monarchy.

The grant of independence to Transjordan by Britain in 1946, was an exercise in promotional packaging. The desert kingdom of the Hashemites, with its mainly nomadic population, and with its strategic situation as its virtually sole natural resource, had been a creature of British imperial politics in the first place. It was now translated into a client of British power, crucially dependent on economic and military support.

British policy and the ambitions of King Abdullah coincided in a resolve to prevent the emergence of an independent Arab state, which would be dominated by the Mufti of Jerusalem, from the approaching partition of Palestine. In the war that followed the end of the British Mandate and the beginning of Israel, much of the territory consigned to the Palestinian Arabs under the partition plan fell to Israeli forces. And of what was left, all but the Gaza Strip, which Egypt occupied, came under the control of Abdullah's Arab Legion. An attempt by the Mufti to establish a Palestinian government got no further than a proclamation; and, by the vote of five thousand picked notables, Abdullah became sovereign over the Palestinian territory that his troops possessed.

From the armistice signed with Israel on 3 April 1949 Jordan emerged a very different state. The number of its inhabitants had enormously increased: not only through the accession of a populous territory, but through the flight of many Palestinians from what had become Israel. Indeed, the Palestinian element now far outweighed the Bedouin among its citizens. Furthermore, the economy was transformed by the inclusion of a rich agricultural area; sites of traditional tourist traffic, particularly the old city of Jerusalem; and communities with important trading and professional components.

In 1951 Abdullah was assassinated by an agent of the Mufti; and in the following year, after the abdication of his son, Talal, his grandson Hussein succeeded to the throne. It continued to be a monarchy rather more of the divine right than of the constitutional kind. The king could appoint and dismiss governments,* dissolve both houses of parliament or simply ignore their determinations, at his pleasure. And he used his power to promote the influence and interests of the Bedouin, on whose loyalty he felt far more confidently able to rely. He appointed them to crucial posts in the army, where they predominated overall, and especially so in the more strategic units; and he encouraged the development among them of an efficient clerical class. Economically, too, the direction of policy favoured the Jordanian hinterland, where most of the industrial progress took place. While Amman swelled into a considerable city, and Irbid and Salt on the East Bank prospered, the population of Arab Jerusalem stayed much the same between 1948 and 1967, as did that of such West Bank centres as Jenin and Hebron.

Yet it is improbable that Hussein would have survived without some important Palestinian support, or at least acquiescence. The source of this lay primarily among the traditional notables of the West Bank, who kept their command of local public office along with their large land holdings; and among a Palestinian bourgeoisie of banking and commerce, which thrived in a Jordanian environment impervious to Jewish competition. For this bourgeoisie, as for the far more numerous petty bourgeois, a favourable economic climate was some consolation for the loss or lack of so much else: and such a climate was promoted by the mounting flow of foreign

* More than forty different governments served between April 1950 and December 1970.

aid;* the existence of what seemed a rare political stability by the standards of the region; and the expansion of trade with other Arab states. Collaboration was further purchased by the very frequency of government changes. Many of the prime ministers and foreign ministers, let alone the lesser fry of office, were Palestinians. And dismissal was so sweetened by payments in cash and in kind,† that the surrender of power proved on occasions even more profitable than the possession of it had been.

The multitude in the refugee camps was largely left to its sullen despair, with police spies to watch for signs of incipient revolt and to identify, for appropriate chastisement, those responsible; while the likely leaders of disaffection among the young were encouraged to pursue their studies at universities elsewhere in the Arab world, or take the lucrative employment on offer in the newly rich oil-producing states.

Above all, there appeared no credible alternative to Hashemite rule in a situation of suspended conflict where the Palestinians looked still to the liberation of the Israeli-held lands, and to the existing Arab armies as the liberators. For Hussein to keep Palestinian opinion in the country compliant, he needed on the whole only to make comforting sounds and gestures, as occasion demanded. And thus, during the 'fifties, the more formal ties with Britain were terminated, with a less overt, and somewhat less popularly obnoxious, dependence on the United States taking their place.

It was the development, initially outside Jordan, of a Palestinian commitment to partisan warfare, that was critically to intervene. Al Fatah,‡ the largest of the organizations involved, claims to have had its beginnings in 1956, when Israel occupied the Gaza Strip in the Suez war. The failure of Egyptian power, even under the leadership of Nasser, to protect the Strip persuaded several young Palestinians there of the need for a specifically Palestinian instrument of liberation. The pre-eminent member of the group,

* In 1958/9, for instance, Jordan topped the list of recipients in foreign aid *per capita*, at \$68·1: compared to \$46·8 for Israel, and such other figures as \$14·9 for Chile, \$3·8 for Pakistan, and \$1·6 for India.

† For example, large cars from the government garage.

‡ The initials of *Harakat Al-Tahrir Al-Falastini* (Movement for the Liberation of Palestine), read backwards to mean 'conquest'.

Yasser Arafat, toured the Palestinian diaspora, recruiting support; and in 1959 the ideas of the movement began receiving publicity in *Our Palestine*, a Beirut monthly. They were ideas that the victory of Algerian nationalism over France in 1962, after eight years of armed struggle, reinforced.

The ideal of Arab unity, so passionately proclaimed by Nasserist Egypt, had held for many Palestinians the promise of their own return. But the collapse in 1961 of the union between Egypt and Syria made a realization of the ideal seem far too remote; and among the young especially, a mood of disillusionment and impatience provided the apostles of an armed Palestinian struggle with a ready response. The Nasser regime sought to control this response, and promoted the establishment in 1964 of the Palestine Liberation Organization (P.L.O.), under a leadership safely devoted to the waging of war by words. The Syrian Ba'athists, confronted by a Nasserist propaganda that blamed them for the failure of the union with Egypt, saw a chance to counterattack and win popular Arab approval by placing themselves in the forefront of Palestinian militancy. Al Fatah set up its headquarters in Damascus and was supplied with military training, weapons and money. In January 1965 came its first strike at Israel.

Fearful of Israeli reprisals, suspicious of the Syrian connection, and alarmed by the possibilities of this new Palestinian militancy, the regimes of Egypt, the Lebanon and Jordan were quick to indicate their opposition to such activity. Nasserism threw its moral weight against it; and Fatah groups attempting to infiltrate into Israel were often intercepted and arrested by Lebanese or Jordanian forces. Indeed, spokesmen of Al Fatah still bitterly recite that its first fatality was suffered at Jordanian hands.

But vindication was near. The Six Day War produced such a defeat for the regular Arab armies that Palestinian faith in this instrument of restoration collapsed. The leadership of the Palestine Liberation Organization, whose rhetoric had raised hopes so high on the eve of battle, emerged on the morrow correspondingly discredited. The regimes to which the Palestinians had looked, at least for protection, had ignominiously failed. The Lebanese had not even risked involvement. Israel was on the Suez Canal and the Golan Heights. And Jordan had exchanged the West Bank, with East Jerusalem, for another multitude of refugees. To many other

Arabs, as to so many Palestinians, Al Fatah represented the one course of honour and hope.

The call to guerrilla warfare was all the more eloquent, for young educated Palestinians especially, in the intellectual climate promoted by the Vietnam war. The literature of revolutionary struggle, from Mao and Giap to Fanon and Guevara, was widely read and discussed at Western universities; and Arab students there eagerly assimilated and communicated its ideas. With the publicity given in the Arab press to the difficulties and setbacks being suffered in Vietnam by the foremost economic and military power on earth, the Palestinian exponents of guerrilla engagement found it easy to persuade themselves that Israel was far from invulnerable, and that they could repeat in the Middle East the Vietnamese experience.

In September 1967, a series of Fatah operations took place, mainly directed at towns on the West Bank, from Jordanian territory. The popular support for the movement was now such, and the Jordanian regime so demoralized since the defeat of June, that even the fear of Israeli reprisals did not provoke effective measures against the guerrillas by the Jordanian authorities. The results fell far short of guerrilla hopes. The inhabitants of the West Bank seemed generally too stunned by the sudden change in their circumstances, or perhaps too bemused by an Israeli occupation regime self-confidently less oppressive than they had expected, to associate themselves with the guerrilla undertaking; while those who did were too often discovered and harshly punished. But the very existence of such an undertaking, whose scope and impact were much exaggerated by guerrilla claims and sympathetic press reports, inevitably increased the popular prestige of the guerrilla movement in the Arab world.

Then, on 21 March 1968, came the battle of Karameh. An Israeli column, with tanks and air cover, crossed the Jordan to chastise the guerrillas and remind the Jordanian regime of Israeli might. The guerrillas, with Jordanian artillery support, stood and fought for twelve hours, and even destroyed some of the Israeli tanks. The Israeli authorities made light of the incident. And to be sure, the military significance was slight. But the emotional impact was immense. 'For the Arab states (King Hussein had his photograph taken mounted on a ruined tank), as well as for the mass of the

Palestinian people, Karameh was an act of *armed propaganda*.'*

Several thousand young Palestinians and other Arabs flocked to join the guerrilla movement, which came to constitute a formidable military presence within Jordan itself. In early November a clash between guerrillas and Jordanian security forces ended in stalemate, despite the use of Jordanian artillery, and a settlement was negotiated between Arafat and the king that underlined the arrival of a significant new force in Jordanian affairs.

Al Fatah itself was becoming a state within a state. It had not only its own substantial army, but its own hospitals, schools, social security system, departmental ministries, tax collectors, and virtually sovereign territory. Its financial resources were considerable, with annual receipts from private and government sources estimated at some £2 million sterling. In February 1969 it gained control of the Palestine Liberation Organization, with the military and financial network, and the official recognition by Arab governments, of which this disposed. But it was no longer alone in commanding the Palestinian guerrilla commitment.

Other organizations had emerged, to reflect old rivalries among Arab regimes, or the existence of a new, deep, doctrinal conflict. The Syrians, for instance, now regarding Al Fatah as too conservative, or too independent, sponsored Al Saiqa as a Ba'athist alternative; while the Iraqis, with their own version, or versions, of Ba'athist purity, backed the Arab Liberation Front. But far more important was the development of organizations professing a Marxist-Leninist revolutionary outlook.

Paradoxically, such organizations were born of the Arab Nationalist Movement, which had so largely been a Nasserist answer to the Ba'ath. With the manifest failure of Nasserism to make much progress in the Palestinian cause, however, the search for an alternative ideology had begun among members of the movement, to produce eventually two noteworthy Marxist-Leninist groups: the Popular Front for the Liberation of Palestine (P.F.L.P.) under the leadership of Dr George Habbash; and, a breakaway from this, the Democratic Popular Front for the Liberation of Palestine (D.P.F.L.P.), under the leadership of Naif Hawatmeh, which had particularly strong links with the Lebanese

* Gerard Challiand in 'The Palestinian Resistance Movement', a report published by *Le Monde diplomatique*, Paris, March 1969.

Left. It was the first of these that was to play a major part in the events of 1970 from which burst the Jordan civil war.

Though itself commanded, like Al Fatah, by intellectuals of mainly petty-bourgeois background, the P.F.L.P. held that the guerrilla war had to be made a people's war, by the mass involvement of Palestinian peasants, urban workers and refugees. Such a war, through such involvement, could only occur if it was directed at more than a mere recapture of the homeland. Its dynamic had to be the socialist restructuring of Palestinian society. Yet this restructuring could scarcely succeed in isolation. The revolution required to be spread throughout the Arab world, the proper context of the Palestinian issue.

Al Fatah, too, had revolutionary socialists amongst its leaders. But for these, the outlook of the P.F.L.P. represented a dangerous misplacement of priorities. They stood, along with colleagues of a middle and even conservative social ideology, for a broad national front, at least at this stage of the Palestinian struggle. The primary objective of liberating the homeland, could only be damaged by alienating the support of Palestinians and other Arabs for whom the doctrines of Marxism-Leninism were either incomprehensible or repugnant. While the leadership of the P.F.L.P. took the Maoist position that only a revolutionary party, 'armed with correct thought', could find and employ finally effective principles and strategy,* Al Fatah declared that party and thought would develop from the course of the struggle.

There were two more major distinctions, related to the doctrinal dispute. The P.F.L.P. emphasized the organization of cells inside the towns and villages under Israeli occupation, with base camps in Arab territory kept as small as possible. And then, in the account of an Arab analyst:

> From the beginning, the Popular Front upheld the principle of total war: if Israel used napalm to kill civilians, dynamited homes in retaliation for commando activity, and engaged in collective punishment, then the guerrillas were justified in refusing to distinguish between civilian and military targets or to limit themselves to a single kind or field of action. The

* *Al-barnamaj al-siyassiyy*, the political programme of the Popular Front, mimeographed, February 1969.

Front, as a result, concentrated on urban sabotage and on 'special' operations, such as plane hijackings and bombings in foreign countries.*

With these 'special' operations, which so spectacularly carried the Palestinian guerrilla commitment into the West and there publicized it as never before, the P.F.L.P. gained rapidly in Arab prestige, influence and recruitment. Relations among the various rival Palestinian guerrilla organizations unquestionably deteriorated as a result; with the increasing pressure on each to assert its particular purpose and efficacy; and with Al Fatah's ideal of unity revealed as the less attainable, the more that it had to be invoked.

Yet this was an especially dangerous time for such divisions. The Egyptian and Jordanian regimes were seeking a settlement in the Middle East that would restore the territory they had lost by the Six Day War, in return for their formal recognition of Israel within its pre-war borders; and they were already involved in mediation attempts by the United States government. It was a search which the guerrilla commitment necessarily opposed. The Egyptian regime of Nasser was too powerful and distant to risk much but a rage of guerrilla rhetoric. It was the Jordanian regime, therefore, which stood, and prepared, to bear the brunt of any real guerrilla challenge.

There were strong reasons why the regime should avoid a showdown. Syrian forces might cross the border, and Iraqi forces already stationed on Jordanian territory might intervene, in support of the guerrillas. The prestige of the guerrilla commitment continued to be such in the Arab world that even the conservative rulers of Saudi Arabia and Kuwait might feel impelled to cancel the financial subsidies that they had undertaken to give Jordan since the Six Day War. There was no knowing how far the Palestinians in Jordan, particularly those who constituted some 45% of the army rank-and-file, would react. And besides, the guerrillas themselves had an armed capacity that was not lightly to be dismissed.

Other factors, however, favoured a confrontation. With his own search for a settlement assailed by the guerrillas, Nasser himself,

* Hisham Sharabi, *Palestine Guerrillas: Their Credibility and Effectiveness* (Center for Strategic and International Studies, Georgetown University, 1970). Reprinted by the Institute for Palestine Studies, Beirut, June 1970, pp. 31–2.

still much the most influential figure in the Arab world, would be unlikely to embrace their cause with ardour. Nor were the guerrillas themselves as popular in Jordan as they had been, or might again become. As some of them would subsequently admit, their conduct there was far from irreproachable. The extortion of funds at gun-point; the theft and destruction of property; the arrogance of local patrols; above all, perhaps, the antagonism and even clashes between the members of different organizations: such had begun to produce, among the more prosperously situated Palestinians at least, a serious resentment. And it was a resentment less and less suppressed by confidence in the prospects of the guerrilla mission. This was not only a consequence of the deepening internal divisions, and of the mounting threat of open war between the guerrillas and the Jordanian army. The extravagance of contending claims to success in action against Israel was sapping the credibility of the mission itself.* And the Jordanian regime was doubtless, through its police spies, kept sufficiently informed of changing public attitudes.

Furthermore, the regime was under gathering pressure to act from leading Bedouins in the army, who saw the display of guerrilla power as an affront not only to the king, but through the king, to themselves. And the regime was promoting this pressure by its own propaganda. An army periodical played on Bedouin fears of Palestinian domination; emphasized the Christian background of many guerrilla leaders; and portrayed a guerrilla rank-and-file given over to rape and pillage.

An outbreak of fighting between Jordanian and guerrilla forces in June 1970 was succeeded by an uneasy settlement, frequently interrupted by incidents. Then, at the beginning of September, shots were fired as the king and his convoy passed from the palace to the airport along a stretch of road controlled by the Democratic Popular Front. The regime claimed an attempt on the life of Hussein; the leadership of the Democratic Popular Front, that the king's bodyguards had fired first. Sporadic fighting followed for a

* With undisguised bitterness, a Palestinian supporter of the guerrilla commitment complained to me later in Amman, 'If you counted up the Israeli tanks destroyed in the various communiqués, and compared the total with the number of tanks supposed to be in the Israeli army, you wondered where the extra ones had come from.'

week, in which over a hundred civilians reportedly lost their lives.*

And it was now that the most spectacular of the Popular Front special operations took place. An American airline jumbo jet was hijacked to Cairo and blown up on the ground. Soon afterwards, a jet from another American airline and one belonging to Swissair were hijacked to Dawson's Field, a desert strip some forty miles from Amman, where they were joined by another hijacked jet, from a British airline. Passengers and planes were held as hostages for the release of Popular Front guerrillas in foreign prisons or custody;† while Jordanian forces, positioned around, were restrained by the guerrilla threat to blow up passengers and planes if they attacked. The central committee of the Palestine Liberation Organization itself demanded the immediate release of passengers and planes; but this only occasioned a display of its impotence. The Popular Front rejected the demand and destroyed the planes.

It is probable that to the sense of humiliation felt by the king, the palace bureaucracy, and the army command, were added powerful promptings from Western governments to act decisively against the guerrillas. And indeed, while negotiations over the hostages were still proceeding, the king formally handed over government to the army, and large-scale fighting broke out between the Jordanian forces and the guerrilla organizations.

How many Palestinian casualties there were remains a matter of dispute. Within a few days, the temporarily united guerrilla movement accused the regime of 30,000; while the regime itself admitted to 1,500. Neither was to do its credibility much good in consequence. The figure was certainly large. The main guerrilla posts were situated in the midst of the refugee camps or of Amman and other towns; so that civilian concentrations came under ferocious fire. And there was a particular element in the assault by the Jordanian forces. Several independent observers in Jordan at the time recall that the soldiers seemed intent on smashing up as much of Amman as they could. 'It was', said one, 'as though the

* *The Economist*, 12 September 1970.

† Guerrillas were held in Israeli, Swiss and West German prisons; and Leila Khaled was held in British custody after her unsuccessful attempt to hijack a jet belonging to El Al, the Israeli airline. The hostages eventually got home, as did, in return, the Popular Front guerrillas held by the Swiss, West Germans and British.

Bedouin were at last getting their own back on a society that they thought so scornfully hostile to theirs.'

Such was claimed by at least one Fatah report.* A captured brigadier at Irbid was asked by the guerrillas how he could have ordered his men to destroy their own cities and people. 'They are not our cities or our people,' he replied. 'We are from the desert, and when we have won we will return there.'

In the event, it was a victory for the Jordanian regime. The Iraqi forces in the country did not intervene; and the Syrians intervened only to be beaten back across the border. The Palestinians within the army remained loyal; and those without were generally too occupied in attempting to survive the cross-fire for any expression of opinion. By early October the Arab governments had jostled the warring parties into some agreement, from which the Jordanian regime emerged manifestly much stronger than before.

Yet the victory was far from complete. The guerrilla movement still disposed of a considerable capacity and might well have recovered. It was in the aftermath, rather, that it suffered its major defeat. 'How easily', a foreign diplomat in Amman observed a few months afterwards, 'the resistance could have played on the king's sense of guilt, and on Arab public opinion, to restore its situation; perhaps with advantage. But in the end it defeated itself. The king has a clear, simple logic. But what is the logic of the resistance? It has several conflicting ideologies. Its unity is again in shreds. And the more plainly unable it has been to make headway against Israel, the more extravagant its claims have become. It is simply no longer believed.'

And to be sure, instead of reinforcing their new-found unity after the September fighting, the guerrilla organizations fell to contending against one another again, if anything, with yet more acrimony; while the leadership of Al Fatah itself was cracked by faction. Moreover, without the means sufficiently to defend themselves, let alone overthrow the Jordanian regime, they provided it with abundant pretexts to strike at them. In the months that followed, sporadic clashes occurred. And then in July 1971, the Jordanian army assaulted and destroyed the last centres of guerrilla resistance in the hills north-west of Amman. The government

* Cited in *The Economist*, 26 September 1970.

claimed 2,300 prisoners, who were held in camps for the separation of 'true guerrillas' from those dedicated to overthrowing the regime. Some of those who escaped, swam the Jordan and surrendered themselves to the Israelis. And if this may not have said very much for their morale, it said still less for the treatment that they expected at fraternal Jordanian hands.

When I visited Amman in March 1971, the palace bureaucracy was already riding high: confident of its control over the country, and contemptuous of the residual guerrilla capacity. 'I was one of the few optimists in September,' said one leading Bedouin official. 'The guerrillas thought that the army would split. But I knew that it wouldn't. We are, in the army, and here in the palace, more and more representative of the country. This is not just because the Bedouin now realize that their own survival depends on the survival of the regime. There is a new Jordanian nationalism.' He looked at me triumphantly. 'It wasn't always so. We used to be as loyal to the ideal of Arab unity as anyone. Many of our prime ministers were not born here. It was the guerrillas who pushed us into a sense of our particular identity.'

The triumph was all too evident in the mood of the soldiers patrolling the city and the roads through the desert beyond. But a Palestinian who had served in several important posts, including the premiership, contemplated the dark side of the mood. 'The regime relies now as never before on the army. And the army knows it. Worse, the army has been put in the cities, to deal, like police, with the people. From a force looking outwards, across the borders of the country, it has become a force looking inwards, at the citizens themselves. How long, under such conditions, will all this so-called stability last?'

Another Palestinian, an engineer in Amman, was more direct. 'We cannot go on submitting to this regime. They talk of allowing a national government one day. But what is the use of a national government when the king sleeps on a pea, and because he has had a bad night changes his prime minister in the morning?'

Such complaints pointed to a major victim of the September events and their aftermath: the alliance between the regime and an influential Palestinian element. There are now rather fewer among the Palestinian bourgeoisie in Jordan willing openly to associate themselves with a regime that has proved so punishing to their countrymen, however deplored the conduct of these countrymen may have been.

And the present condition of the Jordanian economy is such as to permit little purchase beyond support for the material privileges of the bureaucrats and soldiers. It is not only the loss of the West Bank in itself. As a consequence of that loss, and of the intermittent civil strife, the Jordanian Treasury is no longer fat with travellers' cheques. The day I went to Petra, I was the only visitor. 'We used to have two and even three hundred tourists a day,' said the guide mournfully. 'We will be lucky if we have two or three hundred in the whole of this year.'

More than half the country's revenue is now in the form of foreign assistance: compared to a quarter in 1956. The financial subsidies that Jordan received from oil-rich Arab states in the aftermath of the Six Day War have been reduced by the withdrawal of Libya and Kuwait, in protest at the treatment of the guerrillas. And by far the largest supplier today is the United States, which is also responsible for much of the direct military aid to the regime. It is a source of support all too vulnerable to the pressures of Israeli interests. Furthermore, the borders with Syria and Iraq are sporadically closed, with damaging effects on trade. Indeed, without the increasing clandestine traffic through Israeli hands, as in the export of certain agricultural products, the Jordanian economy would be even more stricken than it is.

The regime is dangerously isolated in the Arab world. This does not mean that it has cause to fear the military capacities of Syria or Iraq; or to expect more than expressions of distaste from the Egyptian regime, which has little desire to see a truculent guerrilla resurgence. But the economic consequences must be cumulatively dismaying; and the mental and moral ones, scarcely less so.

Not least, such isolation enormously weakens Jordanian bargaining power in the manœuvres towards a Middle East settlement. Even in the spring of 1971, high officials of the regime revealed, within the elation at their domestic triumph, the fear of a deal in which Jordanian interests would be sacrificed by other Arab states.

Clearly, the regime has lost much of its importance for the Israelis as a likely bridge to an accommodation with the Arab world. And here there has been a further fall-out from the conflict with the guerrillas. It is not only that the end to a serious guerrilla presence in Jordan has deprived the regime of a valuable card to play in negotiations. Paradoxically, Israeli public opinion, far from esteeming the regime for its victory over the guerrillas, was instead outraged by the cost. In the predominant Israeli mood of fervent nationalism, the massacre of Arabs by Arabs seemed a monstrous betrayal of kinship. And perhaps in this there was, too, a compassion for the Palestinians all the greater for having been guiltily suppressed so long by the Jews themselves in the establishment and protection of their state. At all events, the former regard for Hussein, already shaken by his involvement in the Six Day War, gave place among many Israelis to a distaste, even contempt, for the scourge of the Palestinians.*

But perhaps the paramount loss that the regime has suffered in its very triumph has been that of its residual hold over the hopes of its one-time subjects on the West Bank. The Palestinians there might still long and look to escape Israeli rule. But they are plainly not as willing as once they were to change it for the protection of Hussein. They displayed small enthusiasm for his plan, proposed in March 1972, to unite the West Bank and the Gaza Strip with the East Bank, in some federal arrangement under Hashemite rule. And in the unlikely event that such an arrangement were to be imposed upon them, it is all too likely that they would prove to be troublesome subjects.

Finally, the guerrilla movement may be broken in body and mind, but it is far from dead. With the right treatment, self-applied, it may soon enough recover. And its recovery might then prove rather more dangerous to the Jordanian regime than to Israel. For there is a hatred of the regime within the guerrilla ranks now that will lead to a reckoning. As ever, what will happen in Jordan will crucially depend on the Palestinian context.

The story is told of a donkey in the old city of Jerusalem. Its owner was standing in the bazaar when a trader approached and asked if he could hire it for a trip to Damascus. 'Yes, of course,' said the owner. 'A pity,' interrupted a second trader. 'I need it for a trip

* How far he may restore this regard by his condemnation of Arab terrorism remains to be seen. But Israelis pride themselves on being realists. And they know what Hussein has to fear from such terrorism himself. The first notable victim of the Black September group was the Jordanian prime minister.

to Cairo.' And the owner replied, 'Well, then, use the donkey as soon as it gets back.' A third trader stopped and asked if he could hire the donkey for a trip to Amman. 'By all means,' said the owner. 'It is going now to Damascus, and then to Cairo. But afterwards you can take it where you like.' The donkey is the Palestinian people. Everyone wants to take it somewhere, and no one bothers to ask it where it wants to go.

The story, as I heard it, does not say who the owner is. But it is surely the traditional leadership of the Palestinians, which has hired them out to one lost cause after another.

It is a good story. But as often with such good stories, it misses one important point in making another. For the Palestinian donkey has begun to see itself as such; resent its condition; and assert a personality.

'There was no such thing as Palestinians [when the Jews came to Palestine],' Golda Meir, the Israeli prime minister, explained in a celebrated remark. 'It was not as though there was a Palestinian people and we came and threw them out and took their country away from them. They did not exist.'*

There were people living in the country, of course; and it is to be supposed that even Mrs Meir would concede this. Indeed, what is appalling was the implication, the very purpose of her remark, that the displacement of other people in Palestine mattered less, or not at all, because they lacked a specific Palestinian identity. Was it not just such subjugation of a humanist to a nationalist morality that caused so much suffering to the Jews themselves in an exile among assertive nation-states?

Yet this aside for the while, the explicit contention of the remark must be examined. And here Mrs Meir was on somewhat firmer ground. For the weight of available evidence suggests that the indigenous inhabitants of Palestine during the decades of Zionist settlement regarded themselves as belonging to entities both much smaller and much larger than a Palestinian one.

There was a strong affiliation to the immediate context of a town or set of villages. And even today this affiliation, in the very process of being assimilated to a national consciousness, vigorously persists. There is in the United States, for instance, an active association of emigrants from Ramallah, who meet to exchange news of

* Interview in *The Times*, 15 June 1969.

the town and raise funds for public projects there. In Beirut I met an eminent Palestinian whose life is devoted to the advancement of the Palestinian cause. Yet in talking of the lost homeland, he expressed most movingly his attachment to Tiberias, where he had been born and had grown up, and where his family had lived for generations.

The wider affiliation, which for so long pre-empted a sense of Palestinian identity, was to Arab nationalism. This was based on an identity of language, culture, and – for the vast majority, at least – religion. But it became as well, especially for the thrusting classes of land-owners, traders and those in the professions, a political identity, as Western imperial expansion into the Middle East drove the Ottoman empire defensively to impose the Turkish language and culture, with tight centralized government, on its loosely associated Arab provinces. And to this political identity the Palestinian Arabs hopefully looked, when confronted by the development of the Zionist idea.

It was a hope that would be continually betrayed. In the bitter recital of an Israeli Arab:

> The (one-time) Prime Minister of the Iraqi government, Nuri Es-Said, became a millionaire by trading in cattle with the Jews of Palestine while bragging about how he would liberate Palestine from Zionism. Similar attitudes prevailed among many other leaders in Lebanon, Syria, and Trans-Jordan who, in spite of an Arab agreement to boycott the Zionists and not sell land to them, sold their estates in Upper Galilee, Hula, Marj Ben Amer, and the coastal region to Jews. The feudal Palestinian leaders were nearly all collaborators with the Jews for personal economic and political profit.*

The ensuing story of the failures evidenced by Arab nationalism is well enough known. It includes the shabby treatment of Palestinian refugees, so many of whom were placed in special camps at least as much from the reluctance of Arab regimes to bear the burden or run the risk of their decent assimilation, as for the purpose of keeping the issue of their violated rights alive.

* Atallah Mansour, 'Palestine: the Search for a New Golden Age', *New York Review of Books,* 7 October 1971.

There has, thus, developed a sense of Palestinian identity perforce. And who better than the Israelis themselves should see and appreciate this? It was in reaction against the anti-Semitic aspect of European nationalisms in the second half of the nineteenth century that modern political Zionism had its primary impulse. Theodore Herzl himself, the man now revered by Israel as its pre-eminent founding father, was moved by the Dreyfus trial to discard his cosmopolitan outlook and pose an answer to the Jewish question in the establishment of a Jewish state. And, albeit at a horrifying cost, nothing nourished the realization of his objective as much as German nationalism running amok under Hitler.

How ironic, perhaps inevitable, that so many Palestinians should have begun to find a model for their nationalism in the Jewish nationalism whose success was their own defeat. So many Jews, after all, were similarly moved: to make for themselves a nation-state, in accordance with the very concept that had cost them so much. And like it or not, Israelis may see today in the eyes of enmity the reflection of their own past.

A foreign diplomat in Amman, prominent in negotiations for the release of hostages held by the Popular Front at the Jordan Hotel in September 1970, remembers having met Dr George Habbash striding about outside. 'Al Fatah', Dr Habbash had declaimed, 'is the Haganah. We of the Popular Front—we are the Irgun. And that', he had waved an arm in the direction of the hotel, 'is the King David.'*

The eminent Palestinian in Beirut who yearned for Tiberias put it more patiently. 'It is not only the Arab governments that evade any real commitment to the Palestinians; it is public opinion in

* Haganah was the secret Jewish army, founded in the early 1920s, and associated with the Jewish Agency. In 1935 the Revisionists, who stood for a more aggressive Zionist approach towards both the Arabs and the British Mandate, separated from the World Zionist Organization; and two years later, founded the Irgun Tsva'i Leumi (National Military Organization) as their armed force. Though the Irgun co-operated with the Haganah from time to time, it placed a distinctive emphasis on the use of terrorism. And though the evidence suggests that the Haganah was in accord with at least the principle of such action, it was the Irgun alone that was responsible for blowing up a wing of the King David Hotel in Jerusalem, a floor of which was being used as British Army Headquarters, in July 1946. Ninety-one people were killed, and forty-five wounded; with Jews and Arabs as well as British among the victims. One-time Irgun Commander Menachem Begin is now leader of Gahal, the chief opposition group in the Israeli Knesset.

their countries as well. What are we to do? We are the new Jews. And an Arab Zionism is our only hope.' He sighed and shook his head. 'It will take a long time. Perhaps it is for our children's children to do it. They will not forget. They will keep their identity, as the Jews before Israel did. Because they will not be accepted; as we are not; as the Jews were not. In Kuwait, you know, some of us are doing very well. And it is said of us there: "They are loyal, they are good citizens. But still they are Palestinians." And how different is it anywhere else? Where it is different, it is worse.'

But the Jews had a book, I said. It helped to keep them together. It fed their hope, even those who did not believe in Jehovah, with the Jerusalem of the psalms, with the recital of exile and return. 'No, we haven't got the book,' he replied. 'But we have a sort of tribal memory for places: for Jaffa, for Nablus, for Tiberias. We pass it on to our children, so that they should see each place as we saw it. And our children pass it on in turn to theirs. We carry our psalms about in our own minds. And we have our poets, who write of the places they have lost.'

Reality is rather less pat. An Arab Zionism must encounter different difficulties, seemingly even more formidable than those that Jewish Zionism did. The lost homeland is inhabited by a people far more cohesive, organized, self-assured, and politically, economically, militarily, far more powerful, than were the Arabs when confronted by the Jews. Nor does there exist an external suzerainty comparable with the British Mandate, whose strength and weakness might be exploited to undermine the position of the indigenous majority. Indeed, it is impossible to see how, in any at all likely circumstances, an Arab Zionism would triumph.

For such a Zionism is the confrontation of one exclusive nationalism by another; and in this confrontation, the Jews must see themselves allowed a choice only between the survival of their own nationalism and their subservience, individually and collectively, to the nationalism of others. They are certainly offered no alternative by the ideology of Al Fatah.

The Sixth of the Seven Points, proclaimed by the central committee of Al Fatah in January 1969, declared: 'Since Palestine forms part of the Arab fatherland, Al Fatah, the Palestine National Liberation Movement, will work for the State of Palestine to contribute actively towards the establishment of a progressive and united Arab society.'

After that, the Fifth Point, with its promise of an 'independent, democratic State of Palestine, all of whose citizens will enjoy equal rights irrespective of their religion', sounds all too hollow.

Interviewed some months subsequently, Yasser Arafat made matters worse in attempting to mend them.

> A democratic, progressive state in Palestine is not in contradiction to that state being Arab ... Such a state can only acquire stability and viability by forming a part of the surrounding area, which is the Arab area. Otherwise this state with its Jewish, Christian and Muslim citizens would be another alien and temporary phenomena [*sic*] in the area, which will arouse the antagonism of its neighbours, exactly as did the first Jewish state and the Crusaders' state ...
>
> The word 'Arab' implies a common culture, a common language and a common background. The majority of the inhabitants of any future state of Palestine will be Arab, if we consider that there are at present 2,500,000 Palestinian Arabs of the Muslim and Christian faiths [i.e. within and beyond Israeli borders] and another 1,250,000 Arabs of the Jewish faith who live in what is now the state of Israel.*

What is revealed here is both a confusion of concepts and a resolute refusal to face facts. Palestinian Arabs may conceive of themselves as Arabs of Muslim or Christian faith; and of Jews only as Arabs or foreigners of Jewish faith. But the Jewish identity embodied in Israel has been far less a religious than a national assertion. And nowhere is this more evident, indeed, than among those whom Arafat calls the '1,250,000 Arabs of the Jewish faith': those Israelis whose parents, or who themselves, have come from Arab states. Such of them who attach much importance to Jewish religious doctrine represent probably as small a minority as exists among Israelis of European and American origin. But they are in general even more fervently attached to a Jewish national identity that would dissociate them from an Arab one.

This should by itself, surely, be enough to make a dangerous

* Interview published in *Free Palestine*, August 1969.

nonsense of any belief in '1,250,000 Arabs of the Jewish faith'. For identity is at least as much a subjective as an objective realization. But further, by Arafat's own definition of 'Arab', the objective factors are increasingly invalid. Continuously, for these 1,250,000 Israelis, the Arab background recedes, and use of the Arab language diminishes. For a rapidly increasing proportion, born in Israel, the Arab background and language are now totally foreign. And for all, in varying degrees, Arab culture has been vigorously displaced.

But this confusion of concepts and refusal to face facts are faults that run virtually throughout the Palestinian commitment to armed struggle. If the foreign diplomat in Amman was recounting correctly, Dr George Habbash himself provided an extreme example. For how should the Popular Front, with its Marxist-Leninist principles, be equated with the Irgun, which was an organization essentially of the ideological Right in the development of Jewish nationalism? And how should the conditions of struggle by Palestinian Arabs today against another nationalism firmly established in the homeland, be equated with the conditions of struggle by Jews against the infirm imperialism of the British Mandate?

The truth is that this search for comforting parallels constitutes an endemic preoccupation with rhetoric, which itself betrays the failure to develop an effectual strategy of armed struggle. The Chinese communists did not merely repeat the Russian experience. Indeed, the belief that they should was a Russian obsession which cost the Chinese revolutionaries dear while it prevailed. The Chinese made their own peasantry-based revolution, as the course of their struggle dictated. Similarly the Vietnamese have not sought simply to imitate the Chinese revolution, but to develop from their own conditions an appropriate strategy. A Palestinian struggle is nothing if it is not particular, in the problems it confronts and the solutions it must find.

The evasion of such problems or the inability to develop the proper solutions is most evident in the ideological mannequin-parade. With the conspicuous failure of Nasserism in the Six Day War, there began a sort of contest in Leftism to catch the eye of popular support. Leaderships which themselves were predominantly petty bourgeois and till recently Nasserist, displayed a collection of ideas that condemned Nasserism and the role of the petty bourgeoisie.

> The national struggle reflects the class struggle. The national struggle is a struggle for land and those who struggle for it are the peasants who were driven away from their land. The bourgeoisie is always ready to lead such a movement, hoping to gain control of the internal market. If the bourgeoisie succeeds in bringing the national movement under its control, which strengthens its position, it can lead the movement under the guise of a peaceful solution into compromises with imperialism and Zionism.
>
> Therefore, the fact that the liberation struggle is mainly a class struggle emphasizes the necessity for the workers and peasants to play a leading role in the national liberation movement. If the petty bourgeoisie take the leading role, the national revolution will fall as a victim of the class interests of this leadership. It is a great mistake to start by saying that the Zionist challenge demands national unity, for this shows that one does not understand the real class structure of Zionism.

This passage from the 'Platform of the Popular Front'* is a fair sample of ideas whose principle feature is their *extrinsic* quality: the generalizations of developed Marxist revolutionary thought applied to the Palestinian experience, rather than a Palestinian revolutionary thought developed out of the interplay between the Palestinian experience and the general principles of Marxism.

What field-work, for instance, has been done by the guerrilla organizations themselves into the social structure of the Palestinian people? Their publications, and the clichés of their spokesmen, suggest very little. And, if anything, still less has been done to analyse the 'real class structure of Zionism'. Certainly the nature of Israeli society as I encountered it in the talks I had with various representatives of the Palestinian revolutionary commitment, missed far more than it caught of the society that I subsequently encountered direct.

* 'Platform of the Popular Front for the Liberation of Palestine', reprinted in *The Israel–Arab Reader*, ed. Walter Laqueur (Harmondsworth: Penguin Books, 1970), p. 454.

Even Jordanian society, which the Palestinian partisan organizations essentially sought to associate with their strategy against Israel, seems never to have been seriously analysed by those for whom social analysis was supposedly a prerequisite of struggle. There were Bedouin bureaucrats in the Basman Palace whose analysis of social relationships in Jordan, and their political implications, seemed at the time more authentic than that of leading guerrillas in Amman. And subsequent events have scarcely demonstrated that this impression was mistaken.

The reliance on rhetoric has been a refuge from reality. I was taken in early 1970, during my stay in the Lebanon, to visit a Popular Front military training centre and several of the organization's offices in refugee camps. Had the organization itself believed in the trustworthiness of the Lebanese authorities, I would have found the approach to security careless enough. But the Popular Front had repeatedly made clear its distrust of the Lebanese authorities, and the incompatibility of its own aspirations with the nature of the Lebanese regime. It had proclaimed as a central principle the need to revolutionize the Palestinian context, which inevitably included the Lebanon. And there it was, conducting so many of its operations so openly, ostentatiously even, that the Lebanese intelligence services could not but know on whom to swoop as circumstances required. It seemed as suicidal as the hardly less casual talk of turning Jordan into another Hanoi, from a base in the mountains: a commitment which was to prove all too costly in the period that followed.

Of course, this did not mean that all activity was so prepared and promoted. The 'special' operations of the Popular Front achieved their immediate purposes because they were so mounted as to have surprised their targets. And in the Gaza Strip, where a secret network of militants had been developed, the Popular Front long pursued the limited objective of terrorism with a success that Israeli intelligence admitted. But special operations did not, it was soon enough apparent, make a revolutionary war. Nor did the terrorism in the Gaza Strip: a political engagement whose relative success owed much, if not all, to the unique experience and conditions of the Strip's population.

Indeed, terrorism is less an instrument of revolutionary warfare than a substitute for it. Dramatic acts may catch the headlines, but quickly lose them; and merely catching them again becomes an end in itself. The issue may be kept alive; but at the cost of staying where it is.

To be sure, there can be few, if any, organizations in the world dedicated to revolutionary warfare that face such difficulties as do the Palestinian.* And not least among these difficulties is that the Palestinian people, who should be to the revolutionaries as, in the celebrated comparison, water is to fish, constitute three major entities. There are those within the statutory borders of Israel, who possess Israeli citizenship; there are those in the Israeli-occupied territories, with a citizenship in suspense; and there are those, with or without citizenship, in the various independent Arab states. Nor is this by any means the end of the divisions. In an interplay of objective and subjective factors, the Arabs of East Jerusalem, despite their incorporation into the Israeli capital, must be seen as distinct from other Arabs in Israel, while the status of the city remains a serious source of international dispute and credibly a counter in negotiations for a Middle East settlement. The situation on the West Bank is significantly different from that in the poor, densely populated Gaza Strip. The Palestinians in Jordan have had a social experience largely unlike that of Palestinians in, say, the Gulf States. And then there are the social divisions within a single territorial entity: as between the Palestinian merchants or doctors in Beirut and their fellow refugees in the camps near the Syrian or Israeli borders; or, indeed, as between the traditional leadership in the occupied territories and the new proletariat of migrant labour.

The Israeli government has, despite its much avowed devotion to democratic principles, not been beyond making use of local authoritarian precedent. It left to acquiescent officials, previously elected under the Jordanian regime, control over customary administration. In the spring of 1972, it held municipal elections on the West Bank that conformed to the Jordanian law of 1955 and accordingly restricted the franchise to a traditional elite of tax-payers, or some 10% of the population in the relevant towns. Hostile incidents were few, despite the opposition from Palestinian resistance movements abroad; and the voting turn-out suggested a

* See Chapter 1 for an exposition of some of these.

considerable measure of compliance by the social elements involved.

This does not mean, of course, that a common sense of specific Palestinian identity has failed to develop. What it does mean, is that this sense of identity does not everywhere seek to manifest itself in the same way and for the same identified objectives. Nearly all Palestinian Arabs may yearn for the disappearance of Israel and the restoration to them of all the lands that they once inhabited. But experience has taught many of them that this yearning may prove a trap, in which the refusal to accept any less becomes the occasion for losing even more.

The establishment of a viable Israel and its subsequent expansion have largely resulted from an Arab leadership of blind intransigence. In 1922 the British government proposed a Legislative Council of nine Muslim Arab, three Christian Arab, and three Jewish members, all elected; with eleven officials. Given the sympathies of the British officials, and the size of the Jewish community, at the time, the Arabs in Palestine might well have used the Council as the lever to achieve an independent Palestinian state, in which the Jews would have been kept, with the appearance of democratic processes, a manageable minority. Weizmann agreed to the proposal, in the teeth of right-wing Zionist opposition. The Arab leadership rejected it, demanding a constitution that revoked the Balfour Declaration entirely and stopped all alien immigration.

In 1937 the Peel Commission proposed a partition of Palestine which would have given the Jews a state about a third the size of that subsequently granted by the U.N. The Zionist Congress, to save and settle the Jews of Europe menaced by Nazism, seemed sufficiently drawn to acceptance. The Arab leadership in Palestine dismissed the proposal out of hand. Yet such a partition would have produced an Israel so vulnerable that it would have been able neither to expand nor, probably, to survive for very long.

In 1938, the Woodhead Commission again proposed partition, and with a Jewish state much smaller still, or only some 400 square miles in extent. The British government used the report to call an Arab-Jewish Conference at London in early 1939. 'The Jews made it clear that the Peel proposals which they regarded as inadequate, were as far as they were prepared to, or indeed could, go in concession if they were to represent Zionism. The Arabs were prepared for no concessions of any kind ... '* They simply refused to sit at the table with Jewish delegates. The British government, reportedly supported by the French, even considered conceding in return for Arab agreement to a small Jewish state, that long-professed aim of Arab nationalism: the uniting of the area of modern Syria, Lebanon, Palestine and Transjordan in single self-government.

> The prospect of the National Home as a canton in a large independent Arab state, once so acceptable to Zionists ... now filled most of the Zionists with misgiving ... They were in considerable doubt as to how to escape from this untimely gift, but, as on previous occasions, they did not need to place themselves in an unfavourable light by resisting a theoretically reasonable proposition, as the Arabs did the resisting for them.†

The United Nations vote in November 1947 for the partition of Palestine was greeted by dancing in the streets of Tel Aviv; though it provided for a Jewish state of three segments joined to one another at little more than points, and containing an Arab minority so large as to constitute an enormous potential of pressure on the functioning of an Israeli democracy. The armistice lines of 1949 left an Israel with its territory increased, most importantly where the three segments had before so precariously met; and with an Arab population much diminished by flight. After the Six Day War, the 1949 armistice lines, let alone the Israeli borders of the United Nations plan, seemed for many Palestinian Arabs a desirable contrast to their new situation.

And there was another defeat to come: that of the hopes raised so high by the Palestinian guerrillas. It was a defeat all the more harrowing for having been suffered not at Israeli hands, but at the hands of an Arab army, and ultimately with the help of the guerrillas themselves, through their divisions and overreached capacities.

What tendencies are likely to emerge as dominant from Palestinian Arab disillusionment, no one can know. But certainly there

* Christopher Sykes, *Cross Roads to Israel* (London: Collins, 1965), p. 231.
† Ibid., p. 232.

is now a new impatience with postures that promise swift and absolute deliverance. There has begun a questioning that is essentially a creative process. And the answer may well lie in a combination of compromise and struggle, distinct from and involved with developments across the Arab world.

Such an answer will belong to a movement that is quick to learn alike the real resources of its people and the real weaknesses of the enemy; that claims only what it can demonstrate and promises only what it can deliver; that develops an ideology from within the experience of the particular Palestinian predicament; that comes to represent a united commitment, because it emerges from a dynamic communication between leadership and populace, and because its success makes any rival seem merely disruptive.

For the emergence of such a movement, Israel itself will necessarily write part of the scenario. Is there to be a sort of satellite Palestinian state established on the West Bank; its economy dominated by Israel, with many of its citizens driven to commute for employment there; its politics commanded by Israeli demarcations of security? With an economic advance encouraging consciousness of the limitations reflected in its very attainments, such a subservience would be a recipe for revolutionary endeavour. And what of the Arabs living within Israel itself? Will those a present conciliated by rising material standards be thrust into tota disaffection by a Jewish nationalism that concedes the form bu denies the force of equal citizenship?

Will Israelis themselves so react to Palestinian terrorism as t turn it from a substitute for revolutionary warfare into an instru ment? If the terrorists produce an enraged response of repressiv violence; a consideration of all Arabs as collectively to be distruste and chastised; an engagement to revenge and victory rather tha to reason and the search for a compassionate peace: then they wi promote alike the self-mutilation of Israeli society and the revolu tionary challenge to it.

Part of the Palestinian scenario must be written, too, by th independent Arab states. Will their various regimes so fail t accommodate the needs and aspirations of their peoples as t excite a revolutionizing of the Palestinian context? Such a proce would not have to be, and almost certainly could not be, dom nated by Palestinian communities in these countries. But the ommunities would doubtless be influential participants in movements that seemed likely to succour the Palestinian cause.

And this again points to the need for the major impulse: a alestinian movement able to unite the overwhelming mass of the alestinians in their separate communities for a single struggle. The Palestinians are a conservative people,' said one of them in eirut. 'But they are conservative because they look to their aders, and their leaders have always been a conservative lot.' nd perhaps the Palestinian people will remain conservative until aders emerge to make the most radical departure of all, in itiating a real communication with them.

From this communication may even come, to manifest the alestinian identity, a Palestinian Zionism as inclusive as the resent commitment to Arab Zionism is an exclusive one. And om such a development, perhaps, the Jewish identity may be rawn from its own exclusive commitment, towards a sense of ommon Palestinian purpose. For surely in the end only a common lentity, realized albeit by stages in a common society, will romote the free and creative identities of both peoples.

4

Israel between worlds

The Jewish people in their own state are increasingly confronting themselves in a crisis of identity. And first of the choices that challenge them is no less than that between God and Man: between the religious and the secular, ultimately socialist vision.

The very genesis of a Jewish identity was a religious commitment. The original tribes were themselves an 'ethnic conglomerate',* with a culture composed of elements largely borrowed from peoples among whom they had lived and intermarried. The Babylonian, Canaanite, Egyptian civilizations contributed much not only to their technology and social organization, but even to the myths and vocabulary of their characteristic worship.† For it was their worship that essentially characterized them.

The basis of religion in all other cultures of the time was polytheism, or the deification of various natural phenomena. Sun, sea, wind, dawn were gods or goddesses. And such gods or goddesses were true personifications: some good, some bad, some more powerful than others, and most of them more powerful than the most powerful of men; but all with human attributes. They needed food, made love, grew old and even died; though sometimes to be resurrected, as fate required. For it was fate alone that was ultimately absolute; that was the defining force of the universe. This did not mean that events were invulnerable to influence. The practice of magic, which so dominated pagan religion, could invoke divine intervention: to produce rain, heal

* The phrase is Yehezkel Kaufmann's, from his study of the Biblical Age in *Great Ages and Ideas of the Jewish People*, ed. Leo W. Schwarz (New York: Random House, 1956).

† Babylonian myths on the Creation, the Flood and the Tower of Babel, for instance; such Canaanite features as the wine libation and cult of prophesying and even words for the divine, like *'elyon* (most high) and *'adon* (lord); Egyptian influences in traditional wisdom, hymnal literature, magical signs, and of course the whole experience of the sojourn in servitude.

illness, bring victory in battle. The gods themselves were supreme magicians. But no magic could alter the crucial resolutions of fate, the individual nature of god and man alike.

Tragedy is thus the proper product of pagan religion and of the cultures that this religion informed. The struggle of man or god against his fate is the tragic concept. And paradoxically, therefore, the Jewish experience, though surely unequalled in suffering and calamity, has not, in peculiarly Jewish terms, been a tragic one.

For the peculiar Jewish vision was of a universe informed not by fate but by a unique divinity. God was ageless, sexless, timeless and totally free. He was the God of good and the God of evil, since all creation came from Him. Magic was no cause, but only a sign of His intervention. Moses and Aaron were mere agents of the wonders that God employed before the face of Pharaoh. Above all, along with divine came human freedom. God had created man in His image, to do good or evil, by obeying or disobeying His commandments. And history became the drama of free human will: the defiance of God's word by man's pride or greed or impatience or stupidity; with the retributions of flood and fire that this disobedience brought; in a conflict that would end only with the ending of human time. Indeed, as tragedy was the pagan interpretation of human experience, history as a moral record, moving towards a conclusive meaning, was first and foremost the Jewish one.

This new vision of the universe, this new vision of history, had an impact similar to that which Muhammed's religious message would subsequently have on the Arabs. It consolidated the tribes of Israel into a single people, with a formidable, albeit precarious, political and military cohesion. And the vision was not merely the source: it was the flow of identity.

Moses, the first great leader of the tribal confederation, was not a king or a priest but a prophet, the mouth of God. And successors to leadership, as judges or kings, strayed from the moral commitment of Israel only at their peril and to the confusion of the state. The wrath of God would speak against them through prophets, or the plots of priests, or the dissension of the tribes themselves. It was in the name and cause of God that social revolt was raised against rulers whose exactions were intolerably allied with foreign wives, manners, cults, culture.

The people became a Diaspora, but with an identity fixed by the relationship to God. The Covenant at Sinai remained as vital to the survival of the Jew in Toledo or Nuremberg or Vilna as it had been to his presence in Jerusalem. For what was the Diaspora itself, after all, but a retribution for the sins of the people; a retribution to be exhausted by piety, repentance and the grace of God. Secular Zionism based an important part of its case for the restoration of the homeland on the demonstrated attachment of Jews to Zion throughout nearly two thousand years of wandering. Yet the exponents of religious Zionism were and are, surely, right in their claim that this attachment was overwhelmingly based on the religious vision. The hallowed martyrs of the Diaspora were those who gave their lives rather than abandon their God for the simple sanctuary of baptism.

None the less, with the coursing of humanist revolutionary thought through the countries of exile, the religious gave way to the secular vision as the impetus of a Zionist commitment. And the change was the easier for Jews because it did not repudiate but differently charged their sense of history as a progressive moral force. In the place of God was put the liberation of man. The Covenant at Sinai became the socialist society. And the conflict between the divine law and the disobedience of man yielded to the drama of the class struggle.

This does not mean that all Zionists, or even all the more influential ones, were merely circumcised Marxists. A religious element remained, to assume political Zionism in the Mizrachi. Jabotinsky and the Revisionists represented a nationalist Right of the movement. And the two major figures of Zionism, Herzl and Weizmann, were Jewish nationalists of Western liberal genesis and outlook. But the mainstream of settlement was revolutionary socialist, from the source of tumultuous millennial endeavour in Eastern Europe. There, in contrast to the communities of Western and Central Europe, which were proportionately far more middle class in composition, Jewry encompassed considerable numbers of workers: ready for the radical doctrines that came to them through the secularized Jewish intelligentsia among students and those in the professions.

The iron rule of Tsarist reaction fell perhaps most heavily upon the Jews, among the various collective victims. It sought to identify individual Jews, prominent in radical activity, as evidence of the 'foreign' element provoking disaffection. Notably with Tsar Alexander III's chief adviser, Pobedonostsev, autocracy involved a Slavic mystique of ardent anti-Semitism. And, not least, the sporadic pogrom provided an outlet for popular fury and diverted the course of social conflict.

Life in the Pale of Settlement became increasingly difficult, with more and more Jews confined in less and less space; with mounting restrictions on their education and employment; and with onslaughts of pillage and killing encouraged or ignored by the authorities. In 1887 a government commission of inquiry reported that '90% of the Jews are a proletariat of such poverty and destitution as is otherwise impossible to see in Russia'. And elsewhere in Eastern Europe the situation was scarcely less severe.

A majority of Jews concentrated on surviving as they were, with or without the comfort of the divine Covenant. The minority of those who resolved to change their circumstances grew rapidly in numbers and force. Many escaped to the West, mainly to the promise of America. Many caught and carried the excitement of a revolutionary alternative.

Among these last, three major strains of devotion emerged. There were those who held to a Jewish national identity within the struggle for new societies in Eastern Europe. There were those who believed the assertion of this identity irrelevant and even hostile to the struggle; for whom anti-Semitism was no more than a symptom of the basic social disease that the success of the struggle would cure. And there were those who saw an answer to the age-old Jewish problem only in a return to the homeland and the establishment of the new society there.

From the agitation of the 1870s, a specifically Jewish labour disaffection developed, mainly in Lithuania, among hired workers and radical intellectuals. Traditional populism was gradually abandoned for Marxism. The bond with the rest of the proletariat and the all-Russia labour movement was declared 'indissoluble'. But the principle of equal partnership was propagated rather than the integration of the Jewish within the general commitment. The choice was a 'political national struggle' to realize the civic emancipation of all Jews.

Jewish labour groups were represented at the congress of the

Socialist International in London in 1896. In October 1897, at Vilna, with thirteen participants, there was founded the Bund, or General Jewish Workers' Union in Lithuania, Poland and Russia. And of the nine participating delegates at the founding convention of the Russian Social Democratic Labour Party in March 1898, three were Bundists. But the Bund entered the Russian party as an autonomous unit, and held successive clandestine conventions of its own in the ensuing years. During the abortive revolution of 1905 it played a prominent role; but its influence was never to reach as high again.

The Bund borrowed from the Austrian Social Democratic Party a Marxist apologia for its nationalist bias, and looked for a Jewish autonomy within a Russian federation of nations. It even sought to reconstruct the Russian Social Democratic Labour Party on such a basis, but was defeated and for a while seceded in consequence. And meanwhile, within the revolutionary engagement of Jewish nationalism, it was more and more confronted by the Zionist vision.

The Bund, itself under attack from Russian Social Democrats as reactionary in its preoccupation with a particular Jewish struggle, attacked Zionism, including its socialist parties, as reactionary and informed by bourgeois or petty-bourgeois attitudes. Caught between the claims of nationalism and the international proletarian commitment, it was a prey to constant internal dispute and ideological vacillation. Increasingly, the revolutionary fervour of Jews, within both the proletariat and the intelligentsia, attached itself either to the cause of international, hopefully denationalizing, struggle, or to the prospect of a revolutionary Jewish resurgence in Palestine.

Rosa Luxemburg was among the most illustrious of those who chose the first of these. 'Why do you worry me about the Jewish sorrows?' she was to write from prison, during the First World War, to a Jewish correspondent.* She had no room in her heart for the special sufferings of the ghetto. She was drawn to all human beings in pain.

Of the seven members on the founding editorial board of *Iskra* the organ of the Russian Marxist movement, three were Jews

* Quoted in J. L. Talmon, *Israel Among the Nations* (London: Weidenfeld & Nicolson, 1970), p. 45.

Martov, Axelrod and Trotsky. Indeed, it was the conflict between Jewish nationalists and Jewish internationalists within the Social Democratic Labour Party that was to provide Lenin with his Bolshevik triumph. On the rules defining party membership, at the 1903 Congress in Brussels and London, Lenin lost the vote for an elitist movement of revolutionary activists to the call by Martov for a mass party. But the Congress also voted for the fusion of all affiliated independent entities into a single party apparatus. Trotsky and Martov amongst others joined in assailing the nationalist Jewish deviation. Defeated, the Bund withdrew and so produced a majority for Lenin and his followers.

And Jewish revolutionaries gathered to the cause of Zionism as well: in despair at the prospects of ever achieving the full acceptance of Jews as equal citizens, with their distinctive cultural attributes and allegiances, by even a revolutionized Russian society. Too many pogroms had been received with either indifference or delight by Russian populists or other professing radicals; while too many of the new Marxist revolutionaries were apparently prepared to concede, however temporarily, nationalist assertiveness to all peoples but the Jews.

Paul Axelrod, who would himself become a founding father of 'cosmopolitan' Russian Marxism, expressed in an unpublished pamphlet the shock experienced by Jewish socialists at the reaction to the pogroms among their supposed comrades in struggle.

> The Jewish student youth suffered their greatest disappointment when they realized that the Socialist-minded Russian students sympathized with the crusade against the Jewish masses and, worse yet, exhibited their anti-Semitic feelings towards their Jewish fellow-revolutionaries.
>
> Thus, the pogroms made the Jewish Socialist intelligentsia realize that the Jews as a people were in a unique situation in Russia, hated by the most diverse segments of the Christian population ... The Jewish social revolutionaries understood now that they were wrong in forsaking the Jewish masses in the name of cosmopolitanism. The 'native masses' not only lacked cosmopolitan feelings and ideas, but were wanting even in the idea of class solidarity among the poorer classes of Russia's nationalities. These were the conclusions to which

a sizeable part – perhaps even most – of Jewish youth had come.*

For the Zionist socialists, the Bund represented a suicidal illusion: Jews were never likely to get the autonomy, within an association of Russian states, for which Bundism pressed; and the proof might be found in the very fury with which Jewish Social Democrats such as Trotsky assailed a Jewish preoccupation. They accepted the Zionist analysis that anti-Semitism was endemic in the Diaspora; with their own gloss that a revolutionary overthrow of class relationships there would not solve 'the Jewish question'. But they rejected a bourgeois Zionism that ignored or denied class struggle; and agreed with the Bund that the Jewish proletariat should have both a social and a national role of leadership in the liberation of the Jewish people.

Their study circles and secret clubs proliferated in the Pale of Settlement. There were varying degrees of strictness in adherence to Marxist doctrine, and vigorous elements of Populism. But the major strain of the movement was clearly committed to the class struggle. Indeed, the seminal concept was that 'the Jewish question' could not be solved except through the territorial concentration of the Jewish working class; since only then would Jews properly be enabled to engage in the class struggle and produce a socialist society.

'This territorial concentration, however, would not come about as the result of the will of the Jewish people ... but as the inevitable result of the Jewish proletariat's search for a base from which to conduct the class struggle ... ' Marxist determinism lent certainty to the Zionist ideal, 'a fact of great psychological significance to those who had previously suspected Zionism of being Utopian'.†

Seriously dividing Zionist socialists themselves was the issue of which territory should constitute this base. The Uganda scheme appealed to many who saw above all the urgency of starting the struggle and believed that any new territory would do. 'Moreover, it was difficult for socialists to accept the Palestinian orientation of

* Quoted in ibid., p. 37.

† Entry on 'Jewish Socialism' in *Encyclopaedia Judaica* (Jerusalem: Keter Publishing House, 1971), Vol. 15, p. 44.

bourgeois Zionism, since it seemed to be based on mysticism and was unsupported by any scientific, socialist analysis.'* The undying association of Palestine with the Jewish people was far more the preserve of a religious Zionism, such as informed the Mizrachi movement, than of a Marxist commitment. Yet many consistent Marxists, like Ber Borochov, insisted on Palestine all the same; on grounds of pragmatism rather than principle. It was this view that came to predominate and accordingly prevented what might otherwise have been a far more destructive clash between the *national* and the *socialist* engagements.

It was the failure of the 1905 revolution and the terror subsequently unleashed by the authorities that significantly promoted the Zionism of Jewish socialists, and the crucial settlement of the Second *Aliyah*. The endeavour that seemed so calamitously to have failed in Russia: why should it not succeed in the wastes of Palestine? The Zionist revolutionaries, on reaching the homeland, at once established local branches of the political parties that had taken form in Eastern Europe.

The members of the Hebrew Social Democratic Party, Po'alei Zion, in particular, were committed Marxists, considering themselves part of the international revolutionary proletariat, and in Palestine to pursue the class struggle. Its leadership, which included Ben Gurion, the future pre-eminent spokesman of the Yishuv, the Jewish community of the homeland, and first prime minister of Israel, sought public ownership of the means of production in the making of a new classless society.

Almost all these socialists were more than merely indifferent to the ancient Covenant at Sinai that had been so much the dynamic of a Jewish identity in the past; they were passionate atheists. But they invested in the future of a socialist Jewish homeland a similar Messianic fervour. They called their immigration to Palestine *Aliyah* (ascension); and themselves *olim* (pilgrims). *Avoda* means labour, but it means in Hebrew 'worship' as well. And the term *chalutz* (pioneer) originated, with its mood of prophetic exaltation, in the Bible ('to pass over armed before the Lord into the Land of Canaan'—Numbers xxxii: 32).†

* Ibid., p. 45.

† Amos Elon, *The Israelis: Founders and Sons* (London: Weidenfeld & Nicolson, 1971), pp. 111–12.

The various agricultural settlements were hymns to the dignity of self-sufficient labour and the millennium to come. And the vocabulary survives in modern Israeli politics. But the content has gone. The ideals of 'assimilationist' Jewish revolutionaries such as Trotsky, and of the Bundists, who believed in a revolutionary Russia with a national place for the Jews, fell alike victims of Stalinism. The Zionist socialists, not alone to be sure, yet unquestionably as the major element, made a state; but in making and securing it, abandoned the very vision which had informed for them its purpose.

How and why did the new covenant prove no more adequate, and even indeed, less so, than the old? One reason undoubtedly was the disaster of Hitlerism, which reduced the population of world Jewry by more than a third and concentrated the minds of so many among the remainder on mere national survival rather than on some millennial promise for all humanity. And it was not only the acts of Nazism itself which promoted a profound Jewish disillusionment; it was the omissions of the avowedly humanitarian states. On the initiative of President Roosevelt, the representatives of thirty-one countries in Europe and the Americas met at Evian in July 1938 to deal mainly with the problem of Jewish refugees. Only the tiny Dominican Republic offered sanctuary to a number significant in relation to its own size. Most of the participants used the occasion to deplore Nazi persecution, without offering a way of saving its immediate and imminent victims. The United States itself allowed only some 100,000 to enter in the three years 1938–40.

A crucial reason, too, was the conflict with the Arabs. For strange as it may now seem, the early pioneers of a socialist Zionism gave little if any thought to the existence of Arabs in Palestine. Max Nordau is reputed to have rushed alarmed to Herzl in 1897 with the cry, 'But there are Arabs in Palestine! I did not know that! We are committing an injustice!' And as the injustice became more manifest,* with the growth of resistance to Jewish settlement by emerging Arab nationalism in Palestine, the leaders of Zionist socialism sought to convey what they saw as the justice

* That land was being bought at high prices for that time from rich, often absentee, Arab landlords, might have seemed adequate excuse to an avowed capitalist morality. But how should it seem so to an avowed socialist one?

of their own claims not by acknowledging the injustice that was its counterpart, but by denying the injustice altogether. One way was to base morality on nationalism, with the implication that the Arabs in Palestine had no moral claim to the country because they had no national one: in 1917, a half-century before Golda Meir would similarly express herself, Ben Gurion declared that in a 'historical and moral sense' Palestine was a country 'without inhabitants'. A second way was to assume that economic benefits would inevitably reconcile the Arabs to the Jewish presence: though Zionism itself increasingly maintained that for Jews in the more affluent Diaspora material comfort was a poor and ultimately hollow substitute for national realization.

In the event, neither way was effective in deflecting or disguising Arab hostility or Jewish guilt. And the proponents of a bi-national state, that would accommodate the claims of both Arabs and Jews in Palestine, were crushed between the pressures of the two nationalisms. The struggle to establish and secure a Jewish homeland involved acts that the pioneers of Zionist socialism would have declared intolerable, if not incredible. The seizure and effective confiscation of Arab refugee land, on a massive scale; the rigours of a military administration over Arab villages in Israel which the extent of security requirements did not excuse: such were manifestations of a national commitment that had strayed far from the purpose of the early revolutionaries.

Perhaps one event, more than any other, revealed how far the commitment had strayed. In October 1956, on the eve of the Suez war, at the Israeli Arab village of Kafr Qasim, forty-nine Arab civilians, including women and children, were shot dead by Israeli frontier guards for breaking a curfew of whose sudden imposition they were still ignorant. There seems to have been an attempt by the government to hush up the affair; but a campaign in the press led to an eventual court martial. The court found Major Melinki and Lieutenant Dahan guilty of killing forty-three citizens and sentenced them to seventeen and fifteen years' imprisonment respectively; it found Sergeant Ofer guilty of killing forty-one citizens, and sentenced him to fifteen years; and it gave lesser punishments to others held responsible. An immediate public campaign, with the newspapers of Herut and Achdut

Ha'avoda in the forefront, assailed the sentences on the grounds that the convicted had only been doing what they had seen as their duty. On appeal, the Supreme Military court, declaring the sentences 'harsh', reduced Melinki's to fourteen years, Dahan's to ten, and Ofer's to nine. The Chief of Staff then further reduced Melinki's to ten, Dahan's to eight, and those of all others to four years each. The President of Israel intervened, granting a 'partial pardon' and reducing the sentences of Melinki and Dahan to five years only. And the 'Committee for the Release of Prisoners' succeeded in getting a third of all sentences remitted. At the beginning of 1960, little more than three years after the massacre, all those convicted were released. Brigadier Yshishkar Shadmi, the senior commander involved, who had specifically charged Melinki's unit to show no 'sentimentality',* was tried separately, found guilty of a 'merely technical' error, and sentenced to a reprimand and a fine of one Israeli piastre.

One Israeli editor expressed his sense of horror at the implications:

> Now that the instinct for mercy has achieved all it desired, and that the killers have been freed, or on the point of being released, now that compensation or bribes have been paid to the relatives of those who were killed, the time has come to call ourselves to account ... Our integrity, our humanity and our courage have been put to the test, and have been found wanting ...
>
> The main culprit is the press. With the exception of two or three papers, the whole press agreed to compound a conspiracy of silence, and threw a veil over the crime ... When these papers wrote of the 'victims of the disaster', it was not even clear whom they were writing about – the killers or the killed ... In this manner that terrible day has been covered with a cloak of evasive talk. You may be sure of one thing: whenever you come across colourless words, neutral and cautious words, something terrible is concealed behind them ...

* Asked by a subordinate how people returning to the village from their work should be treated, he had reportedly replied, 'That's just too bad for them.'

He blamed the religious leadership, the academic leadership, the 'literary and artistic leadership', which with no or few exceptions were silent. And he continued: 'Where were the parties who sat all that time in the seats of power, mouthing the slogans of peace, justice, and the brotherhood of mankind? Where were the revolutionaries? And where were we, the simple citizens ... Why were we silent?'*

Where, indeed, were the revolutionaries? They had, like the mass of 'simple citizens', become the moral creatures of the very nationalism that they had created: seeing the abstraction and not the individual; the enemy and not the victim of their own exclusive preoccupations. To say that Arab nationalism was no less blind, no less exclusively preoccupied, helps to explain: but it cannot eliminate, and should not excuse, the essential corruptions of such a process. What the Kafr Qasim massacre and its immediate aftermath made clear was that the predominant mood of Jews in Israel had become one crucially informed not by the values of a new society, to pioneer a just mankind, but by the old predatory demands of nation and of state.

It is much protested by morally uncomplacent Israelis today that the Kafr Qasim affair was a mere aberration; passionately to be deplored, of course, but not to be exaggerated into a symptom. The guilty may well have been eventually pardoned altogether, but the essential shock sustained by Israeli opinion did lead to such productive remorse as the more or less express understanding within the armed forces that manifestly improper orders should not be obeyed.

The so different, and yet so similar, affair of the Rafah Bedouin is only the most recent to confront such protest. On grounds of security, an area in the south of the conquered Gaza Strip was fenced off, and the Bedouin inhabitants summarily expelled. Criticism of this from within the political party Mapam,† some of whose 'members on army reserve duty were witnesses to what happened',‡ became involved with a campaign against the whole government programme of Jewish settlement in the Gaza Strip; and from the ensuing controversy it emerged that the military

* *Ner,* August–October 1959.

† Mifleget Hapoalim Hameuchedet (United Workers' Party).

‡ A Mapam spokesman, in the *Jerusalem Post,* 11 April 1972.

authorities were embarrassed by the way in which the Rafah operation had been conducted. Yet, in announcing that the original orders has been exceeded, and that disciplinary measures had been taken against the relevant personnel, Chief of Staff David Elazar told the Cabinet that the Bedouin would none the less be banned from returning to the area; including 'parts which were fenced off in excess of the original orders'.* The Bedouin would be offered a choice between cash compensation and rehabilitation (with housing 'in the vicinity of existing inhabited localities', or 'allocations of land, for smallholdings') sponsored by the Military Government. 'These details, and others which were not reported, were communicated to the Cabinet for their information, not for their approval ... '†

Yet the very triumph of Jewish nationalism that came with the Six Day War of June 1967 seems to have opened more issues than it closed. Were conflict and conquest to be the permanent experience of a Jewish state, in a self-defeating search for peace through strength?

From the writings of some young Israelis came a sense of shame at yet more multitudes of Arab refugees, so reminiscent of the refugee Jews that thronged the history of the Return; at an Israel, however provoked or compelled, now effectively an empire, with armies patrolling its conquests. Yet what credible alternative presented itself? The vision was one of tragedy: paradoxically, a pagan sense of fate. Amoz Oz has thus expressed it.

> Tragedy is not a conflict between 'light' and 'darkness', between justice and crime. It is a clash between total justice and total justice, even though one should not seek the simplification of symmetry in it. And as in all tragedies, there is no hope of a jubilating conciliation based on a clever compromise formula ...
>
> This is our country; it is their country. Right clashes with right. 'To be a free people in our own land' is a right that is universally valid, or not valid at all ...
>
> I believe in a Zionism that faces facts, that ... sees the Jewish past as a lesson, but neither as a mystical imperative

* Report in the *Jerusalem Post*, 17 April 1972.
† Ibid.

> nor as a malignant dream; that sees the Palestinian Arabs as Palestinian Arabs, and neither as the camouflaged reincarnation of the ancient tribes of Canaan, nor as a shapeless mass of humanity waiting for us to form it as we see fit; a Zionism also capable of seeing itself as others may see it; and, finally, a Zionism that accepts both the spiritual implications and the political consequences of the fact that this small but precious land is the homeland of two peoples fated to live facing each other, willy-nilly, because no God and no angel will come down to judge between right and right.*

There is no place in this vision of tragedy for what was the imperative dream of the early revolutionaries. Oz himself lives on a kibbutz; but there is no mention of socialism in his article; no suggestion, such as informed the purpose of so many Zionist pioneers, that a mankind freed of exploitation for profit, and founded on the equal dignity of all, would itself reconcile national conflicts and make of different cultural identities a dynamic process for the moral enrichment of man everywhere.

The Nazi holocaust and the struggle with the Arabs do not alone account for this conspicuous absence. Oz grew up within an avowedly socialist engagement variously divided and dismayed by the course of the Soviet revolution. As were its counterparts elsewhere, but with particular force because of both the Jewish dimension and the dominant Eastern European background, the Left in Zionism was tormented by a series of betrayals: notably, the terror of Stalinism in the 'thirties; the Nazi–Soviet pact, with its hideous relevance for the Jews; the increasingly manifest imperial aspect of the Soviet relationship with the 'people's democracies' of Eastern Europe; the crude show trials, with their element of anti-Semitism; the mounting Soviet support, after the brief honeymoon with Israel, for the Arab cause.

These were shocks that cumulatively drained the Left of vigour, self-assurance and purpose. For it was not as though a powerful Trotskyist movement, or other independent force of revolutionary socialism, existed in the Yishuv. One major component of the early commitment, represented mainly by Mapai and Ben Gurion,

* 'Meaning of Homeland' by Amos Oz; a reprinted article, first published in *New Outlook*.

became openly social democrat and aligned with the liberal leadership of Zionism in the Diaspora.* Another, represented mainly by Mapam, clung to traditional rhetoric and to rationalizations for Soviet conduct, till the first was drained of all credible content, and the second became intolerably inconsistent with the developed imperatives of Jewish nationalism.

In the absence of a revolutionary Left that posed some creative alternative, therefore, the Jewish state came to be informed by several interrelated and mutually promoting dominant forces: the pessimistic, even cynical belief in the primacy of material power; the commitment to nationalism as an end in itself; a virtually exclusive reliance on military means to produce an arrangement with the Arabs. And this in turn involved a foreign policy centred on the American alliance; the continuing necessity for a high and indeed mounting flow of funds from the wealthy Jewish communities of the Diaspora; and a corresponding culture at home.

This correspondence is all too evident in the rampant competitive materialism of Israel today; with consequences of enormous moral as well as social impact. For as does every other society, and perhaps, given the peculiar past of its people, more so than most, Israel regulates the relationships of its members not only by what the law allows or forbids, but by what is traditionally regarded as right or wrong. In Israel, this last demarcation is an amalgam of Biblical and Talmudic morality; of the values developed in the Eastern European Diaspora; of the vision held by the revolutionary socialist pioneers; of the collective involvement which made Zionism the force it has been, and the readiness for private material restraint required by an imperilled state. And by the

* The World Union of Po'alei Zion split in 1920 over the issue of joining the Third (Communist) International. The right wing, commanding a majority in the parties of the United States, Britain, Argentina and the Yishuv, objected that the Third International was likely to obstruct or prevent the independent development of the Jewish homeland in Palestine and ties with the Zionist Organization and with world Jewry. It subsequently associated itself with the mainstream of social democracy in the Socialist International and participated actively in the Zionist Organization.

From the party in the Yishuv there developed Mapai, whose 'approach to socialism was pragmatic rather than Marxist', and whose aim was 'not so much the conquest of power by labour, as a gradual advance, in Ben Gurion's phrase, *mi-ma'amad le-am* ("from class to nation")'. See the entry on Mapai in *Encyclopaedia Judaica*, Vol. 11, p. 912; also the entry on Po'alei Zion in ibid., Vol. 13, pp. 656–64.

measure of this amalgam, the social functioning of Israel today must be condemned; and is, to be sure, giving rise to a critical disquiet among Israelis themselves.

The spread of corruption is an especially challenging symptom: for it reflects the degree to which even the inhibitions of the law are unable to contain the increasing conflict between individual self-engagement and the engagement to collective good. A series of serious scandals exploded in the closing months of 1971, concerned with exploitation of oil in Sinai; with expropriated Arab land in the occupied territories; with the management of certain industrial firms;* even, if only at the level of political intrigue, with the private enterprise of Moshe Dayan in the collecting and sale of antiquities. The impact of the various investigations, or of such as are to be conducted, remains to be seen. But it is already clear that corruption by citizens in official positions of public trust has become a source of significant social anxiety.

All in all, there is emerging in Israel today a sense of moral malaise, manifested as yet in cynicism rather than in any expressions of outrage. But this sense is likely more and more to revolt against the devastating contradiction between the moral mission that Israel was envisaged to be by its pioneers, and the mere pragmatism of material power, for the individual as for the state, that it has become. This pragmatism is a self-defeating process. And indeed, predictably, it is consuming in Israel its own professed purpose. For not the least of its victims is nationalism itself. At no time since the establishment of the state has Israeli society been as divided, as uncertain, as dismayed as it is today.

And how should it be otherwise? By cultural development; by the whole cumulative impact of historical experience, the Jews are a Messianic people. The Zionist socialists of Eastern Europe were no exception. They rejected the particular vision that had preserved and directed the Jewish identity across so many centuries, only to substitute for it their own: a liberator who was not God, but man; a message that was not divine law but the commandment of reason, for the reshaping of society in the image of justice and brotherhood. The agony of Israel today is that of a visionary people without a vision; a Messianic people in search of a Messiah.

* Notably, a large vehicle-assembly plant.

The revolutionary ideas of the pioneers have been effectively renounced. They may attain ascendancy again: in such new form as answers the call of social justice and brotherhood today. And there are those who believe that only so may the experiment of Israel be saved from becoming yet one more horror of Jewish history. But meanwhile the moral bankruptcy of those claiming to speak for Man, encourages the ambitions of those claiming to speak for God.

The three parliamentary religious parties polled 12·2% of the popular vote in 1949, and 14·79% in 1969. Given the minuteness of the shift in party allegiance that usually occurs in Israeli elections, this growth in support for the religious parties is significant.* True, there has been massive immigration of Oriental Jews, with much less substantial a tradition of secular commitment than that among Western Jews in the intervening years. But predominant Israeli opinion holds that the Oriental Jews are not now, whatever they may have been when they arrived, disproportionately orthodox. And in a modern industrial 'social-democratic' state, with rising mass material consumption, such as Israel is today, there has usually been a popular decline in religious attachment.

Furthermore, the religious parties have variously proved far more powerful than their share of the popular vote in Israel would properly warrant. One reason is that successive Labour-led coalition governments have depended on the support of the National Religious Party, the largest of the three, for a secure majority in the Knesset. Agreement to Labour policies in general has been traded by the N.R.P. for Labour agreement to policies that the N.R.P. regard as vital to its own interests. And many would say that the N.R.P. has had the best of the bargain.

The compromise formula of the 'status quo', reached by Ben Gurion and Rabbi Maimon within the Jewish Agency before the establishment of the state, and employed still as the guideline of government, has enlarged the command of religious priorities over the lives of citizens as the society has developed. With more pros-

* It has, to be sure, reached higher. The percentage vote in each election was 12·2 in 1949; 12·0 in 1951; 13·8 in 1955; 14·6 in 1959; 15·4 in 1961; 14·0 in 1965; and 14·79 in 1969. But an upward trend overall seems a reasonable enough conclusion.

perity and leisure, for instance, those without their own cars who wish to travel on the Sabbath must usually resort to the costly hire of private coaches or taxis. Haifa continues to enjoy public transport on the Sabbath; because at the time that the 'status quo' agreement was reached, it was accorded special treatment in deference to its then large Arab population. But the huge Tel Aviv conurbation has no public transport on the Sabbath now; as it had none when only a fraction of its present size. Similarly, though there has been an enormous increase in the travel of Israeli Jews abroad and the visits of Gentiles to Israel, civil marriage still, in conformity with the agreement, does not exist in the state; while conversion to Judaism remains a morally, or financially, exacting process.

Religious law has unquestionably extended its grip. Occasionally it has failed, though not for want of trying. The N.R.P. even got the initial agreement of the Labour leadership to the banning of television on the Sabbath; and was defeated only by a public outcry. But it has also importantly succeeded. In the late 'sixties, a furious public debate broke over the Shalit affair. Binyamin Shalit, a Jew born in Haifa, had married a Gentile Scotswoman in Edinburgh; and returning with her to live in Israel, had subsequently sought to have their children registered as without religion but as Jewish by national identification. The relevant official, in obedience to directives from the Minister of Interior, had written 'no registration' against the item dealing with ethnic affiliation.

Shalit took his case to the High Court. And the Court, in an unprecedented step, advised the government to remove the item dealing with ethnic affiliation from the population registry altogether. The government refused. 'What is a Jew?'—the issue behind the case—divided the Court as it did the country. In the event, the majority of judges found for Shalit on various points of law; such as the competence of the Minister to direct as he had done; and the competence of the responsible officer to refuse the registration of particulars given to him in apparent good faith. In Justice Cohn's words, the courts were not entitled to apply religious law where the legislature had not imported it.

The Court, as several judges made clear in their opinions, was evading the crucial question. The Knesset was forced to take the matter in hand; and in consequence, since March 1970, it is orthodox rabbinical definition that establishes a Jewish national. Golda Meir herself, a lifelong self-professed secularist, and scarcely celebrated for her attachment to orthodox observance, urged the relevant legislation, on 'national' rather than 'religious' grounds. Mixed marriages were endangering the future of the Jewish people, she declared, and should not be encouraged by the state.

The courts now not only caught up with the Knesset, but outpaced it. Dr Georges Tamarin, a one-time senior lecturer in psychology at Tel Aviv University, requested the government registrar to have his nationality status altered from that of Jewish to that of Israeli, on the grounds that he did not belong to the Jewish nation as a religious-racial concept. The registrar refused; the District Court in Tel Aviv upheld the refusal; and in January 1972, the High Court upheld the judgment of the District Court. To grant Dr Tamarin's demand, the High Court held, could lead to a schism of the Jewish people. 'There is no Israeli nation apart from the Jewish people, and the Jewish people consists not only of the people residing in Israel but also of the Jews in the Diaspora.' The identifying mark of all Jews was their feeling of interdependency; and this fact, which had found manifest expression since the Six Day War, contradicted the appellant's contention that Israel was separate from the Jewish people. 'No man can create a new nation with his own breath and say I belong to it.'

The N.R.P., with its own settlements, schools, publishing house, newspaper, banking interests, is a state within a state. But it never makes the mistake of concentrating on the smaller to the cost of the larger engagement. It pays particular attention to the educational system in Israel, and has generally commanded a high post in the department responsible. Above all, it has largely succeeded in projecting its own claims as those of national unity. The threat that it poses is, on the whole, implicit; but none the less potent for that. A break with the government would mean more than a shift in the parliamentary balance: it would divide the citizenry into the servants and the enemies of God. 'We are against the separation of religion and state,' one of the party's leaders rumbled smoothly to me in the restaurant of the Knesset. It was clear what he meant.

The twelve parliamentary seats of the N.R.P. – 10% of the

total Knesset membership—thus represent a disproportionate political force. So, too, do the two other religious parties; Agudat Israel with four and Poalei Agudat Israel with two seats in the Knesset. For theirs are the regiments of fanaticism; ready to demonstrate their intransigence in the streets and invite the rewards of martyrdom. Poalei Agudat Israel has at least a history of involvement with organized Zionism and a commitment to worker interests. Agudat Israel may connive at but ultimately denies the authority of the state.* And both, by flourishing the possibility of tumultuous complaint and even violence, have ensured that successive governments did not ignore their views.

Yet neither the internal pressures of the N.R.P. on government policy, nor the potential insurgency from without by the Agudat parties, sufficiently account for the power of religious opinion in contemporary Israel. The religious leadership is undoubtedly right in claiming a larger popular support for the religious cause than the vote in parliamentary elections would suggest; though just how much larger this support may be, must remain the merest guess. There are many Jews who are more or less strictly observant of religious prescript in their homes but who vote for a secular party that promises more effectively to secure or advance their particular economic interests; that offers a more persuasive prospect of stable government; that looks more likely to promote a settlement with the Arabs. And there are many, too, for whom the leadership of the religious parties seems counter-productively aggressive, or unsavourily cynical and even corrupt. (Scandals have not been the monopoly of the secularists. Prominent figures in the N.R.P. have also been discovered in apparent exploitation of public office for private or party financial advantage.) Such of the believers who vote secularist see at present no significant conflict between their religious attachment and their political adherence. But there is an increasing impulse to the polarization of Israeli society on the religious issue; and the sense of conflict that must accordingly emerge might well drive them to a helpless abandonment of the secular parties.

No less significant are the numbers of those who take little or no part in religious practices and may not believe in any god at

* It long openly opposed political Zionism as seeking to pre-empt the prerogatives of the Messiah.

all, let alone the Biblical Jehovah, but who are assuming a sort of national mysticism that must nourish the religious commitment. The June war of 1967 was crucial in the development of this outlook. Among the conquests were Hebron, the home of the Patriarchs; Shiloh (Khirbat Saylūn), ancient Israel's central sanctuary, where the Ark of the Covenant had been kept; Balātah (Shichem), where Abraham first stopped in Canaan and Joshua took his farewell of the tribes; above all East Jerusalem, with its sacred old city. The Bible and early Jewish history came alive to many Israelis, in particular among the young soldiers, as never before. The Wailing Wall itself, that remnant of the Second Temple, became the supreme symbol of a Jewish striving, victorious and yet still vulnerable. The most passionate secularists caught what they might previously have characterized as the infection. Traditionally Jews had stuck written prayers in crevices of the wall. Dayan, with attendant publicity, deposited a call for peace.

The book *The Seventh Day*,* a celebrated collection of reminiscences and conversations among soldiers of the Six Day War, well reflects this mood. And it is especially relevant here because the soldiers so chosen were from 'the younger generation of the kibbutz'; the bulk of them 'born of a dedicated pioneering generation and educated to live by the principle "from each according to his ability, to each according to his needs".'†

A young paratrooper revealed his horror of war. 'As we grew angrier, we stopped being human beings ... You want to kill and kill. You grow like an animal, you know—no, worse than an animal.'‡ But he revealed too, the ecstasy that had seized him in Jerusalem.

> ... we could see the Western [Wailing] Wall, through an archway. We saw it before, but this time it was right in front of us. It was like new life, as though we had just woken up. We dashed down the steps; we were among the first to get there, but a few had already got there and I could see them, men who were too tired to stand up any more, sitting by the

* Edited by Henry Near, and published by Steimatzky's Agency Ltd. in association with André Deutsch, London, 1970.

† Introduction to the English edition, p. 1.

‡ Ibid., p. 63.

Wall, clutching it, kissing the stones and crying. We all of us cried. That was what we had been fighting for. It goes so deep, this emotion we felt when we reached the Wall. What they did in Sinai and in Syria, sure it was marvellous, but it wasn't the same. Getting to the Wall meant everything.*

Another recited his reactions with dramatic immediacy.

We're surrounding the Old City. Now I begin to understand. Jerusalem the eternal will be ours in its entirety ...

We advance quickly towards the Temple Mount and sprawl there with our weapons, in the shadow of the Mosque. Our eyes dart eagerly towards the Western Wall.

And at this point, I felt it. I became one with the House of David, the Kingdom of Solomon, and the Temple. This is my inheritance ... My heart swells with pride in my people's history ...

We move on from place to place, from the mountains to the plains, from the hills to the valleys. Storming our way to victory, regrouping for another battle in this holy war. Fighting for our homes. I felt as if at that moment we were inscribing a new chapter in the Bible, a chapter of miracles, wonders and greatness like those that preceded it ... The whole of the Promised Land is ours.†

An orthodox Jew wrote in a letter:

I saw my friends, kibbutz-educated towards an attitude of scorn for traditional religious values, now overwhelmed by a feeling of holiness, and as elated and moved as I was. Then I saw the proof of what I had previously assumed, that there is in all of us, religious and non-religious alike, in the entire Jewish people, an intense quality of Jewishness that is neither destroyed by education nor blurred by foreign ideologies and values.‡

The writer Amos Oz was stirred, but rather by the shadow of the Wall.

* Ibid., p. 64.
† Ibid., pp. 74–5.
‡ Ibid., p. 213.

> With all my soul, I desired to feel in Jerusalem as a man who has dispossessed his enemies and returned to the patrimony of his ancestors. The Bible came to life for me: the Prophets, the Kings, Temple Mount, Absolom's Pillar, the Mount of Olives ... I wanted to be part of it all, I wanted to belong.
>
> Were it not for the people. I saw enmity and rebelliousness, sycophancy, amazement, fear, insult and trickery. I passed through the streets of East Jerusalem like a man breaking into some forbidden place. Depression filled my soul.*

It is surely in part to escape this depression, this sense of guilt, that so many Israelis wrap up their minds in this new mysticism. And it is a mysticism with implications that the vast majority of Zionist pioneers would have found all too repugnant. Herzl himself, in his Utopian exercise *Altneuland*, put in the mouth of his protagonist the view that though the state would have a majority of Jews among its citizens, 'Christians, Mohammedans, Buddhists, and Brahmans' would be welcome. 'We ask for no one's religion or race. Let him be a Man, that is enough for us.' And in his seminal work, *Der Judenstaat*, Herzl confined the theocrats 'in their temples, just as we shall confine our professional soldiers to their barracks'. The predominant settler movement even campaigned for a Hebrew rather than a Jewish state, to stress the accessibility of its citizenship to those of other religions, and, by tenable inference, other races as well.

The socialist leadership, indeed, was largely atheist. Ben Gurion refused, on principle, to follow his civil marriage, in New York, with a religious one. By the time that the General Assembly of the United Nations voted for the establishment of the new state, the term 'Jewish', to describe it, seemed proper: in the mood promoted by the tribulations of the Nazi period. But the Proclamation of Independence, on 14 May 1948, pledged 'complete equality of social and political rights for all [Israel's] citizens, without distinction of creed, race or sex'; and 'freedom of religion and conscience, of language, education and culture'. A proposed reference to God was deleted; with 'trust' placed in 'the Rock of Israel' instead.

By the time of the Knesset decision to define a Jew by rabbinical

* Ibid., p. 218.

law, the prevalent outlook had unmistakably changed. Golda Meir's openly expressed hostility to intermarriage based Jewish nationality on the alternative of biological or religious affiliation. And what was Israel but this accordingly confined nationalism institutionalized? Herzl's Judenstaat was, in the view of its own prime minister, built on the two values of race and religion.

'I do not believe', said one of Golda Meir's sharp, smooth young secretaries to me, well before the judgment of the High Court,* 'in the distinction between the Jew and the Israeli. There is only one Jewish people. And this belief is gaining ground. There has been a religious revival in Israel since the Six Day War.'

And how, indeed, should it be otherwise? Those who exulted at the Western Wall; who spoke now of a 'holy war' and 'inscribing a new chapter in the Bible'; who used the phrase 'the promised land', but who denied the demands for religious government; were appropriately answered by a religious leadership which asked: 'For Whom was the Wall built? From Whom does holiness and the meaning of the Bible derive? By Whom was the promise made?'

The escape from depression and guilt may be one impulse to this new mysticism. But another is surely the absence of any secular millennial faith to inform the future: for a people that has always seen history as a moral progression. The surviving pioneer leadership, having abandoned its original vision, needs another to sustain its prophetic presumptions, and has increasingly sought this in a religion of history itself: a sort of Judaism without ritual or, indeed, God. Yet this has inevitably seemed a hollow devotion. The theocrats have pressed their advantage; moving out of their temples to seize control over more and more of the state. For who, in claiming to represent the historical 'inheritance', that 'intense quality of Jewishness' not 'blurred by foreign ideologies and values', can convincingly rival them?

The new assertiveness of the religious leadership is a probing response to the moral vulnerability of the secular pragmatists. The Sephardic Chief Rabbi of Israel went as far as to issue a *psak halacha*, similar to a papal Bull, commanding the government and all Jews individually to refrain from 'even contemplating' the return of any land included in God's promise to His people. This

* See p. 132.

might have been dismissed as the meddling of one old man. But recently, a rather more portentous intervention has followed. The government initiated a scheme for girls from orthodox families to do voluntary national service. A rabbinical court summoned Michael Hazani, the N.R.P. Minister of Social Welfare, to answer for having transgressed orthodox law by his support for the scheme. The lower court withdrew its complaint after the Attorney-General ruled against it. But a Jerusalem rabbi then took the issue to the Rabbinical Supreme Court and was upheld. Government officials reportedly held that by defying the Attorney-General's opinion and by claiming, even without the threat of sanctions, jurisdiction above that of the state, the Rabbinical Supreme Court was challenging the rule of law in Israel.* They wanted a clear declaration by the Court that it derived its authority from the state. But leading rabbis maintained that the authority of the Court came from the Torah, and that the state merely sanctioned such rulings as it made.

In the climate promoted by religious eminences, it was not surprising that there should have been those who sought to advance the religious cause by less measured activities. Increasingly, violent assaults were made on transport infringements of the Sabbath. Pathologists were personally harassed as part of a campaign against autopsies. The liberal newspaper *Ha'aretz*, commenting on the arson at the editorial offices of the vigorously secularist *Ha'olam Hazeh*, declared in an editorial: 'A mood is being created which regards violence as legitimate means of achieving social and political goals. There is no need to explain how dangerous this process is and to what lengths it may go.'† The cases which *Ha'aretz* cited were not all the apparent responsibility of religious extremists. But there is no doubt that religious extremism was in the vanguard of such activities; and was, moreover, justifying the assault on law by reference to an authority not only beyond the state, but beyond essentially human considerations as well.

It is all too probable that the theocratic threat will grow. But a more positive comment is in order. The religious challenge, in revealing the very inadequacies of the present secular leadership,

* *The Times*, 7 January 1972.
† *Ha'aretz*, 28 November 1971.

betrays its own inadequacy to solve the gathering problems of a modern industrial society. By comparison with the multitudes of urbanized Israel, the tribes wandering in the wilderness were wonderfully manageable. Nor does the Covenant at Sinai offer a credible, let alone creative, way of conciliating a hostile Arab environment that otherwise promises repeated wars. A garrison state of Zealots may, indeed, be one possibility. But another is that the very prospect of this will engender in Israel a secularism with a faith in its own fundamental values; give to this Messianic people a movement whose offer of deliverance is once again that of mankind by man.

The clash between secularism and religion is only one, albeit perhaps the most important, manifestation of Israel's identity crisis. Another is the social conflict developing over the resentment among Oriental Jews, especially the young, at the ascendancy, political, economic and cultural, of the Western community. Indeed, public opinion admits the problem, if differing about the extent and significance, by acknowledging the existence of two such communities at all.

The specific issue is urgent enough in itself. But it points to the no less urgent wider issue: of Israel's place in a divided world. For the dominion of the Western community reflects an affiliation to the Western system which contradicts Israeli pretensions to a substantial agreement of purpose with the striving poor of mankind, and in particular to a potential harmonious and productive relationship with the Arab peoples.

The contradiction is implicit in the very character of the help which Israel gives. Israeli technicians abroad advise and direct in the establishment and running of industrial plants; in the encouragement of agricultural development; in the construction of public works; in the equipment and training of troops; while within Israel itself, opportunities for education in a wide variety of fields, from science and technology to trades unionism and the organization of agricultural collectives, are available to visiting students.* Such projects, Israelis claim, differ from the common run of Western aid in several significant respects. Capital investment, from private or public Israeli sources, plays either no part

* See Appendix 4, Tables I and II.

at all, or one clearly inferior to that of the human investment. Israel offers skill and experience and devotion rather than money. And it does so because, even if it had the money to spare, it rejects the role of proprietor or creditor that would result. The principle on which it seeks to operate is the promotion of self-help: so that other countries might efficiently exploit their resources, human and material, for the benefit of their own people. And accordingly it emphasizes such collective or co-operative projects as have had marked economic success in Israel and which grew from the egalitarian commitment of the pioneers.

It is true, of course, that the leading industrial states of the capitalist world also offer technicians for public projects, including military training; and opportunities for visiting students from poor countries to acquire, at the expense of the host government or institution, skills in a wide variety of fields, including trades unionism and co-operative organization. But the emphasis of Israeli aid, with the absence so far of any major direct investment for material profit, does constitute a special case.

Yet if the case is special, it is so only within a general framework. And it is here that the contradiction surfaces. Those countries to which Israel gives aid remain, despite their formal independence, virtual colonies of the advanced capitalist states: their economies are exploited for profit by foreign corporations and the prevailing terms of trade; their governments are composed of the material and moral clients of the Western system. Against this subservience, whose foundations are deep in the past, movements of revolt are increasingly recruiting support from among those citizens who regard themselves as nationally and personally deprived and humiliated. The advanced capitalist states strike back directly by military and intelligence support to the client governments; and indirectly, by technical and financial aid. Their objective is to secure the developed relationship: sometimes by shoring up the government that exists; sometimes by toppling it, for the introduction of a more efficient or less discredited leadership similarly committed. This is not to suggest that those who command the policies of the advanced capitalist states are monsters of greed An amalgam of motives and pressures impels them, including an electoral opinion that demands the dividends of exploitation without being brought uncomfortably close to the mechanism; the irresponsible and recondite operations of national or multinational security establishments; the belief that their own system is basically beneficent and in any event better than any probable alternative. But then a belief in the basic beneficence of the most oppressive social systems has never been difficult to hold, for those who profit from them.

Certainly, almost all Israelis believe in the basic beneficence of their own country's foreign aid programme. But the motives, mechanism and impact of the programme must be carefully considered. The primary motive at least is not in question. Blockaded by its Arab neighbours, and the target of hostility from many other states which for one reason or another identify themselves with the Arab cause, Israel needs friends, for economic links and diplomatic support. Such friends are mainly to be found within the advanced capitalist world. Yet for that very reason, other friends are necessary: to distinguish Israel from the system of advanced capitalism itself, with the enmity it excites; to broaden, accordingly, the base of the state's political and economic relationships; and so to achieve such widespread acceptance as to make the Arab states see the vanity of their ways and acquiesce at last in a reasonable settlement. Furthermore, Israelis, shut off from their immediate environment, and assailed, as an imperialist force, by Arab hatred, suffer from a claustrophobia both physical and moral in impulse. They crave for acceptance in the world outside the West: as an opening up of at least the further environment, with its enhancement of the prospect that the immediate, also, will yield; and as a break in the Arab-led siege of their moral claim to a struggle and social experiment that should inspire the oppressed of mankind.

Yet the mechanism by which these friendships are wooed and sometimes won is the relationship with governments. The proclaimed first principle of Israeli aid is to work through the established authority, without interference in domestic politics.* It is, of course, a principle of patent self-contradiction. For to work through the established authority is precisely to interfere in domestic politics. A notable example is provided by the former

* *Facts About Israel 1971* (Jerusalem: Keter Publishing House, for the Information Division of the Foreign Ministry), cites as a 'fundamental concept' of Israel's foreign policy, 'Friendship and co-operation with all nations irrespective of political, economic, or social regime' (p. 76).

Belgian Congo, now called Zaire. Israeli technicians are active there on various economic projects. But how is the very success of such projects to be isolated from a reinforcement of the Mobutu regime, whose despotism depends on a rapid recourse to the gun and the grateful collaboration of large American, Belgian and other Western financial interests? In particular, Israelis are engaged in developing a transport system that must facilitate the movement not only of merchandise but of forces for civil repression. And, indeed, Israelis are directly concerned in the training of Mobutu's troops. How can they ensure that such training will not be employed to silence protesting students; to force striking mineworkers back down the shafts; or to crush a popular peasant revolt?

The military connection with the Mobutu regime seemed so counter-productively provocative of radical sentiment in Africa that I sought an explanation from an eminent Israeli public servant. 'How can we pick and choose?' he replied. 'Aid to the Congolese government meant such aid as the Congolese government reasonably requested. If we had refused to help in military training, we would have been accused of interfering in domestic matters and kept out of the country altogether.'

By the interplay of motive and mechanism, and by impact, therefore, Israeli aid operates like Western aid: effectively not to promote professed ideals of social justice and eliminate the subservience of the poor to the interests of the rich economies, but to hinder the achievement of such ideals and secure such subservience. To this criticism, the common Israeli reply is: 'What would you have us do? We work in the countries that we do because they are the only ones that will have us; and we work with the governments because otherwise we would not be allowed to work at all. We are a state, and one pressed hard by its enemies. What other state, let alone one so pressed, acts except in its own interests? And all the same, surely we do some good.'

There is some truth in this. Under present circumstances, Israel could align itself with the revolutionary commitment only at enormous risk to its existing relationships and, for the while, at small likely gain in new ones. The subjection of its policies to the apparent interests of the state may offend humanist priorities; but then this is an offence shared by the generality of states. And some good perhaps is done by the Israeli emphasis on self-help and the residual attachment to co-operative techniques. Yet this is very far from the whole story.

Israel is forced into the role it plays by the nature of its own society; and by the related failure to reach an accommodation with the Arabs, or at least to convince revolutionary opinion of its readiness to do so on acceptable terms. Its affiliations with the advanced capitalist states are intrinsic—related to the nature of its own society. It rejects alignment with the revolutionary commitment not only because prudent state accountancy suggests that it would lose more than it would gain, but because the very values in which such accountancy deals are advanced capitalist ones. In short, it rejects the revolutionary alignment because it must; because it is itself, by the scope of its own economy and of the corresponding trade and monetary involvements, an essentially conservative society.

Its search to escape only confirms its challenging state of suspension between what it is and what it needs to be accepted as being. Inevitably, its predicament is sharpest in its crucial relations with the Arabs. Passionately the Israeli leadership argues the case for the advantages that would accrue to the Arabs from an end to the conflict. 'Look what we have to offer you: our technology; even our capital, if you want it; a dynamic trade that will develop your economies.' But an Arab conservatism, feeding on the dividends of the middle ideology, is not allured; it is only alarmed by such a prospect. It may reject war, as carrying a socially explosive potential. But any real peace seems to threaten the ruin of indigenous industry by the technically more advanced Israeli enterprises, or its capture by Israeli capital and superior management; the reduction of Arab economies into mere markets for Israeli merchandise; the spread of social-democratic ideas to confront the beneficiaries of a differently ordered privilege; the triumph of a Western culture that disparages and destroys all values not its own, and humiliates Arab history itself.

But if Arab conservatism is not to be won over by Israeli offerings, how much less so must be the Arab revolutionary commitment. From the failure of conservatism to impose its terms on Israel, with the consequence of yet more military defeats, a mortifying peace, or a resort to manœuvre and threat that waste popular confidence and the substance of the economy alike, the revolutionaries can expect only recruits to their cause. And their cause is certainly not one compatible with the rewards of peace that Israel projects. In all that talk of technical assistance, even capital investment, and dynamic trade, they hear echoes of the Western promise that they reject. Why, they ask, accept Israel for supposed economic advantages that the United States or the European Economic Community can directly and far more generously supply? What is Israel but a minor component of a system directed to secure and extend the power to exploit? For what are the supposed economic advantages but the enrichment of elites for the more effective plundering and control of client states? The struggle against Israel is part of the struggle against the Western capitalist system and is related to the struggle against the indigenous Arab elites, who are ultimately the system's servants.

Israel accordingly represents no such social hope as can draw, to the support of the peace and co-operation it asks, a significant force of Arab opinion. The best that it may realistically expect is some formula for the immediate cessation of conflict that constitutes an acquiescence by the Arab governments principally concerned in a stalemate of strength. Yet what after all would this mean? Such a formula would be the warrant of governments that might all too easily and soon be overthrown; might, indeed, the more easily and sooner be overthrown because of the warrant. And even while this lasted, it would offer no more than the territorial security of a state still sealed off from its proper environment. There would be no dynamic contact to promote the Israeli economy, or lift from the Israelis their sense of confinement in space, time, and the moral dimension. Instead, with the countervailing pressures of military menace sufficiently withdrawn, the evident centrifugal tendencies of Israeli society might well develop to destroy the state from within.

There is no doubt, whatever spokesmen may say from time to time, that the Israeli leadership recognizes this; recognizes that Israel needs not just a cessation of conflict, but a peace such as would permit normal communication with its neighbours. That is why it places such emphasis on direct negotiations with the Arab states and on a peace treaty. That is why Golda Meir herself talks in terms of the opportunity to do her shopping in Cairo.

Y. Harkabi, the Israeli intelligence expert and influential commentator on Arab affairs, believes that any real peace must depend upon a profound ideological change in Arab society. 'I would go far, all the way almost, to make peace, if I could be assured of such a change. A change in outlook towards us, reflected in the content of their education, is what ultimately matters. For what would economic or diplomatic relationships mean without it? We could exchange ambassadors and send technicians. But unless there was an educational change, these other changes would soon be subverted.'

It is not surprising that his own prognosis is therefore dark. 'It is going to be a long conflict. I do not discard the chances of a partial settlement. But the conflict would still continue. We must learn to live with uncertainty, and treat the pathological problems it produces amongst us – a dangerous hatred of the Arabs or a dangerous self-hatred instead. How are we to educate our young under the stress of a seemingly endless conflict? We need an ideology beyond that of mere nationalism.'

There is no doubting that last statement. Yet it is precisely into mere nationalism that Israel finds itself driven, by the failure to approach peace with the Arabs on the terms that the nature of its society dictates. It remains caught between the world that keeps it alive and the world that would keep it from dying.

There is another manifestation of this predicament. Without Israel's material power, the human investment of Jewish nationalism would surely be far more vulnerable to the modern military equipment of the Arab cause. Israeli soldiers may bring to battle a singular cohesion and courage. They also bring a superb military machine. And this machine is not mainly composed of American material; however important, indeed vital, that may be. Even the significant financial flow from the Diaspora supports rather than makes the force that Israel is. For this force is fundamentally the product of the country's advanced industrial capitalist culture: with its abundant capacity for rapid technical innovation; with its infrastructure of transport, communications, developed skills, thrusting attitudes. As Israelis themselves admit, it is in the end their technological superiority that secures them against their enemies.

Yet this particular superiority, in Israel as elsewhere, has a price. The ravages of this culture are all too evident: in the oil-soiled beaches of the Mediterranean coast; in the foam of detergents wherever there is water to convey it; in the fumes that suffuse Tel Aviv and Haifa; in the sheer pressures of people upon each other in the cities, and the self-defeating escape of suburban sprawl; in the noise that the mechanism of such living makes, and that its victims augment with the very protest of their nerves.

More and more Israelis regard this price as intolerable, without necessarily seeing the relationship between price and purchase. The tiny Land of Israel movement, founded by prominent intellectuals, is a compound of territorial appetite and mystic nationalism. Eliezar Livneh, one of its leaders, is a man of far-ranging culture. He knows his way through the literatures of several European languages; but when he moves through the Bible, with his rabbinical gestures, it is obvious that he is at home.

'We do not belong to Western civilization. In the future we will have a closer communication perhaps with the Far East than with the West. Judaism is not humanistic. We are devoted to a defined human being. Our terms of reference are in the past. We are not mesmerized by the present. Three times we have dispersed and three times returned. The future is unintelligible without the past.

'We are passionately of the future and passionately of the past. We see the possibility of the apocalypse: not in the atomic bomb, but in the dead fish of pollution. The modern world, the megalopolis, is impossible. Tel Aviv is hopeless. We have to disperse the coastal population. We were produced to find solutions to such problems. It is our mission: no, not our mission; it is our obligation. We are different from other peoples; not better or worse, as an olive tree is not better or worse than a vine; just different.

'The Arabs have so much land, so much space. Those of them among us must have their full citizenship rights. We are tested by the Arab, by our treatment of him. We are forbidden to hate the Arabs, by our civilization. That is why we have been victorious, because we have not hated. Our behaviour must be almost independent of their behaviour to us. But we must stay where we are. We need what we have.'

The Land of Israel movement is not important in itself. It

received less than 8,000 votes, or little over 0·5% of the total, in the 1969 elections. It is important because it reveals, albeit disfiguringly as through a faulty lens, the national search for a mission; and because, in applying this mission to the challenge of pollution, it projects, in rejecting, the essential dilemma. An Israel that stays where it is, along the frontiers of conquest, needing the space to mitigate pollution, is precisely an Israel that would have to intensify pollution, for the material power to stay where it is.

But the established requirements of a sufficient military posture are not alone responsible. Pollution is the price, too, of the emphasis on recklessly rising material standards of welfare. The Israeli system, with its increasing dependence on the dynamic of competitive consumption, displays the achievements and ravages more or less prominent in other countries of capitalist industrialization. The state capitalism of the Soviet Union, with its own overriding devotion to the growth of the gross national product, has examples of pollution to rival those of the advanced market economies.

If there is a society whose present leadership professes a different measure of welfare, it is that of China. There, with the cultural revolution, was declared the commitment to arrest and even reverse the growth of the major cities, by shifting people and industry away for dispersion among rural communes; to avoid demographic swellings of tower blocks; to reject the dominion of the motor car, perhaps the supreme symbol of self-defeating material progress.* And this commitment inevitably has other features. There are not now in Shanghai, once the most proudly Western of Chinese cities, the ubiquitous banks and bars, the feverish commercial advertising and sexual titillation of Hong Kong and Tokyo, New York and Frankfurt and Tel Aviv. The competitive personal liberties of the market economy are denounced; as are the corporate material prerogatives of Soviet bureaucrats.

Indeed, essential to the whole declared Chinese experiment is the egalitarian emphasis. The avoidance of advance industrial pollution is but a part of a total revolutionary commitment, which does not deny the value of economic growth, but only the distorted

* See, for instance, the series of five articles, 'After the Cultural Revolution', by Robert Guillain in *Le Monde*, 22–5 September 1971.

and distorting ends to which such growth under capitalism is directed. It seeks instead a new, creative relationship between the individual and the community; a subjugation of material to moral values, instead of the reverse or a confusion between the two; a prevailing sense that society should be a probe into the future, rather than a prodigal expenditure of present resources. This is, after all, a commitment not so far from the vision of the socialists among the early Zionist pioneers.

And it has, pertinently, excited opposition in China not only from those of clear bourgeois or bureaucratic outlook, but from some among the avowed revolutionaries in the army, who fear a war with the Soviet Union and believe that China therefore needs the kind of material growth capable of competing with Soviet technology. 'Join them or you cannot fight them' has been the call to the grave of visionary social experiments before.

But whether or not this Chinese experiment continues and succeeds; whether or not the commitment itself can creatively accommodate the development of the individual to the cause of collective realization, the central message is, surely, undeniable: that capitalist systems produce the human and material ravages that they do because they are what they are. It may not be possible for Chinese society to achieve what its leadership claims to desire by means of the system that this same leadership has set out to promote. It is certainly impossible that Israelis should enjoy the material product of their own capitalism without having to pay the corresponding price.

There remains one more crucial choice confronting the Israelis today. It is the choice between the songs of innocence and the songs of experience. And it is for Jews perhaps a peculiarly difficult choice. For what other people in history has had such cause to know the virtue of the simple vision that defies all the reasoning of experience? What was emergent Judaism itself, the Covenant with Jehovah, but a rejection of the real world and its moral meaning as the supreme civilizations of the time had come to see them? What but a defiance of history itself was the Jewish sense of unique mission? And even when, after its triumph in the kingdom of David and Solomon, this defiance suffered corruption, defeat and exile, it survived. It returned to build a second temple; and to see that, too, destroyed. It survived through the decay and collapse of the Roman empire; and through the terrible Christian centuries, when experience argued so forcibly for acquiescence and assimilation.

It survived the hostile rise of modern nationalism in the Diaspora, and became in the process also a different defiance: a Jewish nationalism predominantly secular, with a new sense of mission in the revolutionary socialism of the Zionist pioneers. 'If you will it, it is no fairy tale,' Herzl had declared. And certainly, the establishment of a Jewish state must have seemed a fairy tale among the malarial swamps of Ottoman Palestine.

Yet if Israel was a victory for vision, it is the lessons of experience that inform the present victorious mood of Israelis. For them, history has been a hard school which has taught them the primacy of power. Who listened when the Jews cried, through the seemingly endless age of dispersion, for the right to be treated as other men in their dealings with the world, and otherwise to be left in peace for the pursuit of their own religion? That the Jews should have survived at all was due essentially to the strength of their stubbornness, which no crusade or pogrom could break. Who listened, again, when the Jews cried for a home of their own, to live as they wished, without tyranny or fear? That the Jews should have made a home for themselves at last, in the very land of their beginning, was due essentially to the force of their own endeavours in the face of Arab misunderstanding and British imperial manœuvres.

Who listened when the Jews cried that Nazism aimed at their very annihilation? That some at least were rescued from the horror of Europe was due in large measure to Jewish determination, which no hollow offerings of help or counsels of patience could shake. And finally, when the Jews cried out to the organized community of mankind for protection of the very Israel whose establishment that community had sanctioned, the Jews were left alone to confront their enemies, and to survive by their own armed courage.

When the Jews were the helpless victims of violence, not raising their hands against it but appealing instead to reason and justice and compassion, it was not enough that their appeals were disregarded. They were despised into the bargain. They were denounced as obsequious, wheedling social parasites, whose threat lay only in the impudence of their conspiratorial cohesion. Their vulnerability, itself an impulse to their persecution, was seen as evidence of their cowardice. Cowardice, indeed, was assumed to be their predominant brand.

As late as the 'twenties and 'thirties of this century, in the popular middle-class crime fiction of so professingly liberal a society as the British, the Jew was caricatured: cast in devious, sallow or swarthy, crooked and craven contrast to the frank, fair, straight-limbed courage of the Nordic hero. The Nazi terror and the Second World War made the expression of this contempt at least inadvisable among peoples bearing the banners of democracy and liberalism. But the implicit view of the Jew remained.

There is a different view now. The Israeli has become a symbol of courage. It has even come to be believed that he may look like one of those Nordic heroes of earlier fiction, or in any event behave like one. The prejudices of Western liberal culture have had to find other victims, and with a remarkable irony are finding them in those very Arabs whom they once so romanticized at the expense of Zionism.

But then, the songs of experience continue, that is what the real world is like. And the Jews of Israel have learnt, for their own sakes, to live in the real world. They are accused of being distrustful and even cynical. Perhaps they are. What other people with their experience would be otherwise? They are accused of defying world opinion in their search for secure borders. With what security has world opinion ever provided them? The most extravagant accusations are made against them, of crimes against the Arabs. Why are such accusations so easily believed? There was far less readiness to believe in Arab crimes against Jews, let alone in the Nazi commitment to genocide.

The truth is that Gentiles may have been forced, by the evidence of events, to change their image of the Jew: but they don't necessarily like it. Once vulnerable again, the Jews might all too rapidly become what they were, the despised and persecuted of mankind. And they cannot afford to lose yet another six million. The suggestion that they should be more moral than other peoples, more compassionate, more generous, more trusting, is the old anti-Semitism in a new form. Why should the Jews be different; as though they had some special need to excuse their existence? It should be enough that, given their historical experience, they are as normal as they are.

Perhaps this song would sound more convincing, if it were not sung with quite so much ardour. Cynicism may well be an element in the outlook and conduct of normal societies. But such societies also lay claim to idealism: to a faith in positive, or creative, universal values which informs their sense of purpose. It is the absence of this faith, the very rage of cynicism in the predominant Israeli mood, that stamps the society as abnormal, and, paradoxically, so betrays its real abnormality to be not its peculiar abandonment of idealism but its peculiar submission to it. The songs of experience are so ardently sung to drown the songs of innocence that still sound in Jewish ears.

Indeed, only such a perception can command some patience with the ascendant Israeli mood. For this mood is more than just overweeningly self-righteous. It exploits the historical Jewish agony to excuse whatever outlook or course of conduct present-day Israelis adopt; as though that agony represented so much moral capital to be spent by them as they choose. And it too often resorts to rejecting criticism not by contradicting its content but by attacking its motive. Critical Gentiles are accused of merely displaying their irrepressible anti-Semitism; and critical Jews, of being ashamed that they are Jews. Yet, again, what is this hyper-sensitivity but an expression of profound unease: a tribute helplessly paid by Israeli cynicism to the vital force of Jewish innocence?

The vitality of this force may well be a destructive one. Denied a faith in the future, it may direct itself to a resurrection of the past. But it has, too, a vast creative potential, whose flow may sweep the present social system and political leadership aside, for a recovery of the true pioneering vision. It is unlikely that Israelis can long remain suspended between worlds in the way they are. It is certain that if they abandon the covenant with man, they will be the primary victims. To the measure that the Jewish sense of mission is an inclusive human one, it needs no other excuse for the assertion of a Jewish identity. To the measure that it is exclusive, it must confront the human identity and any corresponding excuse for its own.

5

Israel: the politics of management

I was lunching in Jerusalem with a young political scientist from the Hebrew University. 'Have you noticed', he asked, 'that each new prime minister of Israel is older when reaching office than the one before?'* He stared gloomily at the remnants of the meal. And then he suddenly brightened. 'But it isn't, after all, a process that can go on indefinitely.'

Gerontocracy is an undeniable feature of the Israeli political system. The population itself is among the youngest in the industrially developed world. At the end of 1969, some 75·2% of the total (73·2% of Jews) were under forty-five years old; and 93·4% (93% of Jews), under sixty-five. Yet in both the Knesset and the Cabinet the average age was sixty-three. And a settlement disproportionately old was similarly to be found along the upper reaches of the civil service and the trades union movement.

Nor is this the only remarkable feature of Israel's political elite. Though a clear majority of the Jewish population come from other backgrounds, some four-fifths of the Jews in parliament are Eastern European by birth or parentage. According to Amos Elon's researches, of thirty-five new members elected in 1969, nineteen were Eastern European immigrants, and ten were Israeli natives of parents from Eastern Europe.† And again, the pattern is repeated in other related regions of authority. At a convention of the Israel Labour Party, in April 1971, Mordechai Ben Porat, one of the Oriental Jewish delegates, complained that only 2·9% of the

* There was some poetic licence employed here. But then Ben Gurion may reasonably be held to have begun his tenure in 1934, when he became Chairman of the Jewish Agency. If his subsequent two terms as prime minister, separated by Sharett's period in office, are regarded together, as an extension of his leadership in the Jewish Agency, the course record runs: Sharett older than Ben Gurion; Eshkol older than Sharett; and Golda Meir older than Eshkol.

† Amos Elon, *The Israelis: Founders and Sons* (London: Weidenfeld & Nicolson, 1971), p. 307.

positions in the three top grades of the civil service were held by Oriental Jews; while of the two hundred executives in 'government and public companies', less than 5% were from the Oriental community.*

Taken together, age and culture provide a small enough element from which the political elite is drawn. But the elite itself is far smaller still than this would suggest. For its membership has been very largely unchanged over several decades. Certainly some recruitment has been necessary, as exhaustion or death has depleted the ranks, and ambition combined with achievement have recommended inclusion as the alternative to rivalry. But many members of the elite, not least in the Knesset, were such when the state was established; and some, like the present prime minister, held important office in the politics of Jewish Palestine as far back as the 'twenties.

The longevity of power is nowhere more evident than in the predominant Labour Party. Indeed, Moshe Dayan, still widely regarded as the challenge of youth to age, was born in 1915; was Chief of Staff from 1953 to 1958; and first assumed Cabinet Office, as Minister of Agriculture, in 1959. Pinhas Sapir, Director-General at the Ministry of Defence after the establishment of the state, and subsequently Director-General of the Treasury, was Minister of Commerce and Industry from 1955 to 1963; Minister of Finance, Commerce and Industry from 1963; and Minister of Finance from early 1972: a record of power in both civil service and government, and of continuous responsibility for economic affairs, that must have few, if any, parallels in modern states of formal democracy. But the Labour Party is far from alone in this. Among other major political forces, the National Religious Party, for instance, has virtually the same leadership now that it had, as Mizrachi and Hapoel Hamizrachi, in the dying days of the Mandate. Menachem Begin continues to head Herut, the party that he founded in 1948.

Furthermore, if a high rate of static composition is a notable aspect of the political elite in general, it is no less notably so of government itself. Through changes of name, mergers, splits, and combinations, Mapai has, since its foundation in 1930, dominated the institutions of representative authority in Jewish Palestine and

* Report in *New Middle East,* No. 32, May 1971, p. 9.

then Israel. Indeed, its dominance, through its cast of leading characters, goes further back: at least to the early 'twenties and the rise of the Histadrut, the General Federation of Labour. To be sure, it has not been able to govern alone. But the components of power in the Jewish Agency and subsequently in the successive ministries of Israel have not greatly varied; and it may be said without extravagance that the democracy of the Jewish homeland has had the most consistent command of any in modern times.

The gospel according to this command itself records impressive achievements. It was the settlers, overwhelmingly from Eastern Europe, of the Second (1904–13) and Third (1919–22) *Aliyot** who gave the Jewish community in Palestine the self-confidence and credibility of sufficient numbers, and who conducted its subsequent development. It was they who, unlike their predecessors of the First *Aliyah* (1882–1903), resisted the temptation to exploit cheap Arab labour; whose agricultural collectives and co-operatives, the manifestation of their prevailing socialist commitment, were to prove so crucial to the security as well as the prosperity of Jewish settlement; who accordingly avoided the emergence of a classic colonial system, which would have been so much more vulnerable, materially and morally, to Arab assault. It was they, with some recruitment from among their own children or later immigrants of like background and persuasion, who provided the political and military leadership of the community in the struggle for a state. And victorious against the British Mandate, it was this leadership that went on to defeat the Arab invasions.

Nor was this by any means the end of the challenges. Arab hostility persisted, to constitute a constant drain on resources for military readiness. And meanwhile multitudes of destitute immigrants, with little or no schooling, few skills that the economy could profitably deploy, and a culture inimical to the established political system, arrived from the Arab states. They were fed, clothed, sheltered, trained, employed, and their children schooled, without economic collapse or any enfeeblement of democracy. Indeed, a Jewish population of little more than 750,000 in 1948 grew to one of little less than 2,500,000 in 1969, with nevertheless a remarkable rise in general living standards, and freely fought

* The successive waves of Jewish immigration.

elections that revealed overall small significant shift in voting patterns.

This does not mean that the leadership escaped serious trial. The various parties in coalition were often at loggerheads over important issues of policy; and patience, skill, determination and, above all, a prevailing sense of service were required to prevent the collapse of the whole system. Most dangerously, the main component of government, Mapai, suffered a split which at the time seemed likely enough to produce either political chaos or Caesarian rule. For Ben Gurion himself, who had headed the party for decades and whose person had become virtually synonymous with it, broke away, in a complex conflict that involved a major security scandal; the demand for electoral reform to reduce the number of parties and the need for coalitions; and pressure from among the younger members of Mapai for a larger share in the processes of decision and the responsibilities of office.

Ben Gurion's charismatic appeal threatened to cook the party in its own pre-packed propaganda juices. In the elections of 1961, his picture had glared from hoardings and walls; recent immigrants had been summoned to support the man who had made their immigration possible; and the predominant slogan had proclaimed *Hagidu ken la-zaken* (Say yes to the old man). Yet in the 1965 elections, his new party, Rafi,* polled only 7·9% of the votes: while the electoral alignment of Mapai and Achdut Ha'avoda, a pact between the leadership and the more congenial of its presumptive heirs, received 36·7%.

It was a momentous demonstration that the Israeli electorate, including so many new Oriental voters who might have been expected to follow Ben Gurion anywhere, favoured stability and the group wisdom of an established leadership against the claims of mere change and the risks of a political messiah. And the victorious veterans showed their own readiness to meet the emerging needs of the nation and its labour movement by accommodating in government the worthy of Rafi on the eve of the Six Day War, and by a reconciliation with Rafi itself to form the Israel Labour Party in January 1968. What more convincing evidence could have been provided of their ultimate success in promoting a modern and cohesive society, than the victories of 1956 and 1967?

* Reshimat Poalei Yisrael (the Israel Workers' List).

Yet such, the gospel continues, was never the sort of evidence that they wanted to provide. For theirs has been a leadership seeking assiduously for peace. It has demanded only Arab recognition of Israel's right to exist within reasonable and secure borders. If it has led the nation to war, it has done so only when Arab threats and pressures reached the point at which a failure to strike would have endangered the very survival of the state. Surely, it would never otherwise so have united the nation behind it or secured, despite all the distortions of Arab propaganda, so much understanding and support abroad.

Moreover, it has ensured for the Arabs within Israel vastly improved living standards and, in general, enjoyment of equal civil rights. Security might from time to time have required special measures against particular members of the community. But all in all, there have been few societies which have discriminated so little against a minority that is kin to an intransigent external enemy. Not only do Arabs sit in the Knesset, but they do so even as representatives of a party, Rakah,* which openly pursues policies at variance with those supported by the mass of the Jewish community.

The leadership has surmounted another challenge, all the more formidable perhaps for being largely implicit. Throughout the struggle for a state and subsequently in developing the material strength of Israel, the Western Diaspora has played a crucial role: by the skilled immigrants it has supplied; by the influence it has exercised on public opinion and governments abroad; and, above all, by its massive financial investments and gifts. Much of the influence and most of the money have come from Jews whose personal wealth and political attitudes distinguished them clearly from the dominant character of Jewish settlement in Palestine and the policies followed by the government of Israel.

Yet the leadership in the homeland has never abandoned its resolution to base the Jewish state on broadly socialist principles. Despite the unique difficulties of their development, Israel's welfare services are such as few far richer states can properly boast. Economic discrepancies in the country are among the narrowest in the world; and certainly much narrower than in many states describing themselves as socialist. Even today, with the economy

* Reshima Kommunistit Hadasha (New Communist List).

of Israel in an advanced industrial stage, the after-tax incomes of persons in high public office are low by comparison with those of their counterparts in the vast majority of other countries, and not much above those of most skilled Israeli industrial workers.

In this, as in so much else, the leaders have always led by personal example, as officers in the Israeli armed forces are celebrated for always fighting from the front. They have shirked neither discomfort nor danger. They cleared swamps, planted trees, built roads. They helped defend the settlements against attack. They risked, and some of them suffered, imprisonment by the British authorities. Those who were of acceptable age fought in the army. They bear in their bodies and minds the marks of national struggle: as the crust of the earth contains traces of endeavour and upheaval. They lead not because they were born to do so; not because they have bought their way to power or remain there by imposing themselves; but because they are truly of the people and selected only for the value of their service.

There is fact enough in all this proclaimed record of leadership to carry conviction. But it represents merely one profile of Israel's political face. And the other is rather less alluring. At the convention of the Israel Labour Party in April 1971, Yitzhak Ben Aharon, Secretary-General of the Histadrut and himself accordingly an important member of the leadership, cried out against those who treated their positions of authority as their 'own personal fiefs'. He declared that 'this country can't do without our rule, but we are very, very far from being liked for it'. Above all, he complained, ideological values had been emptied of their content, and social justice made a thing of the past. Economic success had become the predominant measure. 'We live in a spiritual isolation. We give up our lives to create ... bricks, beds, buildings ... '

His remarks were reportedly received with thunderous applause. But applause is not necessarily power. The man who controlled the convention from behind the scenes, and tightened his grip on the party apparatus by getting his candidates elected to pivotal positions, was Pinhas Sapir: the very man who, as Minister of Finance, Commerce and Industry, was more than any other associated with the emphasis on 'bricks, beds, buildings' at the cost of 'spiritual isolation'.

The issue of religion and state, inflamed by recent rulings of the Rabbinate,* was scarcely discussed at the convention, although it was widely considered within the rank-and-file that the Labour Party should assert its secularist commitment. The scheduled debate was simply cancelled at the last minute, because resolutions on the subject might endanger the government alliance with the National Religious Party. One of the delegates, Shulamit Aloni, who had been ousted from parliament by the leadership in repayment for her rebellious views, commented bitterly: 'Our socialism and our democracy are words only, or perhaps meant for export.'†

The gathering labour discontent at the economic policies of the leadership has been evident in the rise of industrial unrest. Yet the leadership has reacted with stubborn lack of understanding. As an article in the newspaper *Yediot Aharonot* declared:

> Instead of asking why the strikes were declared, what is their genesis and of what social disorder they are a symptom, everyone attacked the symptom and completely ignored his own responsibility for the disease. One Minister declared that strikes should be forbidden, another Minister talked about using the army to break strikes, and the Prime Minister emotionally announced that she wants to resign and will not head a government which reputedly 'produces millionaires'. Nevertheless, the government is producing millionaires, and the French newspaper *Figaro* was right when it said that in Israel the rich are getting richer and the poor are getting poorer ...
>
> The use of the law, the army and the police to suppress the workers is something that the generation of the founders of the Histadrut never imagined in its worst nightmares. But the same generation is still living and some of its members are running the Histadrut and the Alignment.‡ This generation

* Jews born of an adulterous relationship were refused the right to a Jewish marriage; and so, since civil marriage does not exist in Israel, to any marriage as Jews. Then, although the Gentile wives of Jewish immigrants from the Soviet Union had been converted by arrangement with the Viennese Rabbinate, the Rabbinate in Israel continued to regard them as Gentiles, declaring their conversions null and void, on the grounds that these had not been conducted in accordance with all the principles of Jewish law.

† Report in *New Middle East*, No. 32, May 1971.

‡ Of the Israel Labour Party and Mapam, with 56 of the 120 seats in the Knesset.

is now talking about taking steps it would have called fascist a few years ago.*

The truth is that the political leadership of Israel is among the most arrogant in the recognized democratic world. Illustrations so abound that it is difficult to select one for introductory recital. But a recent instance merits mention for the self-defeating crassness of the failure to consider, or understand, the popular mood – for its sheer extravagance of gesture. Early in April 1972, Reuven Barkatt, Speaker of the Knesset, died. He was a veteran leader of distinction, but scarcely a folk hero. The leadership took it upon itself to delay the announcement of the death until the end of Passover, apparently so as not to disturb the nation during the festival; and then ordered almost two days of public mourning, with the cancellation of all regular radio and television programmes, from the time of the announcement to the end of the funeral. *Ma'ariv*, a Hebrew daily not celebrated for its vigorous criticism of the leadership, editorially rebuked the imposition of such national mourning 'from on high', and rightly declared that this had prompted instead 'anger and boredom'.†

The arrogance is in part cultural. Ben Gurion referred in 1967 to the immigrants who had arrived after independence as 'human dust' that 'we converted ... into a sovereign nation'. And this attitude was all too evident in the way that the leadership reacted to the protests by young Oriental Jews against what they believed to be their communal deprivations. There was no apparent recognition of the enormous psychic impact which the Eastern European background of the Israeli leadership and the nature of the dominant culture must have on citizens who are incompatibly Oriental in background. To the measure that the leadership at last publicly conceded the existence of a problem, it considered that this was one which the expenditure of enough money alone would solve, through improved educational and employment opportunities. It did not begin to question the sanctity of its own standards. It did not bother to make clear, if it seriously considered the difficulties at all, how opportunities on the massive scale necessary were to be provided. It gave instead every indication of impatience at being

* Boaz Evron in *Yediot Aharonot*, 10 September 1971.
† *Ma'ariv*, 6 April 1972.

distracted from its prevalent concerns; and of affront, even astonishment, that these young Oriental Jews were so ungrateful for what it had done already on their behalf.

But then, to be sure, these Jews had not only their background but their youth against them. For the arrogance of the leadership is also one of age. Criticism from anyone outside its ranks is received with irritation enough; and when not charitably ascribed to ignorance, is denounced as irresponsible or malignant. But criticism from the young is treated with scorn. For how should they know what burdens the leadership must bear? What do they know of the burdens the leadership has borne? In a world where youth is increasingly rebellious, and the leaderships of formally open societies pay at least diligent lip service to the need for promoting among the young a sense of participation in processes of political decision, the Israeli leadership is in general only outraged by suggestions that it may have outlived its usefulness or is essentially unrepresentative of the society it governs.

There may well be in this, even among the supposedly hardened secularists, an element of that emphasis on the respect due to age which belongs to the original tribal culture of the Jews, their developed religious doctrine, and the requirements of distinctive survival in the Diaspora. The rebels of long ago have grown increasingly mystic about the value of Jewish tradition. But then, too, there is no authoritarian quite like the rebel who has succeeded to authority. And so many of Israel's present-day leaders were in their youth rebels themselves, against the wishes, advice, authority of their elders. Their revolutionary ideals, their attachment to Zionism, their departure for the real dangers of Palestine, must all too often have met argument and recrimination from their parents. To be sure, they themselves were proved right. Might this not therefore suggest that a rebellion against their own authority must be wrong?

And this authoritarian self-righteousness has passed, as somehow essential to the process of adoption, from the veteran leadership to its accommodated heirs. The rebels of Achdut Ha'avoda, who raised their independent standard in 1948, and those of Rafi who did so in 1965, seem no less convinced today of the obedience due to leadership, for having been themselves disobedient before.

Self-righteousness itself is, indeed, an important element in the arrogance of the Israeli leadership. And to understand this, it is helpful to examine aspects of the way that Jewish politics operated in the Diaspora of Eastern Europe. For it is not only that so many of Israel's veteran leaders emerged from that experience. The very parties that still dominate Israeli politics had their origins there.

The basis was the *kehila* or largely autonomous Jewish community, within the autocratic Russian empire.* Each such *kehila* functioned on more or less democratic lines, because internal government could scarcely be imposed against the general will, and internal government was imperative. Religious and charitable activities had to be financed by some form of communal self-taxation; officials entrusted to make laws and preserve order. For how was Jewish cohesion, and so survival, to be secured, if the building and running of synagogues, hospitals, orphanages, were to depend on Gentile benevolence; and individual Jews were to seek redress against each other in the Gentile courts?

This does not mean that all the communities organized themselves in the same way. But a few predominant features of functioning should be cited for their relevance to contemporary Israeli politics. I encountered them myself, through the medium of my communally active parents, in Cape Town. Most of the adult Jews there had come from Eastern Europe; and though their material circumstances were now far more congenial, the anti-Semitism that they encountered, especially from the leadership of a resurgent Afrikanerdom, contributed to keeping alive the practices that they had brought with them.

The system involved the existence of the *macher*: literally in Yiddish the 'maker' or 'doer'; by refinement, the big man who could 'fix things', whether necessary papers from Gentile authority or some solution to a local problem. These *machers* were often the richest members of the community, who received a say in collective decisions commensurate with their contribution to the costs of voluntary welfare, their value as emissaries to the Gentiles, and even the respect due to their achievement of material success. For riches were not a source of shame, virtually a sign of sin, in Jewish tradition, provided that they were accompanied by generosity. A whole *kehila* might shine in the reflected light of a notably rich

* Shlomo Avineri, 'Israel in the Post-Ben Gurion Era', *Midstream*, September 1965.

member, rather as the Diaspora itself, if its jokes are any indication, bathed in the light of the Rothschilds.

Yet, paradoxically, in a community whose particular existence was founded on religious or moral factors, the *macher* was also the man of signal virtue: pious, righteous, reticent, humble, self-denying; whose very poverty reflected his spiritual preoccupations and his readiness to serve. Sometimes a rabbi or teacher, sometimes no more than a Jew of ordinary occupation, he was called upon to advise, to judge, to sit on boards of communal management. Several major Jewish organizations in Cape Town, among whose leading members the rich of the city were to be found, were effectively dominated by *machers* of small material but supposedly large moral resources.

Doubtless some of these paragons were no less in substance than in repute. But too close a hold on power for too long left others with an overriding determination to continue enjoying it and a pronounced contempt for riches, which did not preclude a mutually useful collaboration with the rich themselves. The very confinement of the community within so much suspicion, hatred and scorn made acclaim by one's fellow victims at least, the more to be sought.

It is easy to see how this feature of Diaspora politics was transplanted to Palestine and nourished by the endeavour to establish and secure a state. The development of Zionism itself depended upon collaboration between the two types of *macher*, the rich and the righteous. The enormous financial subsidies from Baron Edmond de Rothschild made possible the first firm footholds of Jewish settlement. And it was to another Rothschild, representing the moneyed leadership of the Diaspora and in particular British Jewry, that the Balfour Declaration was addressed. But neither Herzl nor Weizmann, the major figures of Zionism in the Diaspora, had riches. Their ascendancy lay in their imagination, intellect, eloquence; in the vigour with which they served their vision; and in their consequent capacity to command the interest and resources of the rich. They were supreme examples, and with much more substance than many who modelled themselves on them, of the moral boss.

And bossism in the Yishuv was overwhelmingly of the moral type. Palestine was scarcely a place where Jews would settle to amass vast private fortunes; and if a very few did succeed in growing rich there, they were not much honoured for it by the mass of pioneers devoted to egalitarian ideals and self-reliant endeavour. A notable dichotomy in leadership developed between the Zionist movement of the Diaspora, where wealth played so conspicuous a role, and the Yishuv, where moral factors, central among these the determination to create a new sort of society, so long prevailed.

It is a dichotomy that has both more and less substance today. With Eastern Europe under an efficient totalitarianism hostile to the Zionist movement, Zionist organization in the Diaspora is effectively limited to the relatively rich Jewish communities of the West and especially the United States; while aid to Israel is increasingly a matter of money and influence on Western governments rather than of immigration. Inevitably this gives to the bossism of riches a more than ever dominant role. And though Israel itself is increasingly a materialist society, with the appeal and power of money all too evident, its leadership continues to conduct itself as a bossism of righteousness instead.

The pretensions are wearing rather thin. More and more, the leadership is discarding the egalitarian dress of pioneering days for the elitist dignity of ties and suits. And even where the old uniform is kept, the new life style scarcely corresponds. No one would accuse Dayan of conspicuous consumption on his clothes. But his private arrangements, of home and entertainment, are a far cry from the necessities of which the early settlers made such a virtue. To be sure, many of the veterans furnish their persons and their homes little more lavishly than do most of their fellow citizens. Their cash incomes remain moderate. But even on this level, they still live untenably better, for the claims that they make, than a multitude of Jewish Israeli poor. And there is another, disguised level of prerogative. Their free use of cars and telephones, their frequent trips abroad at state expense, provide them with real material standards that fall short only of those enjoyed by the very rich. And the deference that they receive, and do not seem convincingly to discourage, from their official minions is hardly conducive to their promotion of the principle that righteousness should be its own reward.

In short, the bossism is rather more in evidence than the

righteousness, and this in itself may constitute another element in their arrogance. For the leadership has always been largely composed of those who have taken their cause and themselves with profound seriousness. To call them mere hypocrites would be unjust to their motives and manners alike. If they have become so different from what they were and pretend still to be, it is all too probable that they sufficiently suspect this themselves. The very vigour of their claims not to have changed but to be the same self-denying servants of the people that they have always been is a confession of their doubts. They protest altogether too much. Their moral arrogance is a manifestation of guilt.

If bossism was one conspicuous feature of community politics in the Diaspora, party strife was another. The election of a new rabbi or other synagogue official, the organization of some welfare project with the appointment of those to supervise its functioning, supplied ample occasion for *machers* to marshal their supporters and measure their ascendancy. And given the importance of righteousness in the community, faction often became the most vituperative ideological conflict, with rival claims to a monopoly of virtue.

The South African Zionist Federation, for instance, traditionally recruited its executive membership on an individual basis. But several years before the establishment of Israel, and even while Afrikaner politicians were denouncing the country's Jews as a foreign, unassimilable presence, ideological conflict within the Zionist movement, fed by personal rivalries, forced a change to full-dress elections on the basis of party lists. Revisionists, Zionist Socialists, Mizrachi, General Zionists fought each other with posters and leaflets, public meetings and private canvassing; while a non-party party campaigned as passionately, if in the end unsuccessfully, against the parties themselves as these campaigned against one another.

And the party strife in the South African Zionist movement was late on the scene. The World Zionist Organization itself had for many years already been based on the party system: with proportional representation producing several small parties, in whose interest it was to encourage the fervour of conflict among the large ones. But then party conflict was at least as fervent inside Jewish Palestine.

The two main parties of labour, the Marxist Po'alei Zion and the non-Marxist Ha'poel Ha'tzair, disputed with missionary zeal each other's title to the truth. Arriving at the port of Jaffa, an early immigrant proceeded to one of two inns, as his connection with either party proposed. And from there, he was conveyed to some settlement of corresponding ideology. For such settlements, especially the kibbutzim, were not each an eclectic colony, whose members might support both or other parties, but essentially an ideological unit, planted by a particular party to represent and propagate its views.

Thus in 1953, when differences of opinion arose within certain kibbutzim over the nature of the Soviet system and its role in the world, members who had been the closest of friends for years stopped talking to each other. Partitions appeared in dining halls; communal property was split; and at last, those in a minority withdrew altogether, to establish themselves elsewhere.

Nor was doctrinal ardour by any means limited to the Left. The religious parties were scarcely less convinced of their own absolute righteousness, though their differences with one another seemed to suggest that sin was not restricted to secularists. And the Revisionists even broke away from the World Zionist Organization in the 'thirties: not only to pursue their ultra-nationalist policies in distinctive independence, but soon afterwards to form their own military force for the purpose.

In short, the various parties, secular and religious alike, were political sects: concerned not merely with the votes but with the salvation of their adherents, from whom they required a correspondingly total commitment. They were or became competing agencies for the transport and settlement of immigrants; trades unions for those of their members in employment; publishers of newspapers and books; banks and insurance companies; educational institutions for activists, women, the young; centres of guidance and aid; homes within the homeland. And their leaderships increasingly saw themselves, therefore, as priests and prophets; custodians and interpreters of their respective revealed truths; to which, rather than to the fallibility of the faithful, they were responsible.

Their ascendancy and the arrogance that accompanied it were promoted by the development of their common cause. At first, direct democratic practices prevailed, especially within the parties of the Left. Freedom of general discussion was easy enough while the scale of political organization remained small. But as the size of membership swelled, and the character of Jewish settlement in Palestine grew so much more complex, effective decision fell further into the clutch of the leaders; who could meet frequently or at short notice, and persuasively claim exclusive access to the prerequisite facts.

This process was advanced by the engagement against the British Mandate, with the need for secrecy in the planning of campaigns. It was advanced by the relationship between the Jewish community in Palestine and the Zionist movement in the Diaspora, both for particular parties and for the parties in particular unison: a relationship of conflict and accommodation essentially conducted on the leadership level. And it was advanced by the system of proportional representation which structured the Jewish Agency as well as the World Zionist Organization. Indeed, this system became the basis of representative government in the state; and the Israeli voter today selects a party by selecting its list of candidates, whose collective presentation and even order of precedence are determined by the party executive.

The constant necessity for coalition government that this system has produced itself enormously enhances, of course, the domination of the various parties by their respective leaderships. For, given the largely static distribution of electoral support across apparently incompatible commitments, the most unlikely ideological partnerships have ensued. Parties whose identifying passions have been a socialist economy and a secular state have formed ministries with others dedicated to a liberal economy and the advancement of religious law. And it is the leaderships that effectively decide, in the passage between the vituperation of electioneering and the corporate loyalties of government, what proclaimed policies to abandon or adjust as the price of power.

There is a further historical influence on the functioning and attitude of the Israeli leadership; an influence drawn from the Diaspora environment of Eastern Europe, rather than from the Diaspora itself, and primarily, though not exclusively, operative within the predominant parties of labour. This was the involvement in the revolutionary challenge to the Tsarist empire, especially by the Russian Social Democratic Workers' Party. Their Zionism may have cut them off from actual membership, but the Jewish socialists who were to become Israel's veteran leaders could not but be affected by an organization with so much ideology in common. And inevitably they absorbed the Bolshevik emphasis on centralized leadership and rigorous internal discipline.

Yet there is a paradox here that both helps to explain the arrogance of the Israeli leadership and suggests the limitations on its reach. If Diaspora traditions of bossism, reinforced by rival claims to righteousness in party strife and by Bolshevik organization in the Eastern European background, were important influences on the development of politics in the Yishuv, there were others countervailingly at work. The democratic strain in the Diaspora tradition was reinforced by the very process of settlement in Palestine, which demanded so much individual initiative within collaborative endeavour, and which was so much informed by egalitarian ideals.

Social revolt in Eastern Europe was by no means a Bolshevik monopoly. The Narodniks, who commanded the earlier revolutionary challenge, with their emphasis on the potential of the peasantry rather than of the proletariat, were in certain respects closer to the character of pioneering Zionist settlement than were the various parties or factions of Marxist commitment. For it was they who had so hallowed labour on the land. And the strong anarchist element in their thought, which saw in the repressions of all authority the dynamic of evil, was abundantly evident among the recruits to the first collectives of the Return.

Indeed, the whole historical experience of the Diaspora may be said to have promoted a Narodnik approach among Jews to the princes of the state. And it was an approach fostered in Jewish Palestine by the rise of resistance to the British Mandate. Yet the very recognition of this, to them so alarming a propensity, has in turn fostered the Bolshevik approach among the princes of the Jewish state. It is perhaps not extravagant to describe Israel today as a Narodnik populace governed as far as possible on Bolshevik principles.

There is, finally, in the developed arrogance of the leaders an underlying uncertainty. From what they say and do, or fail to say and do, they increasingly betray their sense that they are losing their grip on the society they have commanded for so long. They are accustomed to having all the answers; but now there are new questions being raised for which there are no ready answers available in their background and experience and outlook. How are they to deal, for instance, with the environmental ravages of the very economic growth which they have, like their counterparts in so many other states, so blindly idolized? How are they, in particular, to deal with the social and personal ravages of population pressure, when a major policy, indeed principle, of theirs has always been to promote, by birth or immigration, as large a Jewish population as possible? To be sure, there may be ways of making the state support far larger numbers of citizens in conditions of decent space and quiet and cleanliness. But if Israel's leaders show incipient signs of recognizing that there is a challenge here, they show none of having developed any coherent attitude to meet it.

As industrial, so military success has produced unenvisaged problems. An expansionist, indeed imperial, aspiration, previously limited to more or less tentative commitments among the religious and the Revisionists, has been popularly encouraged by conquest. And the leadership of labour has itself come to raise the threshold of the effectively unnegotiable in consequence. Yet the Arabs no longer flee from Israeli-occupied territory as once they did. Whatever land is kept, with or without a negotiated settlement, the Arabs on it cannot much longer be denied full political rights, whether they demand them or not, except at the cost of denying the professed democratic principles of the state. Yet how is the present complexion of the state to accommodate a correspondingly augmented Arab political force? Again, if the leadership shows some signs of recognizing the challenge, it shows none of knowing how to cope with it. And recent retreats by the avowedly secularist parties of labour, to conciliate religious Jewish opinion, do not indicate much of a determination to learn.

Nor, if there is some understanding of the moral corrosions that the constant state of conflict promotes, is there a considered policy on how to deal with them. What the Kafr Qasim affair in the late 'fifties made clear was not that the leadership at large had a policy, right or wrong, towards atrocities committed by Jewish forces, but that it had no policy at all; that it was caught short by events and, having failed to cover them up, effectively chose the course of least resistance.

Like the massacre of Arab villagers by forces of the Irgun Tsva'i Leumi and Stern group at Dir Yassin in 1948, which brought an immediate apology from Ben Gurion to King Abdullah, the Kafr Qasim atrocity mattered not least for being so marked a departure from the way that Jews believed themselves to be conducting their conflict with the Arabs. But in the development of that conflict, methods have now come unexceptionally to be used, as in the interrogation of suspected Arab guerrillas, and as with the punishment of families or communities for an act committed by a single member, the moral implications of which the leadership has in the main never seemed properly to consider or declare. The issue is not, of course, whether such conduct is common, or indeed commonly regarded as pardonable in the circumstances of the Jewish Israelis; still less, whether Arabs do, or would be likely to, behave with far fewer scruples. The issue is that such conduct contradicts the moral principles proclaimed by most in the leadership. This does not mean that the principles are, therefore, mere camouflage. It is all too probable, given their background and beliefs, that most leaders are morally disturbed by what they increasingly find themselves asked to sanction. But they see, in terms of their overall policies, no alternative. And they accordingly take refuge either in abdicating all responsibility to the army, or in resorting to an ecstasy of self-righteousness. If they themselves, they cry, can accommodate their consciences to methods of this kind, they have no need to fear any moral strictures from others.

They are not, of course, as self-righteous about the financial scandals that sporadically surface and suggest the formidable growth of corruption beneath. For them, the defence of Jewish settlement in the days of the Mandate seems by contrast to have been so much more edifying an engagement. Most of them yearn for the moral priorities of those days. Unmistakably they betray their bewilderment that the cause of the Jewish people is no longer, for Jews in a state of their own, apparently enough.

And in this they betray their bewilderment at what Jewish society itself has become. The highest achievable standard of individual consumption, and hard luck to the hindmost, is far more a mark of the real Israel than is service to the community.

Is it any wonder that strikes multiply, with each group of workers setting out to extract as much from the social product as its particular capacity for economic pressure permits? Is it any wonder that legal tax evasion has become such a feature of employment agreements; or that many citizens should seize opportunities for the reward of illegal enterprise? Is it any wonder that nationalism can no longer disguise the development of riches and poverty, of privilege and resentment?

The leaders, avowedly governing as guides to the promised land of justice and brotherhood, are given to wringing their hands and rebuking the devotion to the golden calf. They admit, under question, to having bent their own principles, but only as circumstances dictated, and for the good of the state. For if they had not encouraged foreign investment and the initiative of Israeli traders and industrialists; if they had not promoted the maximum effort by those in the professions, in skilled management and labour: they would never have been able to absorb so productively such multitudes of new immigrants; to meet the immense defence needs of the state; and yet to ensure so substantial a rise in the living standards of all.

They simply reject the connection between the policies they have pursued, and the popular engagement to private consumption, the strikes, the financial scandals. They will not abandon their own incompatible pretensions, and proclaim a morality that reflects the real processes of their society; and they will or dare not set out seriously to reverse these processes. And so they attempt to square the circle by making their leadership itself the measure of righteousness. Like Jehovah, they ultimately reply that they are what they are.

This arrogance of a leadership that more and more seems responsive only to the intervention of mortality, is for some among the disaffected personified by Golda Meir herself: a maternalism of predatory service; insistently devoted, casually inconsistent, sententious, querulous, plaintively protective and forgiving. With such a mother, it may be asked, who needs a complaint?

But this is to exaggerate the personal ascendancy of Mrs Meir. A rather more apposite analogy is with the governing board of a large corporation whose shares are so widely held that no individual stake comes anywhere near commanding control, though various institutional investments possess considerable implicit influence. Most directors have served, if not on the board itself, then in one or other related executive capacity, since incorporation; and many, indeed, were active long before, in developing the constituent enterprises. It is a sort of family firm: only the kinship is one of background and experience and outlook, instead of blood. The board issues regular reports, and on occasion special ones, that offer morale-boosting messages on the company's impressive growth record, along with admonitions against complacency, and calls for yet more intensive effort; and in submitting itself to the judgment of re-election, is assured that this is largely a ritual, with the result taken for granted. There should be small surprise that the directors seem increasingly afflicted with a corporate arterio-sclerosis; or have come increasingly to conduct themselves as though the sole alternative to their management must be the collapse of the company.

If the arrogance of Israel's political leadership says much not only about the leaders themselves but also about the society they lead, so too does the arrogance of the complex bureaucracy. There are few Israelis without favourite instances of its functioning to cite. One Sabra, a relative of mine, returning after several years in Japan, sought to replace a lost driver's licence. Flatly refusing to believe that she had been out of the country for so long, the relevant functionary demanded to know in what mental institution she had been confined. Realizing finally that the functionary was being serious, she left with such dignity as she could muster, and returned with her passport only to confront outrage rather than apology. She is no longer so sure of ubiquitous Israeli rectitude as she used to be.

In 1965 a study of bureaucratic behaviour at Amidar, a state sector housing agency, revealed that of those officials communicating directly with the public, 60·2% would not greet a visitor or even answer his greeting, while 63·7% would not offer him a chair but keep him standing.

Mrs Meir, in her address to the conference on public administration, supplied a catalogue of failings that, had it come from anyone outside the cloisters of power, she might well have castigated as irresponsible and malevolent criticism.

> It is the normal and regular thing in this country for people to be turned away and told, 'Come back tomorrow, or next week', when a little effort by the clerk or official concerned could take care of the problem on the spot.
>
> It is a tragedy that some young couples, just out of the army and wanting to marry and settle down, cannot find a home or raise a mortgage. But it is much worse that couples who have been approved for a mortgage have to spend six months running around to obtain it. With us, they put a man behind a desk or a window to deal with the public, and he's often amazed by the fact that members of the public actually come to disturb him.*

She lashed out at telephone girls who simply answered 'yes', or, when the caller asked to speak to someone, made no response at all, and left him waiting on a silent line. 'I don't approve of generalizations and criticisms of the entire public administration,' she continued. 'There is no need to exaggerate when so much is in fact at fault.'

An income-tax official at the Treasury, Mr Olesker, then

> took the rostrum to demand that Mrs. Meir meet with him to discuss his proposed 'public council for promoting good citizenship'. He said that he had written to Mr. Sapir, the Finance Minister, a year ago on the subject, but was still awaiting a reply. He had written to ask Mrs. Meir for an interview – and had been referred to the Finance Minister.
>
> He had now written to the new Minister of Commerce and Industry, Mr. Haim Bar-Lev. Mrs. Meir could only explain that she cannot possibly receive all those who want to meet with her. Mr. Olesker should approach the Finance Minister or the Education Minister, she said. That was what they got a salary for.†

Part of the explanation for the outlook and behaviour of the Israeli bureaucrats may lie in the historical precedents that variously influenced them: the Ottoman, the Eastern European, the British mandatory systems, all three of which were conspicuous

* Report in the *Jerusalem Post,* 15 March 1972.

† Ibid.

for the absence of democratic investment and control. And part, surely, lies in the peculiarly Yishuv tradition of *haluka*: the distribution of funds, raised abroad, by officials effectively accountable only to themselves, and impatient at any sign of complaint, or insufficient gratitude, from the recipients. For officials accustomed or appointed to this tradition, the public service in the new state was all too easily seen as creating the society, rather than as developing from and dependent upon it. And the tradition is, moreover, a continuously nourished one: with the reliance of the state on the massive flow of funds from abroad, which the leadership and the bureaucracy disburse as though it were their own. What right has the recipient to criticize the administration of resources that he has not earned?

A prime example of this attitude, for the unplanned edification of bureaucrats who might learn of it through the press, was given by Mrs Meir herself, at a question-and-answer session with students at the University of the Negev in Beersheba. She encountered criticism that immigrants were receiving preferential treatment, while students who had served in the country's armed forces found new housing difficult to get. 'Asking the students whether they had anything against *aliyah*, Mrs. Meir said she never dreamed she would be told by students that *olim** exist at their expense. "All you students at Jerusalem, Tel Aviv, Haifa and Beersheba live at the expense of Jews who are not in Israel," she told the students.'†

For, of course, the bureaucrats tend to model themselves on their masters: displaying the same self-righteousness of service; the same demand for respect and gratitude; the same hunger that power excites by the feeding. And lower down the scale of authority, where the material and psychical rewards are less, the exactions of deference are therefore the more pressed. But there is, connectedly, another element. Given the importance that it is encouraged, by its role in the development of the state and by the example of the leadership, to attach to itself, the bureaucracy is in general poorly paid. Only at the levels which merge into the political leadership do various disguised forms of income, in free services, convey membership in the material elite.

* New settlers.

† Report in the *Jerusalem Post*, 9 March 1972.

Indeed, there is no clearer evidence of Israel's increasingly liberal-capitalist character than the relative material slide which the ranks of the bureaucracy suffer in the competitive pressures of different economic groups. The administrative servants of the state cannot make the same rapid and serious impact on the economy, by strike action, as can other sectors of labour; and are, by the nature of their employment, less ready to take militant initiatives: while the state itself, confronted by the need for retrenchment to reduce the rate of inflationary wage settlements or the momentum of public expenditure, seizes on its own servants to provide an example or a means.

Inevitably, the growing gap in Israel between the egalitarian pretensions that have so long held moral sway and the mounting material inequalities, has made the bureaucracy both more resentful and more assertive. Indignant at sectors of superior consumption whose standards they covet, and by contrast with which they feel socially disparaged, the functionaries parade their prerogatives of office; to chastise the rich where they can, and the poor as a substitute where they cannot.

A survey of adult Jews in 1968 revealed 44% as having had no contact whatsoever with government or public bureaucracy in the previous six months.* But this understates the effective extent of family contact. 'While 70% of the highly educated men report contact, only 55% of their female counterparts do so. The difference for the group with low education is even greater, with 56% of the men reporting contact and only 28% of the women ... Probably women let their husbands take care of many bureaucratic matters, especially if they themselves are poorly educated.'

Of the total sample, only 18% reported 'positive' or satisfactory contact, while 38% reported 'negative'. But this, too, understates bureaucratic deficiencies. 'All groups tend to report more negative than positive contact, but the trend is greater in the higher status groups ... These findings might mean that low-status persons are treated better, or that they are simply less critical (if anything, our

* The survey was based on a random sample of 1,886 adults in the four major cities of Israel—Jerusalem, Tel Aviv, Haifa and Beersheba—and was claimed as 'representative of about 75% of the Jewish adult population': Brenda Danet and Harriet Hartman, 'Coping with Bureaucracy: The Israeli Case' (Jerusalem: the Communications Institute and Sociology Department of the Hebrew University, and the Israel Institute of Applied Social Research, December 1970).

hunch is that they are treated worse). Other findings ... strengthen the second of these interpretations.'

Yet in the politics of management, there is a safety valve in personal contact with the managers themselves. And if the vast intrusive and arrogant bureaucracy is one feature of Israeli society, the widespread exercise of *proteksia*, or personal influence, to avoid or adjust its determinations, is another. It is the enmeshment of these two factors which has led Professor Eisenstadt, the Israeli sociologist, to suggest a simultaneous state of both 'overbureaucratization' and 'debureaucratization'.*

These somewhat heavily described processes have a serious social impact in common. They inevitably favour the better-educated, longer-resident citizens of Western background, who in general display far greater self-assurance, as they possess far greater awareness of their rights, in dealing with the bureaucracy. And that those of Oriental background, in their lesser self-assurance and awareness of their rights, reveal themselves as less critical of the bureaucracy does not contradict but, rather, promotes their relative disadvantage. Furthermore, it is Western Israelis who far more commonly enjoy the personal relationships with management that inform *proteksia*. For theirs is precisely the background from which the overwhelming majority of the managers come. Indeed, their relationship, directly or through their families, is often rooted in the solidarity of struggle that established the state. The cry that 'all Jews are brothers' is the popular appeal to management from members of the Oriental community as well. But the managers themselves are predictably selective in acknowledging the claims of brotherhood. It is certainly not the least notable feature of a liberal capitalist society that to those who have, it shall be given. And the peculiar operations of bureaucracyand *proteksia* in Israel are conducive to the same result.

Yet with the arrogance of the leadership and the state administrative regiments so manifest, it remains to be considered how such management survives. For the Jews of Israel are scarcely a people whose stiff-necked past, variety of background, strong emphasis on initiative, sheer self-respectful refractoriness, would suggest an easy submission to management: let alone to any as

* S. N. Eisenstadt, 'Bureaucracy, Bureaucratization and Debureaucratization', *Administrative Science Quarterly 4* (1959), pp. 302–20.

arrogant as the one described. The leadership itself, of course, ascribes its success to its record of achievement. But the answer is far more complex. And an important part of it lies in the managerial techniques employed.

To begin with, no one should belittle the political skill that the leadership has shown—and is still capable of showing, despite the slowing down of response that age has brought. They are professionals, these: many with training in the hard schools of the Diaspora and early Palestinian settlement; and with decades of practice under the Mandate and independent statehood. There must be few tricks of the established democratic trade that they have not mastered.

They have been adept at just sufficient yielding to just sufficient pressures of social complaint. Despite their sense and, indeed, expressions of outrage, for instance, they did not dismiss the challenge of discontent from young Oriental Jews. Along with their rebukes, they announced their intention of dealing with the problem. And if their indicated measures were unlikely to affect the substance of Oriental deprivation, they provided the appearance of sufficient responsiveness to take the heat out of the issue for the while.

Adeptly, too, they have used the magnifying of minor issues to deflect attention from major ones. The recent controversy over the 'holes in the wall' constitutes a classic instance. Four holes were drilled into the wall of the Old City in Jerusalem so as to insert metal girders and secure two tottering Arab houses some eight centuries old. Religious leaders complained that the Wailing Wall was being desecrated; and a Knesset discussion led to the appointment of a special committee, under Golda Meir herself, to investigate. The holes had been drilled not in the Wailing Wall itself, or that remnant of the Herodian period associated with the Second Temple, but in the city wall built by Arabs and no more credibly sacred or historically valuable than the threatened houses. One might reasonably have supposed, even in the climate of unreason promoted by militant religious opinion, that a clear statement from the prime minister on the facts, supported by a report from some eminent archaeologist, would have been enough. And if creative controversy had been sought, the occasion might well have provoked some remarks on the need to respect the rights of people, even Arabs, to their homes, in the absence of overwhelming considerations to the contrary. As it was, the negative controversy to which the leaders lent themselves, and which fixed on the apportionment of blame, made political sense only in terms of offering some release from other preoccupations.

By a system of seasonable adoption, the leadership has accommodated within its ranks representatives of a discontent that might otherwise prove dangerous. Thus, even before the protest movement by young Oriental Jews, the Labour Party managers had advanced to positions of prominence a few Oriental Jews whose record did not necessarily, in the order of experience and service, merit such treatment. Thus, Mapai formed its alignment with Achdut Ha'avoda for the elections of 1965: taking younger men, like Allon and Galili, into the leadership so as to meet, with their added appeal, the challenge of relative youth and a new dynamism from the rebels around Ben Gurion. Thus, the leading rebels of Rafi were lodged in the Cabinet – Moshe Dayan just before, and Shimon Peres soon after, the Six Day War; and subsequently in the leadership of the reunited Labour Party.

But this skill would be of small moment without the institutional basis of its operations. The alignment of Mapai and Achdut Ha'avoda defeated the electoral challenge of Rafi – and Ben Gurion's charismatic personal image – above all because it constituted an unmatchable mechanism of money, personnel, developed attachments and client loyalties. Indeed, as though to demonstrate this, it went to the polls behind Levi Eshkol, a man who, at least by contrast with Ben Gurion, had a colourless personality, and smacked of machine politics.

Certainly, if all major parties in Israel are political sects, with complex social agencies at their disposal, those that have enjoyed the additional access to government, and especially among them the commanders of the Labour Party, have been able correspondingly to employ state patronage for their purposes. In a society with what must proportionately be one of the most populous public services in the world, the political advantages that may be promoted by a skilful leadership are immense. And the leadership has not been slow to multiply the opportunities for reward, and the accompanying client loyalties, by developing local organizations of manipulative patronage.

Nor has it been slow to exploit the system of proportional representation, with the constant need for coalition government. The leadership of Mapai, and now of the Labour Party, at the centre of real political deployment, has usually been able to play off, for its own advantage, opposing sides on the issues of religion and economic policy. The threat that, driven too far, it is contemplating an alliance with the secularists to the Left and the Right, has concentrated the minds of the religious wonderfully for the while: as the prospect of a necessary deal with the 'bourgeois' parties has been known to reduce satisfactorily the demands from the Left for more energetic socialism.

The leadership of the Labour Party is undoubtedly dominant in Israeli politics. But it is still no more than a part of the Israeli leadership. So far, the option of a solely secularist administration, however it might have been threatened from time to time, has been eschewed by the Labour higher command; and leaders of the main religious group in parliament, now the National Religious Party, have served in successive coalitions of rule. On the conventional Left, Mapam has for stretches enjoyed, as it does now, a share in government; and there has usually been place and a portfolio for some formation, like the present Independent Liberal Party, favouring a freer economy.

Nor should the leadership of the Herut–Liberal bloc (Gahal), the major opposition force, be excluded. It was part of the coalition government in 1967–70; and, whatever the dispositions in the Knesset, may enjoy elective authority at the local level. But in any event, it must exercise a significant pressure on policy by its very choice of the issues on which to confront the uneasy ideological alliance in power. And even the leadership of a minor opposition party, provided that this does not, as Rakah and perhaps Ha'olam Hazeh (the New Force) do, represent policies too far from the developed outlook of Jewish nationalism, may wield influence as the potential constituent of an alternative Knesset majority.

Political power in Israel is, thus, essentially pluralist; with the leaderships of various political sects possessed not only of command over their respective provinces, but of some share, explicit or implicit, in control of the state. And the shares, though unequal, remain real enough to secure the allegiance of each such leadership to the functioning of the system. Indeed, the leaderships have on the whole more in common with each other than with the mass of their own supporters. They are predominantly of common background, age group, experience; and, above all, of common involvement in the actual mechanisms of authority. They have survived separately because they have promoted their common survival.

It is a system which has certain similarities to the Lebanese. And nowhere is this more manifest than in the way that the leaderships exploit the fear of disunity to secure themselves. But if this operates to support the ascendancy of each within its own sect, it operates also to support the system itself against the posed alternative of national disruption. Paradoxically, it is the passionate divisions of Israeli politics which contribute to the stability of the Israeli leadership.

The popularity of archaeology in Israel is celebrated. It reflects a virtual obsession with the history of the Jews before the exile of the Christian Era: because this record fortifies for them their claim to the Palestinian homeland, of course; but also because it declares for them the dignity which they then as a nation possessed and have reassumed, in contrast with the humiliations of the ghetto. Masada, the military citadel where Zealots made a last stand against the Romans after the loss of Jerusalem in 70 C.E., has become a symbol of the ancient heritage, and of national heroism then and now. Yet who in so recollecting the past can neglect the part played by internal dissension in the downfall of the Jewish state?

It had been no easy matter to get the quarrelsomely independent tribes of Israel structurally united in the first place. And when this had eventually been achieved in the reign of David, it did not survive beyond the splendours of his son Solomon. Two kingdoms emerged, Judah and Israel: sometimes combining against a foreign power, but often enough separately seeking the aid of such power against the other, to the eventual ruin of both. Subsequently, with the restoration of a Jewish state, it was the conflict between the Pharisees and the Saducees that opened Judea to Pompey and the Romans. And the revolt against Roman rule two centuries later was that of a people vulnerably divided. Even as Jerusalem was under siege by the forces of Titus, various Zealot leaders were at one another's throats in the city.

There must be few, if any, countries in the world where the far past is so near as in Israel; where its trails are so thronged with indigenous visitors; and where its application to the present is so insistently drummed, in school and army, in politics and religion, in the symbolism of the state. The leadership loses no chance to recite the relevant lesson of history.

Yet patly, Israelis seem so persuaded to relive the past as to repeat the dissension along with the dignity of statehood. In 1966, with economic recession and widespread industrial unrest, the political structure began to look dangerously fragile. It was the resurgent conflict with the Arabs, culminating in the Six Day War of June 1967, that united Israelis so closely behind their government; and the aftermath, of euphoria and continued crisis, that sustained the unity for a few more years. But by 1971, the external threat was again failing to function sufficiently. An Israeli satirist remarked the nakedness of the leadership.

> Ah, if only Sadat would make some small historic mistake already – if only he would block the Straits of Bab el Mandeb, or open fire on us! Doesn't he see that our situation is grave? For what is that idiot waiting? ...
>
> The Government must take things in hand and prevent a disaster before the wave of strikes sweeps the entire country and paralyses all the services; the Black Panthers* begin throwing 'Molotov cocktails' at the homes and penthouses of Israel's elite; the workers revolt and demand that the party functionaries, who serve the interests of the Finance Ministry, which represents the interests of the millionaires, are kicked out of the Histadrut; and before the last emigrant is asked to turn off the electricity at Lod Airport.
>
> The Government must immediately lead the people to a defensive war to preserve our physical existence. Knowing the Arabs as we do, we realize that in this matter it is impossible to rely on them. Their promises are worthless. They won't throw us into the sea unless we throw ourselves into the sea crying to the high heavens: 'Help! They are destroying us.'†

* The name under which young Oriental Jews first demonstrated their disaffection. See Chapter 6.

† Dan Ben Amotz, 'The Panacea', *Ha'olam Hazeh*, 22 September 1971.

It is one thing to say that nearly all Israelis, including the leadership, yearn for peace; if, less and less flexibly, on their own terms. It is quite another to deny that the conflict with the Arabs has had its uses, for Jewish nationalism and the Israeli leadership alike. Apart from territorial gains and the welcome loss of so many Arabs by flight, the conflict has enormously facilitated the assimilation of Jewish immigrants: by the mechanism of the military effort; and by the mental impact of beleaguerment and war. It has inhibited the expression, if not equally the development, of social divisions. And it has significantly assisted a leadership, engendered by a different economic and moral period, to secure itself and its heirs presumptive.

This it has done ultimately by providing that leadership with a plastic politics in the empiricism of saving the state. Do parties avowedly of the Left conduct a government that encourages the expansion of the private sector, by promoting opportunities for profit and the evasion of tax; that even sells established public enterprises to private capital; that confronts the right to strike; that, in partnership with religious interests, erodes the secular state? It is the cause of national security that requires such. Is there a plainly widening gap between the old ideologies still proclaimed, and the effective policies of power? It is a gap which the self-evident need to protect the state from extinction must, merely for the while of course, allow.

And yet this is much more than mere camouflage for the pursuit of policies essentially different from those professed by parties in government, and especially by the dominant Labour–Mapam Alignment. It is itself a response to the very social developments which it promotes; and hence provides perhaps the major reason for the stability of the leadership. For the truth is that Israelis have become increasingly bourgeois in self-identification and outlook.

In a 1962 survey by the Israel Institute of Applied Social Research, a representative sample (1,170 persons) was taken of the adult Jewish population outside the kibbutzim; and another (300 persons) of kibbutz adults: to investigate political and social attitudes. Respondents were asked to select one of five terms as most appropriate to describe their particular social class, in an exact translation of the inquiry pursued by Richard Centers in a

1946 survey of the United States white male population (see table below).*

Social Class	UNITED STATES, 1946 (*White Males*)	ISRAEL, 1962 (*General Jewish*)	(*Kibbutzim*)
Upper	4%	1%	1%
Upper-middle	—	7%	10%
Middle	36%	52%	23%
Working	52%	29%	63%
Lower	5%	5%	1%
No answer	3%	6%	2%
	100%	100%	100%

An Israeli sociologist commented:

> In the bastion of capitalism, over half the males identified [themselves] as working class; in Israel, with its mixed economy and powerful socialist ideology, only 29% of the population do so. It may be argued that the difference is attributable to several factors. First, women may tend to see themselves more as middle class. This is true; considering only Israeli males, 34% chose 'working class'. Second, the inclusion of the additional category 'upper middle class' may have pulled some people into 'middle class' who otherwise might have said 'working class'. Even so, a considerable gap remains. Moreover, it should be recalled that the American sample did not include Negroes, who might well have raised the working-class percentage. It seems to me that this comparison points up something important about the current Israeli scene.†

What comparative surveys for the early 'seventies will reveal must remain mere speculation till the event. But it is all too

* Richard Centers, *The Psychology of Social Classes* (Princeton University Press, 1949). The survey of February 1946 was preceded by one in July 1945 and followed by one in March 1947, both of which gave very similar results.

† Aaron Antonovsky in 'Israeli Political-Social Attitudes', first published in *Amot*, No. 6, 1963.

probable, given the development of both societies since, that the proportion of Jewish Israelis considering themselves 'middle class' would be still higher now than it was in 1962; and at the very least no lower than its contemporary counterpart in the United States.

In short, if the empiricism of national security has supported the effective pursuit of a more or less liberal capitalism by a dominant strain of leadership professedly of the Left, the pursuit itself has reflected prevalent social attitudes within the electorate. There was a yet more direct demonstration of this prevalence in the 1962 survey. The investigators set out to examine the correlation between ideological attitudes among adult Jews and the relative strengths of the corresponding parties. Excluding the peculiar commitments and parties of the religious, and basing their demarcations largely on economic outlook, they found a remarkable discrepancy (see table below).*

	Knesset		*Respondent Identification*	
Left	22·4%	65·2%	9·7%	32·1%
Left of Centre	42·8%		22·4%	
Centre	17·4%		23·4%	
Right	17·4%		18·5%	
Deviant	—		9·9%	
Non-ideological	—		16·1%	

Left – Communist Party, Mapam, Achdut Ha'avoda;
Left of Centre – Mapai; Centre – Liberals; Right – Herut.

Again, there is no similar survey by which to measure the current situation. Still: excluding from the present Knesset the representatives of the religious parties (18); the virtually all-Arab Rakah (3); and the Arab lists affiliated to Labour (4); a rapid calculation would give the Jewish conventional Left, composed of the Labour–Mapam Alignment (56) and the Israel Communist Party (1), exactly 60% of the remainder, or 57 out of 95 seats. And there is no evidence to suggest that the adult Jewish population has moved ideologically to the Left in the past decade. If anything, it has

* Cited in Aaron Antonovsky, 'Political Ideologies of Israelis', first published in *Amot*, No. 7, 1963.

moved much further to the Right; so that the discrepancy between its outlook and the avowed commitment of its representatives in the Knesset is almost certainly no less wide and probably wider than it was at the time of the 1962 survey.

Why, then, should the bulk of the Israeli leadership none the less continue to proclaim its traditional attachment to the Left? Part of the explanation may well lie in sheer intellectual inertia. The veterans and their adopted heirs go on using the vocabulary of ideas that they acquired at the outset of their careers, because it is the only one they can project as distinctively theirs. They are too old or tired to set out once more as intellectual pioneers; and perhaps too fearful of what they may discover, about themselves and the real impact of their social role. But then, among established political leaderships in the world, they are far from singular in this.

But there is another, connected, reason. The creation of Israel, it cannot be sufficiently stressed, was for the majority of Jews in Palestine and, above all, for the mainstream of the leadership, more than a mere exercise in nationalism. It was to be a moral instrument for the realization of a socialist society. And subsequent events have scarcely diminished the need to portray the state in this light. For how else should the Arab accusation be met that Israel is essentially a capitalist emplacement: an agency for the domination of the Middle East by Western technology, in the service of material profit? And even aside from the conflict with the enemy, is the whole vision of the Return to come in the end to this: a Jewish version of the modern Western state, with the prerogatives of wealth and the deprivations of poverty? What meaning would there be to the long struggle of the Jewish identity, if Jews, again in their own homeland at last, were to be exploited by their fellows and so turn one day in fury against them?

One member of a celebrated Zionist family in Britain always earmarks for kibbutz development part of the substantial sums he gives to Israel. In British politics he is an unflinching Conservative; with all that that generally conveys. But the Israel that he seeks to promote is a society of which the collectivist commitment is an influential feature. Israelis cannot thus divide themselves on the map; and so many divide themselves in the mind instead. They express outrage at the irresponsibility of those who, by resorting so readily to strikes for higher incomes, endanger the economy and very survival of the state; yet they will themselves strike readily enough to preserve and even raise their relative standards of living. Collectives continue to proclaim both the wickedness of exploiting labour for profit and their own contrary objective of an egalitarian society; yet will themselves use the surplus value of hired labour to advance a prosperity for their own members already higher than that of most Israelis.

Of this moral schizophrenia, the leadership of the Israeli Left and hence the bulk of the political leadership in the state has proved accommodatingly representative. While it brandishes still the vocabulary of its old ideological commitment, the content of its policies bears less and less relationship to the words. Many citizens may thus soothe their moral anxieties with the promise of socialism, while confident that social performance will continue to reflect liberal-capitalist priorities. Small wonder, then, that the Labour Party today, as its predecessor, Mapai, did previously, attracts so large a proportion of young managers and technicians; of those in the liberal professions; and even of traders and industrialists: a constituency for which the social ideals of the pioneer tradition might reasonably be considered unalluring.

And this points to yet another important reason for the persisting contradiction between promise and performance by the bulk of the Israeli leadership. Quite simply, the contradiction has so far effectively pre-empted serious challenge from both the Left and the Right. For to the Left this leadership talks in the old ideology, and so denies room to an appeal based on the letter; while to the Right it acts with suitable policies, and so denies room to an appeal based on the spirit.

The empiricism of national security and the interplay between socialist talk and liberal-capitalist conduct together account for the particular ascendancy of the Labour Party and its leadership. To the Left, Mapam may be uneasy at the social policies pursued by its senior partner in government, and may even contemplate ideological challenge; but so overwhelming is the issue of national security that it prefers, under more or less muted protest, to share in the responsibility, and in the power, of protecting the state. Loyal, therefore, to the Alignment with Labour, it makes the more difficult any challenge from the Left based on the old ideology.

Indeed, by any real definition, the vast bulk of the Left in Israel should be seen not as the Left at all, but as the Centre. And to identify the residual Left is to see why it is so ineffectual. There is Rakah (the New Communist List). But its attachment to the Kremlin line tars it with the brush of a disreputable regime; while its own policies, on peace or anything else, are further discounted by the mass of Jewish public opinion as no more than might be expected from a party all but entirely dependent on Arab votes. The maverick Moshe Sneh, who was the single Knesset representative of the Israel Communist Party, enjoyed widespread respect for his personal qualities. He was, as a former commander of the Haganah, an important figure in the struggle for the state. But few took his subsequent politics seriously. He pressed for the values of a worker's society; and he assailed the government for its failure to display enough imagination, enough generosity, in seeking peace. But in the end, his own imagination and generosity were confined by an old nationalism, as his social policies were confined by an old ideology: and both properties had sitting tenants. Now, with his death, his successor in the Knesset seat is a party worthy, caught in the same predicament but without Sneh's national distinction or personal flair.

Then there is Ha'olam Hazeh, with its two representatives in the Knesset at loggerheads, to the obvious glee of the professionals in the Centre; and with its popular magazine of the same name, which mixes good muck-raking journalism and tabloid sex with a crusade for secularism and peace. And if any substance remains to the Left in Israel, this crusade must constitute some small part. The leader and editor, Uri Avneri, busily explores such possibilities for a settlement in the Middle East as a Semitic federation between Israel and a Palestinian Arab state, or a common market for Israel and the Arab countries that would include a Palestinian Arab entity; and meanwhile denounces the policies of the government as at best self-defeatingly fearful and at worst no more than a cover for clinging to conquests. In pursuit of his attack on the compromises of the Labour–Mapam Alignment with the religious interests, he even went so far as to propose in the Knesset homosexual law reform, on the British model. The representatives of the religious parties reacted in a way which indicated their regret that Biblical forms of punishment were no longer acceptable. And the mass of a Labour–Mapam Centre, which seemed stuck somewhere between Leviticus and orthodox Soviet morality, either abstained or voted against the proposal.

Yet such assaults do not constitute a serious challenge because they are accompanied by no essential alternative to the economic policies, let alone the cobwebbed ideology, of the Centre. 'Uri's a good guy,' said one of his assistants, 'but he's no socialist. And this means that he's cut off from the major potential force of disillusionment. I remember in the last elections talking to young members of the Labour Party, especially in the kibbutzim, who claimed that they would not vote for the party again because it had betrayed them. So I asked them to vote for Uri instead, if only as a protest. But they said, how can we vote for someone who isn't a socialist? And they didn't vote at all.'

And there are, too, movements on the Left, albeit minute, of Jewish and Arab radicals working together outside the political system. But again, the issue of national security is so dominant as to suggest small potential support from within the Jewish community for organized unconstitutional endeavour that seems merely to deny Jewish nationalism for a cause all too compromised by the nationalisms of others. Only a movement that sought rather to transcend this nationalism, for a society of creative economic and cultural experiment where Jewish and Arab identities would be the material of a truly socialist commonwealth: only a movement that fitted a new revolutionary vision to the facts of the Arab environment and of the advanced industrial age might succeed in transforming the political system itself.

Meanwhile, the predominant pressure on the Centre comes from the Right, since it is the Right which constitutes the vast bulk of constitutional opposition. Gahal (the Herut–Liberal bloc) has over a fifth of the national vote (21·67% at the 1969 elections), and probably a quarter, when combined with splinter groups of like-minded outlook; while the three religious parties received a total of almost 15% at the last polls. It would be surprising indeed, therefore, if the Labour–Mapam Alignment at present looked anywhere else for its major electoral antagonist; or if those of the Right inside the Centre did not fortify their pressures with the warning represented by the Right outside.

The warning comes essentially from the dynamic of liberal capitalism. For, paradoxically, just as the Labour Party attracts so much support from the richer sectors of society, it is from the poorer that Gahal, and in particular Herut, has achieved remarkable recruitment.

It is by no means a phenomenon peculiar to Israel. In other countries where liberal capitalism seemed for so long so successfully to function, the promotion of poverty which the promotion of riches entails has been nourishing a challenge from the Right amongst those who feel themselves not just materially deprived but, in a climate of prevalent material values, socially despised. Many, among the elderly on fixed incomes or slow-rising pensions, among small-scale businessmen and public employees, who are hurt by inflation or otherwise left behind in the race, might be expected, as a matter of course, to manifest their disaffection on the Right. But there are others, in the lower-paid and even anxiously middle ranks of industrial labour, who turn to the Right because the constitutional Left is itself closely associated with the system, and especially with the organized pressure of the more highly skilled industrial workers, the technicians and managers. They look to the Right for a government that will protect them against the strong in their own society, by imposing a corporate settlement of conflicting interests; and that will compensate them for their sense of personal failure by a corporate engagement to national pride.

Thus, Gahal called in the 1969 elections for 'extension of state sovereignty to the "liberated areas"; ... liberation of the economy from continual dependence on officialdom; obligatory mediation in labour disputes and arbitration in vital public services'.* It scarcely represents a coherent programme of convincing action to counter the ravages of the competitive society. It does represent a mood which, for all its genuflections to freedom, reflects an authoritarian commitment. And it is a mood the more dangerous in Israel because the leadership of the Centre is effectively so authoritarian already; because there exists the additional authoritarian pressure from the Right of religious interests; and because the continuing conflict with the Arabs is so congenial to the encouragement of an aggressive nationalism.

It is a mood to whose development the leadership of the Centre

* *Facts About Israel, 1971* (Jerusalem: Keter Publishing House, for the Information Division of the Foreign Ministry), p. 70.

cannot safely be indifferent. To be sure, the record of economic growth has been impressive. But it has not disguised the cost, through inflation and the disproportionate advances in real income, to important sectors of the population. Still another large currency devaluation in August 1971 was accompanied by measures that promised some profit to the rich, from the increase in value of stocks, or private income from abroad, but a decline in living standards for many without commensurate wage rises. And the government made clear its intention to prevent as far as possible these last, if necessary by new legislation against strikes. Yet it was clear, too, that simply more repressive government would not suffice.

The call to the national battlements was still eloquent. In a major public opinion poll, some 70% of respondents expressed support for the government on 'foreign affairs and security'. But only some 30% did so on 'internal issues'. And some 80% answered 'no' to the question: 'Has enough been done for the Oriental Jews and families with many children?'*

Nor did security problems dominate public thinking as before. A public opinion poll in the spring of 1972 revealed only 33·4% of respondents (compared to 68·4% in December 1971) who regarded these as the most pressing issue; while 18·5% (6·8%) chose Housing; 16·6% (6%), Education and social questions; 15·5% (–), Immigration; 9·1% (11%), Economic Affairs; and 4·5% (2%), Labour Relations.†

To be sure, such polls vary widely, even at short intervals, as events and policies interact. But overall there has been an undeniable movement of the public mood, to concern with 'domestic' issues. And though a flare-up in the conflict with the Arabs would be bound to reverse this, it is far from certain that the old medicine will be available just when needed; or, when available, work always as well as it has.

Towards the end of 1971, the particular issue of the high defence budget had openly divided the Labour leadership. The party organ, *Ot*, demanded reductions in military expenditure to service social and education needs. 'For 23 years we have been accustomed to regard security as a sacred cow ... We should revise our social

* An article in *Ha'aretz*, 10 September 1971.

† A report in the *Jerusalem Post*, 22 March 1972.

attitudes about the security problem lest we unintentionally follow the example of Sparta or Prussia and establish an apparently successful political structure devoid of social content.'*

It was an issue reflecting the conflict between hawks and doves inside the party's command. And this conflict itself was by no means a simple one. The most influential dove was without doubt Pinhas Sapir. And his disposition followed in part from his belief that the addition of Arabs in the occupied territories to the ranks of Israeli citizenship would seriously endanger the survival of the Jewish state; while no less serious a danger would lie in keeping the occupied territories but denying Israeli citizenship to their inhabitants. 'He has the ghetto mentality,' grumbled a political opponent on the Right. 'He does not want Arabs in a Jewish state. And if he must have them, he wants the fewest possible.' There is much truth in this: not altogether to the discredit of the ghetto. If its products in the pioneering days had wishfully thought themselves able to establish a state without Arabs, they had also, on finding the Arabs unmistakably there, set their faces against exploiting Arab labour. Sensibilities about exploiting Arab labour have since grown a great deal less delicate. The fear of there being too many Arabs within the Jewish state persists.

But at least as important, Sapir was increasingly concerned at the social costs of the hard military posture. He was concerned, as principal operative of the Labour Party machine, at the rising discontent among the rank-and-file and the electorate at large with the evidence of poverty and its moral implications. He was concerned, as Minister of Finance, at a rate of inflation which the combined demands of military and now urgent social expenditure threatened to drive out of control, or in any event raise to a point of unmanageable social damage. He was concerned, as overlord of the economic relationship between Israel and the outside world, at the mounting pressure on the balance of payments. And not least, as the single most influential figure in promoting the liberal-capitalist accommodation, he was concerned at the social conflict which the system was producing, in its shortage of resources for the demands it variously excited.

The reply came in a speech by Defence Minister Moshe Dayan,

* Quoted in *Ha'aretz*, 29 October 1971.

delivered on 6 November 1971, the fifteenth anniversary of the Sinai Campaign.

> A flag has been hoisted in Israel lately. There is nothing wrong with the flag of social reform, housing for young people and a solution to the Panther problem. In itself the flag is desirable. In my opinion, it is impossible – and therein lies the mistake – to wave two flags at one and the same time, because the State of Israel does not have the strength to support the flag of war and the flag of all the benefits to the customs workers, longshoremen, the Panthers, the young and the not-so-young.
>
> These two flags cannot exist in the State of Israel; and no country in the world can simultaneously wage war and also institute social and economic reforms ...
>
> The two flags contradict each other. Consequently we must choose one or the other. It is impossible to choose social reform, because another front has priority ... *

The Board of Management is engaged in a contest of policies. And involved, certainly, is a contest of politicians, for succession to the post of chairman. For not even Golda Meir, whose enjoyment of the office seems to have produced so remarkable a rejuvenation, is supposed likely to last for ever; and she may even be driven to resign by the momentum of her own threats. Already Israel's large political class is engaged in intrigue and speculation over who will then preside and exercise the accompanying prerogatives: Sapir or Dayan; or a compromise candidate closer to one or the other.

Superficially, it is a contest fraught with enormous implications. Will there be a retreat from the hard line on the borders, into interim security arrangements and the primacy of social reform; or a digging in, with political trench warfare at home to match the military commitment? But essentially the situation will not change beyond matters of emphasis; until the issues themselves reach far deeper than so far they have done. No candidate for command within the predominant party, and no other party, yet constitutes a credible challenge to the liberal-capitalist character of the society

* Quoted in *Yediot Aharonot*, 7 November 1971.

and the corresponding politics of management. The opposition Right offers only to secure this character by making the management more authoritarian yet.

And it follows from this that government in the foreseeable future must continue to promote the social stresses inseparable from the functioning of the system: the competitive pressures for higher private consumption; the widening of the gap in living standards between those whose capital, culture, skills are at a premium, and others less useful to an economy of profit. It follows, too, that a leadership directed by the values of such a society, and seeking escape from the consciousness of its gathering difficulties in a nationalist mystique, will have neither the imagination nor the will to see security except in terms of dominant borders and armed capability. Measures of social reform will do no more than advance the problem by both pretending and failing to solve it. The proportionate expenditure on the military may lag for a while, in response perhaps to adjustments of strategic imperatives; but overall it will keep pace with the failure to make a convincing, dynamic peace. The system allows no choice; only, an intrinsic dilemma.

Yet this must, surely, open rather than close politics in Israel. The very sterility of the Centre must increasingly polarize opinion; and the remedies of the Right raise a commitment from the Left against the system itself.

Liberal capitalism is everywhere becoming more repressive, as its competitive pressures increase, and the state moves to impose arbitrary adjustments. Measures to discipline the society seek impossibly to provide with an inclusive commitment a system whose very basis is an exclusive preoccupation with his own interests by the individual citizen. Radical opposition, unable to move the managers, takes to assailing the management itself; and the management comes, more and more manifestly, to depend on the company guards. Law and order, or national survival, seems less and less adequate an excuse for the ravages of the social and natural environment; the subjugation of the person to profit; the protection of authority by prisons and riot police. As the very existence of a Jewish state ceases to be a source of intimidating wonder, more and more of its citizens must more and more ask for whose good the state really operates.

With the Babylonian conquest of Judah and the destruction of Jerusalem in the sixth century B.C., Jews were deported in their multitudes to exile in Babylonia. But the Babylonian empire fell to the rise of Persian power; and by the middle of the fifth century Jews were back in Jerusalem with the protection of the Persian king. Under the Zionist leadership of Nehemiah, governor of Judah from 445 to 433 B.C., they set about rebuilding the city walls. The work encountered much opposition from Judah's neighbours. But there was opposition, too, from among the Jews themselves.

> Jews were not behaving like 'brothers'. Short of food to eat and money for taxes, many were forced to take costly loans, mortgage their fields, and sell their children into slavery. Even Nehemiah and his servants were guilty of extorting heavy interest and taking pledges. Demanding interest from a brother in need was incompatible with fear of the Lord (Neh. 5:9; cf. Lev. 25:36) and would not be conducive to God's blessing on the newly occupied land (cf. Deut. 23:20–21). If the building of the wall were to be brought to successful completion, all debts had to be cancelled and pledges returned. Nehemiah convened an assembly of the people and forced his reform through.*

This time round, perhaps, Nehemiah will be not a man, but an idea; and an idea that sees in the rebuilding of old walls itself a corrupting exercise.

* *Encyclopaedia Judaica* (Jerusalem: Keter Publishing House, 1971), Vol. 8, p. 621.

6

The economics of inequality

Tel-Hai (Hill of Life), in Upper Galilee, is a symbol of the egalitarian endeavour which informed the dominant strain of pioneering Zionism. Established as a pastoral settlement in 1917, it came under Arab attack in 1920; and among the eight Jews who died defending it was Josef Trumpeldor, the founder of the Jewish pioneer movement in Russia. There is a museum there now, where among the exhibits are examples of the crude agricultural and domestic articles that these pioneers used. And nearby is the cemetery where the eight lie buried and memorialized.

Every day, on Tel-Hai Day, 'youths from all over the country make a pilgrimage to this site, to pay tribute to the fighters: "courageous and true, men of toil and peace, who followed the ploughshare and sacrificed their lives for the honour of Israel and for its soil".'*

And little over a mile away stands today Kiryat-Shemona (Town of the Eight), on the site of the Arab village from which the attackers had come, and named in memory of those who were killed at Tel-Hai. With a population of over 15,000, it houses those Jews who go as hired labour to several of the kibbutzim around. For these last are no longer mere agricultural settlements. They have expanded into industry and the services.

Ayelet Hashahar (Morning Star) was founded in 1915† by pioneers from Russia. For many years it had a lean time. Subsequently, with the establishment of the state and the development of a national water supply system, the kibbutz has become a successful producer of fruit and honey, fish and cotton. But agriculture is not the compass of its enterprise. A four-star guest house, with a celebrated restaurant and with shops selling, on a

* Zev Vilnay, *The Guide to Israel* (Jerusalem: printed at the 'Hamakov' Press, 1971), p. 518.

† 1915 according to literature distributed by Kibbutz Ayelet Hashahar itself; 1916 according to *The Guide to Israel*, p. 512.

commission basis, a multitude of luxury goods from cameras to perfume, has prospered. And the kibbutz has marked such prosperity with the building of a splendid auditorium, at the cost of some $230,000.

It is far from unique. Afikim, to the south of Lake Kinneret, has not only intensive agriculture but one of the major plywood factories in Israel, thrivingly engaged in the export trade with the help of hired labour. Indeed, kibbutzim account for only some 4% of the total population, but over 30% of the country's agricultural, and around 7% of its industrial, yield. Half of the workers in these kibbutz industries are hired labour. And 80% of these hired labourers are employed by the 10 largest of the 180 kibbutz factories.*

'We are', said a senior member of Ayelet Hashahar, 'good socialists with bad consciences.' And he hastened on to tell me of the latest contemplated venture, into insurance. The following morning, at the nearby kibbutz of Neot Mordekhai, a man who had served Israel in several important official capacities, open and secret, dismissed such talk of conscience with a smile.

'There may be kibbutzniks who worry about the meaning for socialism of all this, but I haven't met them. The main issue now in Israel is how to modernize education and train the special advanced skills that we need. And the kibbutz is on the way to meeting the need. Its very prosperity allows it to send its gifted children for proper training.

'Anyway, all this talk of bad conscience is phoney. With the equipment available today, we can easily calculate just how much we have to pay a hired labourer so as to avoid exploiting him. Of course if you pay the minimum wages laid down by the Histadrut, you can make a profit from the workers you hire. But why not pay the margin that amounts to such profit, as well? All this agonizing about the moral dilemma: it is only a cover for not paying a hired worker what he should get.'

The senior police officer in Jerusalem, whom I had been besought to meet as a representative of the best in Israeli administration, was conscious of the irony. A member of Mapam, he saw the contradiction between what the early pioneers had set out to

* Information provided by Menochem Rosner, of the Center for Social Research on the Kibbutz, Givat Haviva.

make of a Jewish homeland, and what the very survival of that homeland now seemed to demand.

'The men who came to this country when it was so backward: they said, we must develop it so that we will never have a society of class differences. And a society of class differences is what we are becoming. But then what else are we to do? We have to put a premium on quality, on talent. For the moment that we lose this lead in quality, in talent, we are lost in the Middle East. We are the military power that we are because of our economic power; because we have the skills and the enterprise to compete successfully in world markets.

'But then what follows is also true. Egalitarianism is out of the question for the next few generations. There cannot be equality between the trained engineer and the man who carries your bags at the hotel.'

The occasion of our talk was not irrelevant. That afternoon a demonstration was to be held in Jerusalem, to protest against police brutality, by the Black Panthers: a group of young Oriental Jews who had taken to demonstrating in the streets against the gap between the circumstances of their own community and those of the dominant Western Jews.

The Black Panthers chose their name deliberately to shock Israeli public opinion; and shock it they did. It was not only, or indeed mainly, that, for the majority of Israelis who believed that they knew something about them, the original Black Panthers of the United States were hostile to the Israeli cause and critical of the American Jews. The name was a symbol of racial revolt against a white ascendancy. And there was just enough validity in the implicit parallel to make of it a distressing challenge.

The average immigrant family from 'Asia-Africa', as the Israeli Central Bureau of Statistics identifies the Oriental category, had a gross annual money income in 1969 of IL 8,300; the average 'Israel born family', one of IL 11,900; and the average immigrant family from 'Europe-America', one of IL 12,000. And the trend was scarcely encouraging. Whereas the average family income of Oriental immigrants was IL 1,600 below the national average, or some 20·5% less, in 1965, it was IL 2,200 below, or, given the increased national average, the same percentage less, in 1969. (See Appendix 3 for details.)

In the year 1969, according to a survey conducted by the Ministry of Education and Culture, some 18,000 Jews between the ages of fourteen and seventeen – or some 9% of the total 207,000 in that age group – were neither at work nor at study.* Given that no less than 70% of all Jews in Israel between the ages of fourteen and seventeen are now Oriental, and that the poor are generally Oriental as well, it may reasonably be inferred that few, if any, of these 'idlers' come from the Western category.

There are obvious social consequences outside the manifestations of organized protest which the Black Panthers represent. An Israeli writer, himself an immigrant from Iraq, has recited some instances of these.

> It is from the ranks of these marginalised youths that most of the young delinquents hail – the youth gangs who recently wantonly rioted in the development town Sderot, wrecking shop windows and molesting passers-by; the under-privileged young men and women from the slum areas of Ramat Hasharon who make life unbearable for the inhabitants of the nearby Neve Sharett, a new and relatively luxurious quarter built for new immigrants hailing largely from Eastern Europe; the youths who daily invade Tel Aviv night-clubs and refuse to pay their entrance fees.†

But the communal argument disguises as it reveals an essential issue. To be sure, Western Jews in Israel are economically privileged, by collective contrast with Oriental Jews. But this should not deflect attention from the central and simpler fact: that Israeli society contains a substantial sector of poverty. And though this poverty may in large measure correspond to immigrant origins, it is by no means identical with these. Just as there are Oriental Jews who have risen to riches in Israel, so there are Western Jews who have stayed at or fallen to manifest levels of poverty.

Employing the approach of Victor R. Fuchs, the American economist, who defines the poverty line as equal to half the median income in a society, the Research and Planning Bureau of

* Of the rest, some 66% were at study; 6·6% were both at work and at study; and 18% were only at work.

† Nissim Rejwan in *New Middle East*, No. 52, May 1971, p. 21.

Israel's National Insurance Institute has produced its 'Preliminary Findings' on 'Patterns of Poverty in Israel'.* These fixed the 'poverty line' at a level equivalent to approximately 40% (or exactly 38%) of the median disposable income possessed by a family of four persons; and the 'near poverty line', or that level of low income at which a family is 'near poor', at approximately half (or exactly 51%).

The conclusions are startling for those nurtured on the myths of a devotedly egalitarian Israel. Out of some 614,000 urban families in 1969, as many as 68,400, or approximately 11%, 'subsisted on an income whose level was below the poverty line'. And the number of persons in these families amounted to some 253,000, out of the total population (2,250,000) surveyed.

An additional 63,400 families were 'near poor'; so that there were some 132,000 families, or 519,200 persons, with low incomes in 1969. 'It may, therefore, be stated that in fact every fifth family and almost every fourth person in the urban population live in poverty or near poverty.'

More startling yet for those who have been led to believe in the superiority of Israeli to American standards of social justice, was the comparison in the 'preliminary findings' between the incidence of poverty in Israel and that in the United States.

> A comparison ... with corresponding data in the United States is likely to create the impression that the incidence of poverty in Israel is relatively limited ... But this impression is a basically erroneous one and originates mainly in the fact that the poverty line in Israel has been fixed at a lower level in comparison to the United States. The poverty line in the United States in 1959 was fixed at a level corresponding to half the median income for a family of four persons, and 22% of the inhabitants of the country fell below the line at the time. The poverty line in Israel, on the other hand, was fixed at a level of approximately 40% of the corresponding median in Israel, in other words 20% lower than the United States level. Had the line been fixed at the relative level of the United States in 1959 ... and had the Israeli scale been

* By R. Roter and N. Shamai; first published in *Social Security*, a Journal of Welfare and Social Security Studies, and published in English by the National Insurance Institute, February 1971.

adjusted with regard to a number of other items to the American one, the Israeli line would also then have delimited 21%–22% of all persons. The conclusion is thus that there is no significant difference between [*sic*] the incidence of poverty in the United States.

Given this measure of poverty in Israel, it would be reasonable to expect a corresponding sector of significant wealth, with various differential levels in between. And this is evident from the various statistics available, not only before but after the application of Israel's supposed steeply rising tax rates. Income estimates, at 7 February 1971, of the Finance Ministry, give both the before-tax and after-tax situations, by percentage share in income, of the ten income groups (see table below).

Rank of Decile (from the poorest)	*Range of monthly income (in IL)*	*Share of gross income (before tax)*	*Contribution to tax revenue*	*Share of net income (after tax)*
1	–160	1·1%	—	1·5%
2	160–325	2·9%	0·1%	4·1%
3	325–460	4·7%	1·0%	6·2%
4	460–590	6·2%	3·0%	7·6%
5	590–725	7·8%	4·5%	9·2%
6	725–840	9·2%	6·6%	10·5%
7	840–970	10·6%	8·7%	11·6%
8	970–1160	12·5%	11·4%	13·3%
9	1160–1520	15·4%	17·4%	15·2%
10	1520–	29·6%	47·3%	20·8%

SOURCE: a private interview with a senior official of the Ministry.

Admittedly, as government spokesmen are quick to point out, neither poverty nor riches in Israel attain the extremes evident in the vast majority of other countries. But this is ultimately beside the point. The poor in Israel do not compare themselves with the poor in Morocco or Iraq, even if they once lived in these countries and remember the conditions there. They compare themselves, and properly so, with the rich, and with the middle income groups, in Israel.

The survey of poverty by the National Insurance Institute recognized this in the very definition of its terms.

> ... 'Minimum needs' were fixed at a level which would also take into account accepted social norms with regard to a reasonable standard of living. Families accordingly defined as poor on the basis of such a standard do not necessarily suffer from hunger or malnutrition.

> Poverty, thus, is defined as a standard of living which deviates to a considerable extent from the common and accepted standard in the conditions of a certain time and place. It is possible for a person defined as 'poor' in American society to have a standard of living which is likely to place him among middle-income groups in India.

By the measure of economic differences within Israel itself, the poorest tenth of the population possesses a disposable income between a *sixth* and a *seventh* of that attained by an income tenth in the middle; or the poorest fifth of the population, one that is between a *third* and a *quarter* of the middle fifth. And at the other extreme, the richest tenth enjoys a disposable income *fourteen* times that of the poorest, and *twice* that of a middle income tenth.

Such rich, like such poor, are numerically important. The top 10% of the population encompass over 20% of the total disposable income; the top 20%, well over a third, at 36%. And their income is not in general secretly saved, but conspicuously spent in an acquisition of goods and services that make those who cannot enjoy them feel deprived in consequence. For Israeli society is in the full flow of competitive consumption: with shop windows and advertisements beckoning the citizen to get ahead of his fellows, or at least keep up with them, in the priorities of the market-place.

Indeed, the income statistics give only part of the picture. In order to evade the relatively high tax rates that apply to the upper reaches of income, more and more Israelis demand and get more and more of their pay in what are known as fringe benefits—forms of income exempt from tax. Thus electricians go on strike for a higher 'clothing allowance', among other pay demands. And government hospital doctors strike for benefits similar to those enjoyed by doctors in Kupat Holim, the health service run by the Histadrut.

Dr Gideon Manelis, head of the government hospital doctors' group, complained that although government and Kupat Holim doctors received the same basic salaries, 'there is a wealth of difference between the fringe benefits. I receive a IL 25-a-month car allowance; my counterpart in a Kupat Holim hospital receives IL 250 a month, net, for his car. A Kupat Holim department head receives IL 4,000 a year clear for working in an out-patient clinic; we do the same work without receiving any extra money.'

And he charged that there were 'many other "under-the-table" benefits which we don't even know about'.*

These benefits can reach such lengths as to constitute far more than the formal income after tax. One doctor in Jerusalem, working for Hadassah,† gets a salary of IL 1,800 a month, or IL 898 after tax. But he gets as well, free, the use of a costly car,‡ which is replaced every five years and for which all repairs and petrol are paid: a benefit that he values at some IL 650 a month. His telephone is paid for, at an equivalent of IL 100 a month. He receives a special 'representation allowance', for entertainment and other job demands, of IL 565 net a month; and a monthly net, after tax deductions, of IL 195 for being on call. Then he has a 'specialization' or foreign travel allowance of IL 210 net a month, and is due to receive a monthly teaching allowance of IL 400 gross.§ Leaving aside the last item, therefore, he has an untaxed additional income of IL 1,720 a month; or more than twice his after-tax salary. With his wife's net IL 730 a month, after taking her own fringe benefits into account, the family has a net income of IL 3,348 a month: or some *twenty-four* times the maximum old age pension for a couple, at IL 135.¶

* Report in the *Jerusalem Post*, 17 June 1971.

† A medical organization in Israel, founded and maintained by the American women's Zionist organization, Hadassah.

‡ According to the Secretary-General of the Histadrut, only some 40% of all cars in Israel are taxed as private; the remainder are taxed as company equipment. Interview with the author.

§ An interview with the author in May 1971.

¶ The following report in the *Jerusalem Post* of 2 June 1971 provides an illuminating contrast.

'Old age pensions have been raised from IL 82·5 a month for a single person to IL 96 and from IL 123·7 to IL 135 for couples, Labour Minister Yosef Almogi announced at a press conference in Tel Aviv yesterday. This means that National Insurance pensions, which cover 90,000 old people, now amount to 14·3 per cent of the national average monthly salary of 1970 as compared with 12·3 per cent ... It was also noted that this increase of 16·3 per cent is the largest single pension increase since the 16·6 per cent increase granted just before the 1969 elections ...

'However, in spite of yesterday's official gratification, some reporters noted that the Welfare Ministry's basic allotment for single persons – IL 102 a month – is still above that of the new pensions.'

Members of the government claim, in defence of their allowing such practices, that the poor have fringe benefits, too: as in subsidized housing and food. But the comparison is absurd. The subsidies to the poor are meant openly to prevent the more corrosive consequences of economic inequality; the fringe benefits enjoyed by the better-off are meant more or less covertly to maintain and promote their condition of privilege.

There is, inevitably, much juggling with the law. As one eminent member of the Labour Party admitted, far fewer millionaires appear in the tax returns than any half-observant Finance Ministry official would regard as credible; and, on the evidence of estate duty, rich men never die in Israel. The supply of credit is far behind the demand, and private loans, at 15% interest and more, are arranged without informing the tax authorities. The share of services in the national income has enormously grown; and there is relatively little effective control exercised by the tax authorities in this sector.

One surgeon in private practice is reputed to have furnished much of his home by arranging to have his bills paid in kind rather than cash. And there is a current joke about the dentist, a certain Dr X, who tells one of his patients, 'Don't give me the money; just pay my lawyer's bill.' But the lawyer, too, refuses money: 'This is what I owe the architect; pay him instead.' The architect says, 'Look, my wife owes this to her hairdresser, so just give it to him.' And the hairdresser tells the patient, 'I'd rather you paid my dentist, Dr X, instead.'

A professor at the Haifa Technion explained how such practices were reaching into the middle-income groups of the skilled artisan. 'Plumbers, electricians, painters, who run their own businesses or are given sufficient discretion by their employers, do the same. I had to get some books bound. And the binder said, "Must you have a receipt? Because if you don't need one, I'll charge you less than half."' He paused. 'Well, did you demand a receipt?' I asked. 'I had to,' he replied. 'The Technion was paying.'

But such fiddles, considerable as their cumulative impact must be, are still less important than the scrupulously lawful ways by which wealth may be accumulated or maintained. Short-term government loans have offered an 8·5% tax-free return on a single year's investment: or the equivalent of around 45% gross for those investors in the highest tax bracket.* And since even this may be inadequate to allay the alarm at inflation, there are bonds with both the capital redemption and the interest rate linked to the official cost-of-living index. (For those investors more concerned with the exchange rate of the Israeli pound, there are also dollar-linked bonds.)

That such inducements were proving a profitable proposition for the rich, was demonstrated by the very doldrums in which the equity market was long caught, despite notable increases in the profits and dividend payments of quoted companies. To be sure, one reason was the very tight market in equities. The companies themselves preferred to raise money by bonds than by increases in their ordinary shares; and many prices were accordingly nominal, with rapid rises at any substantial order to buy. But at least as significant was the counter-attraction of bonds, with their less precarious returns and their link to foreign currency or the cost-of-living index. On the Tel Aviv stock exchange alone, some IL 4 billion of local money had been invested in such linked bonds; while the market for equity transactions had shrunk from some 86% to some 13% of the total during the previous ten years.†

It was a movement spectacularly reversed as the profitability of companies in the private sector, and the rate of inflation, gathered manifest force. In its issue of 4 March 1972, *The Economist* of London published a letter from a certain Y. Greenberg in Tel Aviv.

> Whilst believing that it is only right to take pride in one's own achievements, I feel that I must comment on your statement (February 19th) that: 'London is the only stock market in the world (with the exception of Hongkong) to come close to a 50 per cent improvement in its capital value over the past year.'
>
> I would like to point out that the stock exchange here, in Tel Aviv, has been enjoying boom conditions for the past six

* In June 1971. Nine months later, the rate of net return, on a new short term loan, had risen to 9·125% a year for eighteen months, and 9·0% for twelve.

† Information from the head of the Tel Aviv Stock Exchange in a private interview, June 1971.

> months or so, which has taken the general index of industrial shares up from 169 before devaluation last August to a level this week of 303, making a rise in this period of 78 per cent (the rise over one year has been no less than 115 per cent). At the same time, the 'all share index' has risen 63 per cent during the last six months and 83 per cent for one year.

There is no mystery over which sector of the population benefited from this particular boom. And what an irony it is that the exploits of the early pioneers, like Josef Trumpeldor and his companions at Tel-Hai, should still be sung; as Tel Aviv outstrips the other cities of the world in the euphoria of its stock exchange.

The prosperity of the private sector is, indeed, a much emphasized aspect of government policy. Considerable advantages are offered, for instance, to those enterprises promoting exports. The *Israel Investors' Manual* states the objectives clearly. 'The Law for the Encouragement of Capital Investment is designed to attract foreign and local capital that will develop the productive capacity of the national economy, increase exports and reduce reliance on imports, absorb immigrants and populate the undeveloped areas of the State. An investment project which assists in the achievement of these aims may enjoy special benefits and financial assistance.'*

Cash grants amounting to 15% of the cost of equipment; medium- and long-term loans at subsidized interest rates; exemption from various taxes for varying periods, including exemption from income tax on dividends paid out of profits; exceptional depreciation allowances; a five-year tax concession on chargeable income, involving a maximum personal rate of 25%: these are among the benefits offered to resident investors.

In order to encourage building for rental, the government offers substantial concessions to approved property projects. Thus, new buildings, where at least 70% of the area is rented, and at least 66% rented for housing, are exempt from 80% of the property tax. Moreover, they enjoy depreciation allowances, for income tax purposes, over a shortened period of fifteen years; and are liable to a 'maximum income tax rate of 25% for individuals and 33%

* Published by the Government of Israel Investment Authority, 1971, p. 21.

for companies'. For 'sizeable rental projects', where the apartments are leased for a period of fifteen years,

1. The government will extend a 20-year mortgage amounting to 50% of the cost of the apartment, up to a maximum of IL 30,000.
2. There will be no rent control.*

Such opportunities, and others yet more alluring for export industries and investment in special development areas, have been readily exploited. Large personal fortunes have been made, with the risk of relatively little personal capital, by successful ventures; and many unsuccessful ventures have been made successful by the government's taking a direct share in their ownership and management.

There is a capital gains tax of 40%. But it does not apply to gains from the sale of shares and debentures listed on recognized stock exchanges, or from the sale of bonds issued or guaranteed by the state of Israel.† It is easy to see how an entrepreneur could exploit government inducements to establish an industrial enterprise; then float his company on a recognized stock exchange; and make a large, untaxed capital sum by selling shares to the public.

Similarly, capital has been often hugely augmented, with no or very little tax liability, by the possession of the right chattels or land. Moveable assets 'held by an individual for his personal use' and 'real property used for residential purposes' are exempt from all capital gains tax; though in most advanced capitalist countries, the augmenting of capital by the first method at least, is liable to such taxation. Further, the capital gains tax on the sale of other 'non-depreciable' assets is reduced by 5% for every year that the asset had been held by the seller, and disappears altogether on assets held for eighteen years or more. Certainly, considerable private fortunes, free of tax, have been made in recent years with the soaring prices of urban land and property. And for those who do not effect reductions in estate duty by timely dispositions, the maximum rate is 60% for assets of over IL 1,000,000 (a rate on very large fortunes significantly lower than that in Britain).

* Ibid., p. 33.
† Ibid., p. 55

Two further important sources of private wealth exist. The first applies to new immigrants, who for *three years* enjoy various income tax concessions on earnings inside Israel; and for *seven years,* pay no income tax on income from abroad, and no capital gains tax on the sale of assets held abroad before immigration. They are entitled to retain foreign currency brought by them to Israel or received by them abroad, for *ten years* from the date of their arrival; and during this time may carry out transactions abroad with foreign currency held in a local or foreign bank.*

They may import all personal and household effects free of duty or purchase tax; pay a much lower tax than generally applies on imported cars; and may import the tools of their work without customs duty or purchase tax up to the value of $25,000. Various loans from the 'Fund for Middle Class Olim' are available 'to middle-class immigrants and professionals, for the purpose of setting up light industries, factories, businesses, services, private farms, etc.'† And an immigrant wishing to acquire housing in the private market is entitled to a mortgage of up to IL 40,000 (IL 50,000 in Jerusalem), provided that this sum does not exceed 75% of the purchase price.

Immigrants from the more affluent areas of the Diaspora, with substantial capital already, and advice from a competent accountant, have accordingly been enabled to retain and even augment their private wealth in the supposedly more socialist climate of Israel. And their success is all too evident in areas of luxury housing, like Savyon and Herzlia-on-Sea, where some have chosen to settle. A HOME WHERE YOUR HEART IS announces an advertisement in the *Jewish Observer and Middle East Review,* published in London.

> Exclusive homes for sale at Golden Beach, Herzlia-on-Sea. Golden Beach is designed to be one of the most exclusive, most beautiful housing areas in the whole of Israel ... On the famous Herzlia beach by the blue Mediterranean, set in its own extensive and superbly landscaped gardens, Golden Beach homes are ideally situated near the Accadia and Sharon hotels and close to the shopping centre, cinemas, restaurants,

* Ibid., pp. 62–3.

† Ibid., p. 60.

> hotels, banks and the International Airport which serves Tel-Aviv ...
>
> No expense has been spared to create homes as splendid as rare jewels in a precious setting. Two and Three Bedroom villas, designed by Israel's leading architects, built by craftsmen to the highest standards, wait for you to claim them ...
>
> Golden Beach homes create an immediate impression of ultra-modern styling and are designed to ensure trouble-free, gracious living. An outstanding example of Israeli skill, art and purpose ... Prices from £22,000 (IL 184,000) ... *

On other pages of the *Jewish Observer and Middle East Review* reports may be read, more or less regularly, on the continuing military threat to the very survival of Israel; on the terrible lot of Soviet Jews who yearn to reach Israel; and even, since the issue has, at last, become prominent in Israel itself, on the distress of the Israeli poor.

The second further source of private wealth has lain in the various restitution payments made by the Federal German Republic to victims of Nazism. Such payments have differed widely, according to a logic compounded of capitalist priorities and the graduations of guilt accepted by the German authorities. Some Jews have received lump sums for loss of liberty, at the rate of DM 5 for every day spent in a concentration camp.† Others have received compensation amounting to several hundred thousand deutschmarks for property confiscated or sold under pressure for less than its then market value. A former German judge has been receiving a pension that now runs to DM 2,000 a month and rises alongside the equivalent civil service pension rate in Germany. Similar payments are being made to those who lost senior posts at German universities. There are differences, too, in restitution for suffering or loss by former citizens of Germany, and by former citizens of other countries under Nazi occupation. At one extreme, there are between twenty and thirty Israelis of former German citizenship who have received capital payments of some DM 500,000 each; and a few instances of capital payments reaching as

* Now, since further devaluation of the Israeli pound, over IL 220,000.

† Information provided by an Israeli official concerned with restitution payments.

high as DM 1 million. At the other, some immigrants from Rumania have received restitution of DM 1,000 each for having been forced to wear the yellow star.

Still, the number of recipients and the extent of many payments have been such as to have had a profound impact on Israeli society. Since 1954, when the flow of restitution money began, the equivalent of some $1,800 million has been disbursed; to more than 400,000 Israelis (including their immediate families as well as the recipients themselves). Indeed, since new claims are still being decided by the German courts, and many of the successful old ones involve regular payments tied to pension rates in Germany, the total flow of funds a year has significantly increased, albeit with intermittent declines, from some $129 million in 1965 to some $205 million in 1970. (The rise in the exchange rate of the deutschmark has contributed to the rise in the dollar delimitated total; but it has also made such remittances worth more in Israeli purchasing power, and this last benefit has been further advanced by successive devaluations of the Israeli currency.)

With payments exempt from Israeli income tax, many Israelis have enjoyed an addition to their earnings which has effectively placed them in the upper ranks of consumption; while some have attained substantial riches. Not all the money due has, of course, been transferred; and funds well, if covertly, invested abroad have produced further sources of wealth. But in order to prevent just this, the Israeli government has offered special inducements to those depositing their remittances in Israel. The right to hold certain percentages in foreign currency, which might be used to buy foreign securities, has been conceded; and this in turn has led to possibilities of augmenting the Israeli value of the sums involved, with the premium existing for the investment dollar.

According to those, both in government and outside, who have studied the expenditure patterns, the recipients of restitution have in general employed their funds carefully. Capital sums or regular remittances have gone into housing first, and then into consumer durables; while the wealthier have invested in equities and bonds.

But individual recipients and their families have not been the only direct beneficiaries of German restitutions. Apart from the state itself, which has accordingly had far less trouble with its balance of payments than it would otherwise have faced, two groups in particular require mention. Many Israeli lawyers have been well rewarded for representing claimants; with some charging between a fifth and a quarter of any award made. And several kibbutzim have mightily thrived with the help of restitution money: investing it in new branches of agriculture or in establishing industry. Relatively few kibbutz members have, in consequence of receiving such payments, chosen to leave communities in whose midst they have lived for so long; and though allowed in some kibbutzim a little private indulgence, recipients have always been expected to let the collective kitty have the bulk of their restitution money, if they were to stay.

On the evidence so far assembled, it is plain that Israel today is a long way from being that new commonwealth of social justice which the dominant pioneering commitment set out to make, and which the Labour leadership of government has consistently claimed to be promoting.

The fact of inequality is, to be sure, generally admitted. What the leadership itself generally denies* is that the overall trend since the institution of the state has been one of increasing inequality. Yet just such a trend emerges from a study of official statistics.

One relevant analysis was made for the Falk Foundation by Giora Hanoch, an Israeli economist, at the end of the 'fifties. It carefully examines why income differentials in Israel were so narrow at the time that the state was established. Relatively new as the Jewish population was, there had been 'no chance for a large group of property owners, deriving their income from the capital they have accumulated in this country, to develop. In addition, very few of the Jewish residents came with a considerable amount of property accumulated abroad.' And then, the Zionist movement had considered it necessary to nationalize the land and retain in public ownership most of the large development enterprises. The egalitarian ideology of the pioneering movement itself had looked upon work as 'a supreme value in

* With notable exceptions, like the present (1972) secretary-general of the Histadrut, Yitzhak Ben Aharon. In a recent speech (29 March 1972), to the first world conference of Jewish emigrants from Morocco, he blamed Israel's 'economic and social leadership' for the widening in the social gap. 'This situation is not an act of God, but the outcome of a political decision.'

itself and, therefore, did not agree that there should be inferior types of work for which a very low wage should be paid ... The desire for a system of equality and non-exploitation was part of the general atmosphere in the country before the establishment of the State, and the desire for a high standard of living and for the accumulation of wealth was not viewed favourably by the public as a whole.'

Further, many of those in the pre-state Jewish community had been well educated, so that the premium placed on such skills by their scarcity had not been significant. And finally, 'a considerable measure of uniformity in the cultural, social and ideological background of the immigrants' had promoted these processes and 'prevented the development of well-defined classes'.

But, Hanoch continued, 'since the establishment of the State, things have changed considerably.' There was the massive influx of Jewish immigrants; most of them from a background of poverty and repression. And the declining importance attached to the values of pioneering and egalitarianism was accompanied by a soaring demand for advanced skills. This promoted the growth of a considerable social and economic gap between 'the veteran settlers ... and the new immigrants ... most of whom lacked education, technical training and a cultural tradition that would enable them to be fully and immediately absorbed, economically and socially, in Israel's modern and developing economy'.*

And reinforcing these trends was 'the increasing tendency to adjust the levels of wages and incomes to that prevailing in a competitive economy. The factors of supply and demand began to exert greater influence on prices and wages, while there was a decrease in the importance of ideological factors and of social intervention in economic processes.'†

Hanoch went on to compare the changing pattern of income distribution from 1950 to 1957/8.‡ And he found that the index of inequality, or Lorenz curve, by which absolute equality is expressed by zero and absolute inequality by the number one, had risen in the period from 0·172 to 0·220.

* 'Income Differentials in Israel', published in the *Fifth Report, 1959 and 1960*, of the Falk Project for Economic Research in Israel (Jerusalem, August 1961).

† Ibid., pp. 43–4.

‡ See Appendix 5, Table I.

Using different data, he then compared the distribution of disposable income for urban wage and salary earners by income units in 1954 and 1957–58.* And here he found that the index of inequality had risen from 0·230 to 0·270 over the period.

Hanoch concluded: 'it may be said that the trend towards wider inequality after the establishment of the State was a definite and all-embracing one, and it brought the inequality in Israel closer to that existing in other countries.'

Employing the albeit somewhat different data available, an analysis clearly shows this trend to have continued to the end of the 'sixties (see table below):

DISTRIBUTION OF DISPOSABLE INCOME BY DECILES

Deciles	*Savings survey, 1954* (urban families)	*Savings survey, 1963/4* (urban survey units)	*Family expenditure survey 1968/9* (urban families)
Bottom 10th	2·7%	1·8%	1·8%
2nd	5·0%	4·0%	3·8%
3rd	6·8%	5·6%	5·6%
4th	8·1%	7·2%	7·1%
5th	9·4%	8·6%	8·4%
6th	9·4%	9·7%	9·9%
7th	11·4%	11·2%	11·3%
8th	11·9%	13·1%	13·3%
9th	14·5%	15·6%	16·2%
Top 10th	20·8%	23·2%	22·6%

the index of inequality rising from *0·265 in 1954, to 0·324 in 1963/4, and to 0·330 in 1968/9*. And were the relevant tables to take adequate account of fringe benefits and the opportunity enjoyed by the rich to make untaxed income by profitably manipulating their capital, the inequalities revealed would doubtless be a good deal greater.

Indeed, mounting political agitation and argument over the growth in the gap between richer and poorer led early in 1971 to the appointment of a special committee, with David Horowitz, Governor of the Bank of Israel, as chairman, 'to examine the development that has taken place in incomes and their distribution and in social inequality during the past decade'.†

* See Appendix 5, Table II.

† Report of the Committee on Income Distribution and Social Inequality, Tel Aviv, 1971.

The majority of the committee found the degree of inequality, by the income per 'standard equivalent adult', little changed over the period. The pattern for the years 1957–70 according to gross income distribution was as follows:*

Year	1957/8	1963/4	1967	1968/9	beg. 1970
Inequality index	0·367	0·369	0·413	0·372	0·368

while the pattern according to net income distribution was:†

Year	1963/4	1968/9
Inequality index	0.323	0.334

This would suggest that, on the most indulgent interpretation of the figures, what had become by 1957/8 a far from trivial degree of inequality, had not diminished by the start of the 'seventies.

By being required to examine developments only 'during the last decade', the committee, of course, escaped the need to admit the substantial increase in inequality over the whole period since the establishment of the state.

But there is further criticism to be made. The majority report made much play with the mitigation of inequality produced by progressive taxation. Israel Kessar, a committee member whose various published reservations constitute a challenging minority report, commented: 'There is room for the presumption that precisely in recent years the difference between the official system of taxation and the effective system has widened.'‡ He cited chiefly the growing practice of payment in 'invisible wages', or fringe benefits. Neither he, nor the committee as a whole, considered masked income from capital manipulation or other well-known devices employed by the rich to reduce their tax liabilities.

Still more important, the report was completed at quite the most favourable time for the government case. Had the committee sat earlier, with the figures for 1967 as the terminus of the trend to be examined, its conclusions would have been rather different.

* Ibid., pp. 21–2.
† Ibid., loc. cit.
‡ Ibid., p. 54.

And had it sat later, with the figures for all of 1970, for 1971 and for early 1972 at its disposal, its findings might, unavoidably, have been alarming indeed.

In the pages of the *Jerusalem Post*, Dr Moshe Ater, Economic Editor, commented on the 1970 survey of employee income by the Central Statistical Bureau.

> The 'Lorentz Index' [*sic*], a tool used by economists, shows that inequality in the distribution of wage incomes declined between 1968–69 and 1970. However, compared with the previous period a rising trend of inequality is evident, and it stands to reason that it has gained further ground in the past year.
>
> To be sure, this development has been partly caused by high wages which owner-workers – members of transport co-operatives, shareholders, managers, etc. – pay to themselves. But one may doubt whether this factor has been of major importance. It seems that wage differentials have been increasing under the pressure of potent economic and social forces which have not yet been adequately studied.*

It is a pattern similar to that in other advanced industrial societies under liberal capitalism. Wealth and poverty promote themselves and each other; with a steady shift in the distribution of income from the lower to the upper levels.

Such trends indicate a society that is intrinsically unequal; a society whose inequalities are not due to some sudden immigrant influx or the demands of a soaring defence budget, but to the nature of its functioning. The peak year of new and largely unskilled immigration was in 1949, with some 240,000 arrivals; followed by some 170,000 arrivals in 1950 and 175,000 in 1951. In 1952 the number of immigrants fell to some 24,000, and only in 1957 topped 70,000 again. Nor have fluctuations in military expenditure been reflected in trends of income distribution.

It may well be that the influx of so many immigrants from culturally backward areas, at least by the prevalent values of the settled Jewish population, excused and reinforced the impulse to the development of liberal capitalism. And the insistent demands

* *Jerusalem Post*, 26 March 1972.

of military expenditure may well have done likewise. But there is nothing self-evident in the proposition that enormous numbers of immigrants can be absorbed, and the reasonable requirements of defence credibly met, only by the development of such a society. The truth is, rather, that just such a society is what the interplay between leadership policies and the predominant public mood in Israel produced.

And how may such a society solve the specific problem of poverty among Oriental Jews? It essentially perpetuates and promotes the problem, in perpetuating and promoting the problem of poverty itself. Professor Arthur Hertzberg of Columbia University, a rabbi and one of the seven American representatives on the executive board of the Jewish Agency, publicly attacked the political and religious leadership of Israel for what he called their 'apathy and insensitivity' towards the existence of poverty in the Jewish state. He warned that Israel was in danger of repeating the South African experience, or the mistaken policies that American society had pursued towards its black citizens a decade before.

He firmly rejected the conventional argument of the Israeli leadership that the country's resources had had to be diverted from social welfare to defence expenditures.

> What is most incomprehensible to someone who looks at contemporary Israel with love and deep involvement from the perspective of contemporary American experience is the lack of sympathy, comprehension and identification of Israeli religious leadership, intellectuals and the middle class as a whole with the outcry of the Israeli poor.
>
> As of this moment, there is not a single rabbinic figure of public consequence in all of Israel who is publicly pleading for that one-fifth of its population which is abysmally and well-nigh hopelessly poor.
>
> There are few professors to make the point that a country in which 70% of those who start elementary school are of Oriental origin and only 16% who finish high school come from the same background, has something radically wrong with it.
>
> This society was created from the beginning with a passion for human dignity and social justice. That remains its essential commitment. Yet if it condones even the beginnings of

two societies co-existing in tension, it is untrue to its own deepest meaning.*

The warning against a repetition of the South African experience is doubtless in this context inapposite. There is no statutory economic domination, by one set of Jewish citizens over another; nor is there any real risk at present of any such developing. On the contrary: it is precisely the absence of this that makes the other analogy, with the American experience, so apt. For in the United States, the conceding of equal rights has not produced equal opportunity; because equal opportunity is denied by the functioning of the competitive system and in particular its perpetuation of the past. The blacks are in general poor because their prevalent social conditions and their related attitudes preclude the acquisition of the equipment successfully to compete, on the terms that the dominant ideology imposes; and, unable successfully to compete, they remain poor.

It is, of course, possible to envisage that the political leadership in Israel, sufficiently alarmed by the identification of poverty with a cohesive minority of particular background and culture, would institute substantial measures of discrimination in favour of such a minority. There are already in operation pilot programmes for taking promising candidates from among Oriental youth in the army and giving them crash courses for entrance to higher education. But it is scarcely possible that such measures should have, in terms of the economic system, more than a marginal success. And such success would, above all, merely be bought at the expense of other Israelis, who would slither into poverty as some of the existing poor were assisted to climb out of it. The problem would not be solved, but shifted; and the shift would be accompanied by social stresses surely no less serious.

For the truth is that the economic system of Israel is fundamentally one of competition for differential rewards. And that is why the sort of criticism which Professor Hertzberg's cited remarks represent skirts the issue. For it is concerned not with the basic issue but with the manifestations. Poverty (whether Oriental or any other) does not exist because rabbis or professors or 'the middle class as a whole' are deaf to the outcry of the Israeli poor.

* *New York Times* report from Jerusalem, 15 June 1971.

It exists because the economic system essentially makes such poverty; makes the deafness of the rabbis and the professors, and of the 'middle class as a whole', in making a middle class itself.

There is another claim, false but carefully fostered by the leadership: that Israel remains at least structurally socialist, and any incompatible manifestations are the consequence of temporary difficulties. Has not the state, ever since its establishment, been advancing its role in the economy? Is the Histadrut—with its affiliated co-operatives commanding important areas of agriculture and public transport; its ownership of major industrial enterprises, its own health service, Kupat Holim, the dominant medical organization in the country—not far more than a mere federation of labour unions on the usual social-democratic pattern?

There is surprisingly little detailed analysis available on the developing relations of the private, public and Histadrut sectors of the economy. And what is widely regarded as still the best study of these relations was done by Haim Barkai, in the early 'sixties.* He included in the public sector all concerns of whose voting shares a public authority held, directly or indirectly, at least 50%. He defined the Histadrut sector as consisting 'of all units in which one of the Histadrut groups has at least 50% ownership, unless the other 50% is owned by a public authority'. And he saw the private sector as consisting of all economic units not thus encompassed in the public or Histadrut ones.

On this basis, and recognizing that his definitions would lead to some underestimate in the contribution of the private sector, Barkai examined the developing share of each in the net domestic product from 1953 to 1960 (see table below):

Year	*N.D.P.*	*Public sector*	*Histadrut sector*	*Private sector*
1953	100%	19·4%	18·0%	62·6%
1957	100%	20·9%	20·6%	58·5%
1958	100%	20·0%	20·0%	60·0%
1959	100%	21·6%	20·3%	58·1%
1960	100%	21·1%	20·4%	58·5%

His evidence pointed, thus, to a small overall increase in the share of the public sector, over the period; a rise in the share of the

* First published in the *Sixth Report 1961–1963*, of the Falk Project for Economic Research in Israel.

Histadrut sector concentrated in the years up to the end of 1957; and 'a decline of some significance' in the relative contribution of the private sector. He then produced tables to show how the increase in the share of the public sector had been entirely due to the growth in the activities of public enterprises such as Israel Railways and the Bank of Israel, and especially of the corresponding corporations in utilities and manufacturing. Indeed, these corporations had contributed about a fifth of the sector's total share in 1952; and were contributing about a quarter in 1960. Within the Histadrut share, the companies had moved from accounting for some two-fifths, to accounting for about a half; while there had been a continuous rise in the relative product of the kibbutzim.

Turning to the origins of the contribution made by each sector, Barkai examined the data for 1959.* And on such evidence, the private sector contributed less than three-fifths of the net product; the Histadrut sector, about a fifth; and the public sector, slightly more than the Histadrut. The traditional emphasis of the Histadrut sector on agriculture (notably through the kibbutz movement), on construction (through its building and housing firms), and on transport (mainly through the commanding position of its bus co-operatives), accounted for its share of around a third in these three categories; while its health services were the major factor in its significant share of trade and other services. The considerable share of the public sector in construction reflected the large public housing programme, with much of the work undertaken by public corporations. And Barkai commented on the figures for manufacturing: 'The government sector's role ... seems surprisingly small at first glance, in view of the considerable public resources channelled, through the development budget, into this industry. But these funds were given largely in the form of loans and were not used for the acquisition of titles of ownership by the public sector.'†

Barkai's basic thesis was the 'significant bias towards socialized elements in the sectoral structure of the Israel economy'. Indeed, comparing the proportion of the public sector product in Israel

* See Appendix 5, Table III.

† Haim Barkai, *The Public, Histadrut and Private Sectors in the Israel Economy*, the Maurice Falk Institute for Economic Research in Israel, December 1968, p. 34.

with that in advanced Western societies, and considering the lower level of Israeli economic development (with the lower level of government expenditure on services that this should normally have entailed), he placed Israel at the top of the list as 'a welfare state *par excellence*'. And he concluded: 'The contribution of private firms proper to net product in Israel is significantly smaller than in other non-Soviet-bloc countries, because of both the relatively important place in production occupied by the public sector, and the existence and size of the Histadrut sector, which is a unique phenomenon.'*

Now the welfare state, whatever the excellence of its Israeli manifestation—and the analysis of poverty previously given scarcely confirms such a judgment today—is not at all the same thing as socialism.† It is, instead, plainly a product of liberal capitalism, by which the system of private profit—the free market—has promoted both its efficiency and its popular support. It involves a massive measure of state intervention: to ensure conventionally decent standards of health, housing, education, mobility, security, for the vast bulk of the population; and so to manage the economy as to promote industrial growth and a high level of employment.

But the function of the state is essentially residual. The objective is not to extend, however gradually, the confines of the public sector until there is no private sector left. It is for the state to take over such parts of the economy as the private sector does not find it sufficiently profitable to operate, or would operate only on terms incompatible with the prevalent view of the public interest.

Thus in Britain, where the concept of the welfare state was initially expressed, the public sector encompasses not only the gas and electricity industries, the bulk of public transport, the post and telephone services, but coal-mining and, for the present at

* Ibid., p. 74.

† As Barkai's study itself acknowledges, in an early footnote: 'The welfare state is neither in fact, nor in theory, identical with a socialized economy. The significance of this distinction may be realized if one considers the possibility that a government may supply services free of charge, not by granting the services but by issuing coupons entitling the holder to obtain them from producers in the private sector. An example of this system is the supply of medicines by the British National Health Service. Comprehensive public ownership of production units is evidently the distinctive feature of a socialized economy.' Ibid., p. 16.

least, by far the bulk of steel production. Indeed, by Barkai's own table of comparison, the public sector accounted for 24% of the British net domestic product in 1957, but only 22% of Israel's in 1959.* And it is doubtful if the figures for Britain followed Barkai's definition of public sector concerns: which would then, for instance, have included British Petroleum, with government ownership of half its shares.

British Petroleum is, in fact, a significant instance of the welfare state at work. The British government holding was bought for reasons of national security when Winston Churchill, hardly an adherent of the socialist cause, was in power. And though its holding would have enabled a British government to exercise effective control over the company whenever it chose to do so, the company has instead been permitted, by both Labour and Conservative governments, to operate essentially as though it were altogether in the private sector.

What Barkai calls 'the unique phenomenon' of the Histadrut does make a difference. This does not mean that Israel has the only federation of labour which owns and operates substantial economic concerns. Sweden and the Federal German Republic are notable instances of other countries where such exists. What distinguishes the Histadrut is the sheer scale of its membership (1,079,000, or 57·4% of the adult population, in 1969), and of its direct share in the net domestic product.

But this makes for a difference of degree rather than of kind. Ultimately, as do its counterparts in Sweden and the Federal German Republic, the Histadrut operates in accordance and not in conflict with the capitalist system. Barkai claims that, '*in theory at any rate,*† the activities of the Histadrut production units are not exclusively motivated by considerations of profit. In this respect they resemble publicly-owned rather than privately-owned production units.'‡ But he gives the game away in the initial qualifying clause. In practice the activities of such firms must be dominated by the profit motive, since they exist within the context of capitalist competition.

Of course they are not 'exclusively' motivated by considerations

* Ibid., p. 70.
† My italics.
‡ Ibid., p. 15.

of profit; but then neither are most large companies in the private sector of Israel or of any other liberal-capitalist state. There are considerations of public interest, as in pricing policies and the treatment of environmental pollution, which they can sacrifice to the full possibilities of profit only at their peril. The importance of a favourable image with the public at large encourages an expenditure on public relations that cannot altogether be dismissed as offset in the balance sheet, by the prospect of public contracts or increased sales. That profit remains the primary impulse is not to be doubted for a moment. But who can equally doubt that this is true, too, for the professional management of Histadrut companies?

Indeed, these Histadrut companies may be so different from one another in process and product, and some of them so large and complex, that a significant distance is inevitably set between ownership and management. The Hevrat Haovdim, or General Co-operative Society of Jewish Labour in Palestine, the form in which the Histadrut organizes its production units, appoints the management of the companies it owns. But once appointed, such management is likely to exercise increasing independence of decision, at least in the large companies: on the pattern of large private companies elsewhere, whose ownership is so diffuse that management may reasonably expect displacement only in consequence of marked failure. And how is success measured if not by the profit record? The Histadrut companies are, in essence, private companies owned by a particular corporate entity: functioning in effect as do other private companies under capitalism, and especially like the constituents of a major 'conglomerate'.

There are, to be sure, also the individual service and production co-operatives, which are in principle based on self-employment. But hired labour is used in many of them; surely sufficient in itself to deny a socialist character and function. And even where hired labour is totally eschewed, what are these, if not private corporations of a specific type, dominated by the motive of profit for their respective shareholders? The members of the two huge bus co-operatives, Dan and Egged, for instance, have repeatedly shown themselves directed to getting as high as possible a return for their labour and capital investment, regardless of the impact on other workers or on consumers in general. The kibbutz increasingly functions, in production and marketing, with its members having their own benefit in mind; while the benefit of other kibbutzim, let alone of the whole society, is left to look after itself.

Of course, kibbutzim in the same movement collaborate; as do the various kibbutz movements; and the kibbutz movements themselves, with other co-operatives, with trades unions, and with industrial and commercial companies, in the Histadrut. But it is a collaboration that each constituent pursues only so far as seems to serve its own interest. And the collaboration itself is, after all, only the exclusive interest of the participants writ correspondingly large.

In short, the Histadrut should properly be placed in the private sector of the Israeli economy. And once this is done, the size of this sector is much the same as in other liberal-capitalist societies.

No analysis such as Barkai's has been done for the decade of the 'sixties. But the available evidence suggests that the pattern of productive ownership in Israel has significantly been altered only by the overall fall in the share of domestic production enjoyed by the Histadrut. The growth rate of the real gross national product has continued among the highest in the world: at an annual average of 10·3% in 1961–5; then sliding to 1·3% and 2·4% in 1966 and 1967 respectively; before soaring to 15·3% in 1968, and 11·3% in 1969.* And the liberal-capitalist formula of development may be traced in the contributions made by the various categories.† The relative increase in the contribution of the public sector during the recession years of 1966 and 1967 is evident. So, too, is the overall growth in importance of the industrial contribution. Indeed, the structure of the economy is of the sort displayed by the advanced industrial states of Western Europe.

In the absence of adequate detail, the precise shares of the public, the Histadrut and the private sectors in industry cannot be established on the basis of the definitions used by Barkai. But one source claims:

> The great majority of enterprises – 93% – belong to the private sector and in 1965 employed 76% of industrial workers; 5·5%,

* An annual increase of over 9% from 1950 to 1969: compared with 3·3% for the United States; 5% for Denmark; 5·3% for West Germany; and 9·6% for Japan. *Facts About Israel 1971* (Jerusalem: Keter Books), p. 90.

† See Appendix 5, Table IV.

> with 15% of total employment, were in the Histadrut sector; only 1·2% belonged to the public one.
>
> Public sector enterprises are large and concentrated in capital-intensive industries, such as mining, chemicals and petroleum refining, and transport equipment. Most Histadrut plants are big, too; they are mainly in such industries as basic metals, non-metallic minerals, wood and wood products and quarries. The relative importance of the Histadrut sector has been declining.*

This last statement was abundantly confirmed by the Histadrut itself, with a survey published in the middle of March 1972 by its Institute for Economic and Social Research. In 1966, the survey showed, Histadrut companies were responsible for 21·4% of the net domestic product; but in 1970, for only 18·9%.

The trend was not uniform for all major economic activities. From 1966 to 1970, the share of Histadrut enterprises in the country's agricultural product rose slightly, from 71·3% to 72%. And there was almost no change in the share of the banking sector. But in industry, the fall was pronounced: from 19·5% to 16·4%. In construction, the Histadrut's share dropped from 28·9% to 22·4%; and in transport, from 24·5% to 20·3%.

With all the caveats, it emerges that no less than 91% of Israeli industrial workers were, during 1965, in the private sector, proper and Histadrut-controlled; as were 98·8% of the individual establishments. And it seems unlikely that the share of the public sector in banking, industry and trade grew much, if at all, from the small percentages in 1959.

To be sure, this does not dispose of the massive role played by the public sector in the economy. For such a role has become intrinsic to the operation of capitalism in its liberal development. In his formative work, *The General Theory of Employment, Interest and Money*,† Keynes propounded the need to grant the state 'an ever greater responsibility for directly organizing investment'; since, unlike the individual businessman, it was in a position to 'calculate the marginal efficiency of capital-goods on long views and on the basis of the general social advantage'. Some three and

* *Facts About Israel 1971*, p. 112.

† Published in London by Macmillan in 1936.

a half decades later, a Republican President of the United States could unflinchingly proclaim himself a Keynesian, and receive the plaudits of the American business community for doing so. In Israel, as in the United States, or Britain or France or Sweden, businessmen expect the state to act for a 'general social advantage' that has consistently served their private interests so well.

In Israel, the state has provided large credits to new or ailing industries under private control; and, where considered necessary, imposed its own more competent managers, all too often without taking commensurate title to ownership. Indeed, even when it has taken such title, through the acquisition of voting shares to secure its investment and control, it has been known to sell back the relevant enterprises to private ownership, sometimes at an overall loss, as soon as these had become profitable.

Of course, the role of the state has been expanding at a unique rate in Israel because of the uniquely large expansion in defence expenditure. This last consumed some 12% of the gross national product in 1967, and some 25% in 1969. Of the combined Ordinary and Development Budget, 'Security' took in 1969/70 no less than 39·3%; and 39·8% in 1970/71.* Yet this has been very far from a source of unmitigated distress to the business community. Private industry has been given considerable help from the government to establish new or augment existing operations that would advance the domestic manufacture of defence equipment; related activities, as in construction for strategic purposes, have been similarly encouraged; and, by common account, the extent of resultant profits has not been too closely examined by the government departments involved. In particular, given the instances cited by the State Controller (Israel's equivalent of the Scandinavian Ombudsman) in his twenty-first annual report,† it would seem that the Ministry of Defence has been rather too accommodating in its attitude to prices and terms of payment.

Inevitably, also, the boom produced in defence industries has spread into other areas of the private sector. The twenty-two major industrial companies listed on the Tel Aviv stock exchange reported earnings of some IL 60 million in 1969/70, compared to

* *Facts About Israel 1971*, pp. 90, 95.
† Published April 1971.

IL 15 million two years earlier.* But then it was Keynes himself who suggested, in declaring the virtues of public expenditure at a time of economic recession (such as Israel itself experienced in 1966/7): '... pyramid-building, earthquakes, even wars may serve to increase wealth.'†

Indeed, the extent of public expenditure as a percentage of the gross national product was until recently much less in Israel than in Britain.‡

Year	*1965*	*1966*	*1967*	*1968*	*1969*
Britain	28·2	29·6	31·6	31·4	30·6
Israel	19·9	22·1	29·5	30·5	30·3

And it is the soaring costs of defence that have produced the spurt in the Israeli percentage.

Year	*1965*	*1966*	*1967*	*1968*	*1969*
% of public sector consumption in Israel G.N.P.	19·9	22·1	29·5	30·5	30·3
Public sector security expenditure as % of Israeli G.N.P.§	9·1	9·8	17·3	19·2	19·6

SOURCE: *Bank of Israel Annual Report 1969*, p. 105.

This thriving of the private sector on nourishment from the public one has other manifestations. As elsewhere under liberal capitalism, there is a significant traffic in personnel between the upper reaches of the business community and those of government: though in Israel the movement seems especially strong from the second to the first; and within this direction, from the top

* Information from the head of the Tel Aviv Stock Exchange in a private interview.

† *The General Theory.*

‡ Excluding defence expenditure not classified as public consumption.

§ For Britain, this item is described as 'Expenditure on goods and services as percentage of gross national product at factor cost'; source: *Social Trends No. 1*, A publication of the Government Statistical Service (London: Her Majesty's Stationery Office, 1970), p. 45. For Israel, the description is 'Weight of Public Sector Consumption in G.N.P.'; source: *Bank of Israel Annual Report 1969* (Jerusalem, May 1970), p. 105.

ranks of the defence forces. Military distinction has become a well-known route to the boardrooms of the larger companies.

It is a traffic which has provided occasion for considerable abuses. The twenty-first annual report of the State Controller complained of how the Ministry of Finance had bailed out failing industrial companies and bankrupt banks and covered up the folly of officials. And it cited instances of state employees who had been party to the award of privileges to private firms and crossed over immediately afterwards 'to the other side of the table, becoming directors of projects set up by these firms in line with their own decision or recommendation'.*

In an editorial on the report, the *Jerusalem Post* commented:

> We have prided ourselves for many years that unlike the region in which we live, we have escaped the banes of bribery and outright corruption. Reading the nine hundred pages of the State Controller's twenty-first annual report, one is not certain that this is any longer true. We have not yet reached the level of our neighbours and other developing countries whom we try to teach good administrative practices. But if the present trend remains unchecked and unreversed, then the road to becoming a real Levantine country is short.†

'Levantine' has long been the term used by the Western cultural leadership of Israel to describe that blend of despotism and corruption supposedly characteristic of the immediate (Oriental) environment. Yet the abuses to which the State Controller referred are of the rather more refined kind all too well known in the United States; and practised, to varying extents, in other societies of liberal capitalism.

Related to this, there is emerging in Israel, also, the massive private corporation: involved in such a multiplicity of activities, and disposing of such large resources in terms of the economy, as to constitute a source of considerable social power. The Histadrut has a mass membership to which it is, if more in principle than in practice, responsible for the management of its various enterprises. But to what constituency is a company like Clal, in principle let alone practice, responsible?

* Comment on the report in *Hatzofe,* 21 April 1971.

† *Jerusalem Post,* 22 April 1971.

With its control reportedly shared by the three major Israeli banks, commanding together some 40% of the company's voting stock, but with a large participation of private capital from Latin America, Clal in 1970 had twenty-four affiliated companies (compared with ten in the year before): among them a major textile concern, several real estate enterprises, and the country's largest publishing house (headed by a former general in the Israeli army). According to the Economic Editor of the *Jerusalem Post*:

> The 1970 operating profit was IL 9·1m., more than double the 1967 figure. The net profit (after tax and write-off of capital-raising costs) was IL 10·3m., one sixth more than in 1969 ... The consolidated profit per share was 15·5 per cent, and the consolidated operating profit was up almost 30 per cent compared with 1969 ... The group's aggregate assets are now probably not far below IL 500m. ... Its financial force, its liquidity (IL 43m. of current assets, against IL 26m. current liabilities, at the end of 1970), and *its excellent connections with the Ministry of Finance*,* enable it to go on increasing its hold of various business ventures.†

This is a far cry, indeed, from what those early pioneers believed, and so many of Israel's present leaders still claim, the Jewish state should be. Even the Economic Editor of the *Jerusalem Post,* scarcely renowned among the country's newspapers for its opposition to capitalism, expressed some disquiet.

> At this juncture one is tempted to raise another, more basic question: what actually is Clal's economic function? When it was set up, nine years ago, high hopes were entertained concerning immigration from Latin America, and the company was expected to blaze the trail and to act as a trustee in this field. However, this role is by now of lesser importance. Instead, it has become this country's major conglomerate, of a size which already does not fit easily into Israel's rather small national economy.‡

The excuse for all this indulgence of the private sector, when the indulgence itself is not merely denied, is that beggars can't be

* My italics.
† *Jerusalem Post,* 25 May 1971.
‡ Ibid.

choosers. As in Washington or Paris or Budapest, the cry is that the production of wealth must take precedence over the distribution: with the added argument in Jerusalem that an Israel which has to spend so much on defence in order to ensure its very survival has more pressing priorities than the ultimate commitment to socialism.

A high official in the Treasury explained how a large capital inflow had enabled Israel to develop the economy and raise the general living standards of the population, while so many immigrants had been absorbed and so much, especially since 1967, spent on defence.

'We need vast amounts of investment capital. And we have to compete. Not against Brazil and the Congo', and he waved away a multitude of clamorous backward states with precarious regimes, 'but against Britain and Italy and Canada. Do you know the inducements for capital investment in Quebec? Sure, they've got a problem there, of English and French. But look at us! We could be at war again tomorrow morning. We should only have *their* problems!'

I clucked encouragingly. And his voice dropped, as though he were communicating a confidence. 'You see, it is simple. The choice is between our all being poor, and some of us becoming rich with the poor becoming less poor in the process. You go to a rich Jew abroad, and you tell him that Israel must have money. He will open his cheque book and give you, say, fifty thousand dollars. But if you want a million or two for investment, then he wants to know what return he is going to get; what the tax officials are going to take; how safe his investment will be. Go!' he said, pointing a formidable finger, like those bronze statues of celebrated pioneers who advanced the frontier, 'And ask such people yourself.'

A few days later I was in Haifa, on my way to interview a professor at the Technion who is an expert on industrial relations. The taxi driver spoke an easy English and pressed his complaints.

'My wife and I have been working and waiting two years for an apartment. We have saved ten thousand pounds [Israeli] and we need forty thousand. Don't laugh, but we are thinking of leaving.' 'Where for?' I asked. 'Germany perhaps. I have family there, and in America. My parents came from Russia twenty years ago.'

He brooded for a few moments. 'They used to talk to me about socialism. But this talk of socialism is only talk. Here, when your neighbour gets a car, you must get one as well, even if it means that you don't feed your kids properly. My friends pay month by month for television sets, and here a television set costs much more than in America.'

Haifa is not a bad place to look at the consumer society. It has a topographical neatness. At sea level, near the port, where industry spews its waste into the air, live the poorer of the citizens. Then the city climbs, up the slopes of Mount Carmel, through middle income groups; to where, with a generous view of the bay, the rich have their homes.

Near the top, to the side, stands the Technion, where the technological elite of Israel is trained. What the expert had to say about industrial relations was all too predictable.

'It's getting like Britain and Sweden now, with a growing gap between the trades union bureaucrats and the shop floor. Practically every small group uses what power it has to take what it can; and blames others for doing the same. The teachers are angry with the port-workers, the port-workers with the nurses, for striking. Often it is just a tiny group of technicians who ignore the advice of the elected committee on the shop floor, and bring the whole plant to a standstill. The electricians shut off the power and much of the country. In Haifa there are 70 or 80 port pilots, out of some 2,500 permanent employees. If they don't bring in the ships, that's that. Of course the Histadrut doesn't approve. But so what? Everyone complains of what is happening to the country. Everyone is against strikes: except for himself.'

Just before leaving Israel, I spent the evening with a Cabinet Minister. 'These Arabs,' he said. 'They are so stupid. Why don't they declare peace and watch us jump at each other's throats?'

Not for the first time under liberal capitalism, a government dominated by those professing to represent the interests of labour, blamed the high wage demands of workers for the tribulations of an economy based on competitive greed. Finance Minister Pinhas Sapir, talking to the Labour Party Young Leadership Circle during a wildcat strike at El Al, the country's civil airline, warned of catastrophe for the nation if the government did not crack down on such behaviour. And he angrily defended the government against criticism for not spending enough on social welfare, and for lacking any concerted social policies.

'I am very much against encouraging people to live in a permanent hothouse of social welfare, where they prefer to live on the dole rather than to do something constructive.'*

The newly appointed governor of the Bank of Israel, Moshe Sanbar, offered his own recommendations in a report to the Cabinet.† All new state-financed development projects should be shelved for six months; and all new construction of public buildings, with the sole exception of hospitals, for a year. Interest on all forms of subsidized loans at present ranging from 6% to 12%, in comparison with *a free market interest rate of 16% and over*,‡ should be raised by 2–3%. Zones designated as development areas should be reduced, so as to cut the number of corresponding loans and investment grants. And the authorities should slash tariffs, in an accelerated drive to liberalize imports. It was not a course of treatment that seemed to disturb the stock exchange, where prices continued for the while their hectic rise.

Certainly the government had manifest cause for concern. A massive conversion of foreign currency, along with substantial deficit financing, was threatening runaway inflation. In 1969, the money supply advanced 7%, or not much more than the gross national product; and the cost of living, 2·5%. In 1970, the money supply rose 5%; and the cost of living 6%. Then in 1971, the money supply rocketed 27%, more than three times the growth of the gross national product; and the cost of living, 12%. During the first ten weeks of 1972 alone, the money supply increased by 7% (more than 35% at an annual rate), about as much as the gross national product was expected to increase over the entire year. Yet with general elections to be fought before the end of 1973, this was no time for drastic retrenchment. The system of liberal capitalism has well-tuned political rules.

What this inflationary process reflects is, in the first place, a dangerous amount of high living on unearned resources. Despite the considerable sums donated by the Diaspora, the country's foreign debt increased by 50%, to $3,500 million (a figure well

* Report in the *Jerusalem Post*, 13 April 1972.
† Ibid.
‡ My italics.

over half the value of the annual gross national product), in 1970–71.* And the heavy demands of defence supplied only part of the reason (see table below).

In the year	*Foreign trade deficit, including invisibles; and excluding total defence spending: in millions of U.S.$*
1966/7 (average)	195
1968	310
1969	461
1970	457
1971	488
1972 (forecast)	540

> Israelis are accustomed to thinking that the economy must depend on foreign loans and charity because of the crushing military burdens, but the fact is that the dollar gap is increasing steadily quite apart from the defence effort ...
>
> Since 1970 Israel has been subsidized by the U.S. Government to the tune of over $300m. a year (covering about 40 per cent of defence expenditure in foreign currency).
>
> But can, and will, this last forever? Even German restitutions will peter out over the next decade or two. Israel may still go on borrowing abroad on a huge scale, but only up to some limit, and the wisdom of doing it for financing domestic spending is rather doubtful.†

Israel may continue to demand from other countries consideration as a developing state. Yet, according to Pinhas Sapir himself: 'The economic resources at the disposal of slightly more than 3 million inhabitants of Israel nearly equal those of the 34 million inhabitants of Egypt, or of the 20 million inhabitants of Iraq, Syria, Lebanon and Jordan combined.'‡ And it still needs to borrow enormously abroad to meet its expenditure. But then a fever of consumption is coursing through the society: sucking in ever more luxury goods for the abundant shops; ever more private cars for the already cluttered roads.

* Speech by Moshe Sanbar, Governor of the Bank of Israel, on 15 March 1972.

† Dr Moshe Ater, 'The Economic Time Bomb', *Jerusalem Post*, 11 April 1972.

‡ From an article in *Davar*, 2 February 1972.

The future is being recklessly mortgaged, and not only by the proliferation of debts that must be serviced and repaid. The very dependence of such feverish consumption on unearned income, from borrowing and from foreign charity, promotes a widespread attitude of mind scarcely compatible with the competitiveness that the international context of the economy requires. The reputation of Israelis for efficiency, in carving out export markets despite the pressures of the Arab blockade, is not what it was. And there are simply not sufficient resources left available for building a balanced industrial infrastructure to meet the likely demands of the future.

Above all, the system must continue to foster, by its competitive commitment, social inequalities. Those who can exploit it for profit, by manipulating their capital or exploiting the demand for their labour, may find themselves carried to new heights of material consumption. Those whose peculiar talents or temperaments, skills or corporate organization, culture or age, do not fit them for the conflict, must find their relative circumstances relentlessly reduced.

Nor, of course, are the victims of such exploitation only Jews. More and more, the competitive society is sucking in others: for the supposed material needs of the Jewish state, and effectively for the material advantage of particular groups within it. Apparently it is not enough that so many Arabs from the conquered territories are being employed in Israel at wages which, like those of Israeli Arabs, and of Jewish immigrants from Arab countries indeed, are well below the average.* There is increasing official reference to the necessity for importing labour from further afield. In a speech to the Jerusalem Trade Union Club *(sic)*, Moshe Sanbar said that there were 25,000 unfilled jobs in the country; and that since this was seriously hampering economic development, the state might have to import labour from countries with which it had economic and trade ties.†

How long ago was it that the employment of non-Jewish labour by capitalist enterprise in a Jewish homeland was regarded as both morally repugnant and nationally suicidal? But then nothing is

* Central Statistical Bureau sample survey of employee income in 1970; a report in the *Jerusalem Post*, 26 March 1972.

† Report in the *Jerusalem Post*, 16 March 1972.

more certain than that a state in which some citizens exploit their fellows for material advantage will as far as possible engage in exploiting the citizens of other states. It is a perilous pursuit; and a terrible irony that the homeland which the heroes of Tel-Hai set out so differently to build should have chosen to adopt it.

7

The perspectives of peace

'Policy in Israel is not long-term, but a matter of manœuvre through the next few months,' the foreign correspondent in Jerusalem complained. 'The old lady plays for time. She won't take risks. And so there is a see-saw of rhetoric between Cairo and Jerusalem. When Sadat seems flexible, Golda is rigid; and when Sadat seems rigid, she becomes flexible herself. It's a failing of the imagination, that comes with old age.'

The old lady gets the blame, and she doubtless deserves some of it. But the government is far from being Golda alone. There are Cabinet hawks with still harder dispositions; and the doves are odd creatures, whose coos are intermingled with harsher cries, and whose claws seem incompatible with their feathers. Beyond, the opposition is dominated by a Gahal which withdrew its representatives and support from the government in August 1970, on the grounds that the decision to accept the United States negotiating initiative portended Israel's withdrawal from the 1967 cease-fire lines. And Jewish public opinion in general reflects the policies of the leadership.

The *Time*–Louis Harris poll of April 1971 revealed 85% of Jewish Israelis as satisfied that the government was doing all it should to negotiate a peace treaty. Only 7% felt that it should be more flexible. Some 73% were prepared to give back part of the conquered territory for an overall settlement; 18% preferred to keep the present borders; 3% actually wished to expand them; while only 4% favoured total withdrawal. But more detailed expressions of opinion suggested that the willingness to trade territory for peace was scarcely a generous one. No less than 93% approved Israel's annexation of East Jerusalem; 86% wanted annexation of the Golan Heights; 72% wished to keep Sharm-el-Sheikh; and 47% even wanted to keep Eastern Sinai. Some 49% would annex the Gaza Strip (with 13% for neutralization; 16% for returning it; and 10% for using it to create a Palestinian state): while 39% would annex the West Bank (with 16% for neutralization; 18% for returning it; and 12% for using it to create a Palestinian state). 'About the only territory that significant numbers of Israelis are generally prepared to let go is the sandy western Sinai desert. Yet even here, only 18% are willing to give the captured desert back to Egypt, while 29% favour annexation, and 38% propose neutralizing the territory as a buffer zone.'*

First among the explanations for the general hardness of outlook is, undoubtedly, fear. After three wars, the Jews find all too close the possibility of having to fight a fourth. It is impossible to know how many of them really believe that their national existence would then again be at stake, or at least their numbers calamitously reduced. Certainly their own government, in pursuit of both domestic and foreign backing for its policies, takes care to emphasize the dangers. But in any event, the fear of any casualties at all looms the larger for the smallness of the Jewish population. Who can be certain that he, or his child, would escape?

It is this fear that clings to the conquered territories as providing strategic advantages in war; diminishing the cost of a surprise attack; and meanwhile augmenting the difficulties of conflict by attrition. Holding the Golan Heights, the supposition runs, protects the northern settlements from Syrian guns and makes Damascus itself edifyingly open to Israeli ground attack. The West Bank is a buffer against Jordanian strikes and any resurgence of guerrilla activity. The Gaza Strip under Israeli rule is no longer the potential bayonet thrust of Egyptian power or a connivance at terrorism. Possession of Sinai keeps Egyptian tanks so many more miles, and Egyptian planes so many more minutes, away, while keeping Israeli forces so much closer to Egyptian targets. Sharm-el-Sheikh commands the sea route from Eilat. And the reunification of Jerusalem not only secures the former western sector from immediate assault, but is unnegotiable for other reasons.

Along with fear, there is distrust of Arab promises. Yet here the factor seems rather less formidable than is conventionally assumed. Although in the poll previously cited, 56% considered that Sadat was not sincere in offering to recognize Israel's sovereignty as part

* *Time*, 12 April 1971.

of a settlement, no less than 30% were willing to take him at his word, while 14% were undecided.

But the factor of sheer pride in the public outlook ought not to be excluded. After so many centuries of being despised, not least for supposed physical weakness and even cowardice, the Jews see in their 1967 conquests the embodied vindication of themselves before a world that still values physical strength and courage so highly. To give up all or nearly all their conquests: is it not to give up the very symbol of their new-found dignity; and, along with it, in the eyes of the world, the substance as well?

For many, with the ranks of the religious now swollen by recruits to a new national mysticism, this is not pride but the mere assertion of right, the fulfilling of the promise. What is Israel if it is not, for instance, Hebron, the resting place of the patriarchs? And where Jehovah was regrettably imprecise, history can supply pretexts for claiming one or other place as no more than due restoration.

For most, probably, distrust and pride together are the response to the pressures of the world at large. The Arabs, after all, had no responsibility to protect a Jewish state; and had, indeed, clearly and frequently enough expressed their determination to destroy it. But what did the United Nations do to prevent Nasser's reoccupation of Sharm-el-Sheikh, and consequent stranglehold on Israel's shipping route through the Straits? At a stroke, the guarantees for which the conquests of the 1956 Suez war had been so trustingly traded were revealed as valueless.

How should one suppose that guarantees now would prove any more reliable? The Security Council could not move over a Soviet or Chinese veto; and a General Assembly dominated by hostile opinion would support no further initiative to defend Israeli interests. Nor should much confidence be placed in the increasingly canvassed prospect of a four-power guarantee. The Soviet Union would eagerly betray Israel to Arab purposes, as occasion served.

France has shown since 1967 what little weight Israelis should attach to its protestations of neutrality; and Britain would always place the security of its oil supplies and investments above any pledges made to Israel. Certainly, to suppose that either state, or both, would commit sufficient military force to intervene effectively for the defence of Israel defies the facts of their developed policies and interests.

The United States alone carries some conviction as a guarantor: but how much? In the 1967 crisis, Israel looked to speedy action from Washington and was fed instead on words. Nor have sudden somersaults in American policy since, as towards China, encouraged confidence in the longevity of commitments. Besides, a gathering public mood of disengagement, promoted by the course of the Vietnam war and the troubles of the dollar, bode ill for American readiness to take military action on Israel's behalf. There is, it is true, an influential body of American opinion behind Israel. But it is by no means the only pressure group, actual or potential, concerned with conflict in the Middle East. And its influence has demonstrably succeeded better in discouraging unfavourable activities by the American government than in encouraging favourable ones. In short, the celebrated Zionist lobby might prevent American power from being employed against Israel's interests: but to assume from this that it could ensure the employment of American power to save Israel from its enemies, would be a dangerous mistake.

They must, Israelis accordingly believe, rely on themselves to guarantee the provisions of any settlement. And in this resolve, they have nothing to fear from the recriminations and threats of so-called world opinion. They have successfully defied resolutions, protests, demands from the Security Council itself, and have no cause to suppose that further defiance would encounter disciplinary action. The United States would not allow economic sanctions of any kind; and in any event, the Rhodesian experience does not suggest that such sanctions have much bite to accompany their bark.

Given this attitude among the leadership and public at large, the endless games played by Israelis over what they would or would not give up for a peace treaty are too often counter-productive. For they reveal to themselves, to the immediate Arab environment, and to the world beyond, how much more powerful in Israel at present is fear than faith; distrust than generosity; pride in courage than the courage of compassion.

I played the game with a foreign correspondent for whom Israel has become home. 'I take a minimalist position,' he said warily. 'I would agree to a federal borough system for Jerusalem; some leasehold undertaking for the Golan Heights; even give up

Sharm-el-Sheikh; but I would insist upon a demilitarized Sinai and West Bank.' And then he went on to list the combination of ministers that would be necessary to sell such a settlement. But no such combination existed: or, in his judgment, seemed likely for the foreseeable future.

And, indeed, what is left to negotiate? Government spokesmen continually cry that everything is negotiable. But they have variously laid claim to one or other part of the conquered territories as beyond concession, till only the meaningless remains for them to yield. Indeed, the double-talk would be ridiculous if the issues involved were not so serious.

Speaking to the Knesset on 27 March 1972, the Minister without Portfolio, Israel Galili, defended the policy of fostering Jewish settlement in the Gaza Strip. 'There is no contradiction between settlement and negotiation with the Arabs,' he claimed. Israel had stated on more than one occasion that it would not return to the pre-1967 lines, but it had also stated that everything was negotiable, he noted. He asked whether the Arabs, who had been defeated in war three times, expected to come out of the conflict 'without a single hair out of place'.*

On 16 March 1972, in a resolution passed by forty-four votes to four, with twenty-seven abstentions, the Knesset supported the government in dismissing Hussein's proposals for a federation of the East Bank with the conquered West Bank and Gaza Strip. In reiterating willingness to negotiate 'without prior conditions from either side', the resolution also 'determined that the historic right of the Jewish people to the Land of Israel is beyond challenge'. The abstentions were largely those of the right-wing Gahal opposition; and given both the context of the debate, and the high emotional charge that the phrase 'Land of Israel' has come to carry for those who see the conquered West Bank as inalienably part of the Promised Land, it is clear that the abstentions concealed a great deal of glee.

A reader of the *Jerusalem Post* wrote to express himself 'stunned' at the Knesset declaration. 'What has happened to the previous pledge to strive for negotiations "without prior conditions"? Is not "beyond challenge" a prior condition? ... I fear this is a grave

* *Jerusalem Post,* 28 March 1972.

breach of policy and a dangerous obstacle in the road to settlement ... This is also just what our enemies need to prove that we have no serious intentions of entering any settlement.'*

His astonishment was understandable. But, unhappily, it was rare. The hardening of the Israeli government line has hardened Israeli public opinion accordingly: and this in turn has made the government still less flexible. Professors disturbed by the annexationist direction of policy are refused a meeting with the prime minister. A group of high-school students, representing an attitude of precocious imperialism, is received for amicable exchanges.

'Do they not see what they are making of Israel, with their counting in kilometres—our leaders with their minds like tiny slide rules?' an anguished professor at the Hebrew University asked me rhetorically. And, to be sure, they seem like people building a dam of sand, with their backs blindly to the sea.

It is not that they want war, unlike those caricatures of them that sometimes glare from pages of the Arab press. It is not perhaps even that they want to keep as much as possible of what they have won in war. It is that war, with its habits of fear and distrust, its definitions of interest, has become their home. They can find their way on the military maps; but peace requires a journey where the map is largely blank.

They simply do not have the will to search through the unknown for peace. Their minds are attached to the past as mountain climbers to a rope. And they see mountains everywhere. They have consistently magnified the influence of the Soviet Union in Egypt as an obstacle to any settlement: as though Soviet interests themselves never changed; or Arab interests could not change, to force corresponding changes in the Soviet outlook.

They have consistently underrated the need of the Sadat regime for a reasonable settlement with Israel: so that they often seem to speak as though nothing important had happened in Egypt since the death of Nasser, or even the abdication of Farouk. For if a continuation of the Arab–Israeli conflict confronts Israel with profound social problems, the problems with which it confronts the Sadat regime are yet more menacingly immediate. In the mood of Egypt today, failure to solve the 'national problem' of the occupied land, together with the costs of military preparation

* Ibid.

for some engagement to seek a break in the deadlock, must feed only disaffection on both the Left and the Right. Is this then what the Israeli leadership awaits: the fall of Sadat before a revolutionary force of the urban underpaid and unemployed allied to a peasantry aroused by nationalist passion; or, more likely in the near term, a military coup with Muslim Brotherhood undertones? Yet neither is calculated to present a better opportunity for a settlement with the essentially liberal-capitalist direction of Israel today than does a Sadat regime of essentially liberal-capitalist aspiration and petty-bourgeois support.

The Israeli politicians and gcnerals speak with such authority and application to detail: and only the apparent absurdity of a settlement on any but their own terms emerges. Yet the doubt persists. And confirmation comes occasionally from remarks passed by the mighty themselves.

Haim Bar-Lev, former Chief of Staff and recently appointed Minister of Commerce and Industry, told *Ot*, the Labour Party weekly: 'I believe that we could reach a so-called peace arrangement today, on the basis of the former boundaries; and if I believed the old lines were the best we could achieve, I would agree to them. But I think that if we stand fast today, we will be able to get more secure borders.'*

Private interviews yield further evidence.

'We are not stronger but weaker for having our forces along the Canal,' declared a high-ranking officer on the reserve list. 'An artillery barrage would cost us many lives. And how much deeper must we strike into Egypt as our reply? We can take out the Soviet missiles, but it won't be cheap. And, above all, our hard line has lost us the tolerance abroad for our most powerful weapon, the preventive strike. Why do we need all that sand?' I asked him what he would set as terms for withdrawal from Sinai. 'We must be allowed to keep a force there, mainly of planes, to discourage attack; just a sufficient force somewhere across the border.' 'And would you agree in turn to a similar force of Egyptians on the Israeli side of the border, as their insurance against Israeli attack?' He seemed momentarily startled. 'Of course not.'

But how should a settlement essentially unequal stand much chance of success? 'The victorious and the defeated are not to be

* Report in the *Jerusalem Post*, 9 March 1972.

treated alike' is a frequent reply. Yet such is the framework not of a settlement, but of a stalemate temporarily imposed. Is it really ridiculous to envisage an arrangement by which trust may be explored and developed through the positioning of military forces from each side on the other's territory? Would such not effectively constitute the protection which Israelis and Arabs demand?

Yet only an insensate Arab nationalist would see inflexibility, and the failure of imagination, as solely an attribute of the Israelis. If Jewish nationalism is a moral nonsense, what is to be said of Egyptian or Syrian nationalism; or Jordanian, Lebanese or Palestinian? Even the wider compass of Arab nationalism will not bear too close a moral examination. If Israel is a product of conquest, the Arab world was scarcely established by prayer. And the present separate Arab states emerge from a past, near or remote, which adapted the map to the arbitrations of power. In the end, justice is reduced to a matter of chronology. And this is moral quicksand.

Such is not, clearly, an argument for confusing what is right, or what is compassionate and creative, with what is strong: for mocking morality by making it the instrument of the nation, or rather the particular regime which commands for the while the national identity. It is an argument against the propaganda of double standards, which ends only by defeating itself.

To ask, therefore, that the Arab states should recognize the sovereignty of Israel is to ask that they act consistently within their own framework of vision. The criterion then is one of a political calculation: of how much is to be gained and how much lost by one side or the other. And by this criterion, the formal recognition of Israel within its borders prior to the Six Day War, as an earnest of realism rather than a bargaining counter, would achieve three important purposes. It would promote the productive adaptation of Arab opinion to the facts of nationalist power in the Middle East; it would confront the fear of annihilation in Israel, which so strengthens the cause of obduracy and even expansionism; and it would make much less tenable the claim of Israel to retain the conquests of 1967.

It is generally supposed easier for the victorious to be generous in initiative than for the defeated. And, doubtless, imaginative concessions, to change the mood of negotiation, would seem more appropriate from the strong than from the weak. Yet generosity itself can be a strength, as obduracy a weakness; and the concessions of the defeated can be a formidable challenge to the fastnesses of the victorious. For as long as the Arab states refuse to face the fact of Jewish nationalism, so long, self-defeatingly, they must continue to sustain that nationalism in its own fantasies, its own refusal to face the fact of the nationalism confronting it.

But, of course, neither side, immediately strong or immediately weak, may reasonably expect to promote a settlement by being generous at the expense of the Palestinians. For Palestinian nationalism also is a fact; and no arrangement that denies this will itself be any more than a fantasy. If it is a nationalism that must come to terms with the existence of Israel, the existence of Israel must ultimately depend on coming to terms with it. Certainly it is political, not to say moral, nonsense for Israel to suppose that it can successfully dictate, beyond the borders of its own survival, how Palestinians should manifest their identity. Had the Jews themselves submitted to such dictation, there would not be a state of Israel now to secure. And Israelis can scarcely move Arabs to abandon the deceit of double standards by confronting it with their own.

Given sufficient imagination, generosity and will, the realization of a viable Palestinian nationalism might come from a radical redrawing of the map on the basis of concessions made not only by Israel, but by the Arab states around. The present Palestinian calamity may in large measure be a product of Jewish nationalism. It is far from being entirely so. Egypt, Syria, Jordan, the Lebanon: each in its own way has used the Palestinians as an instrument; encouraging their hopes, exploiting their conflicts, betraying their cause. The degradation and the misery of the Palestinian refugees are the outcome not just of resurgent Israel, but of the particular recalcitrant nationalisms in the Arab environment. The divisions and failures of armed Palestinian resistance owe at least as much to the rival ambitions and ruthless manœuvring of Arab regimes as to the reply of Israeli power.

It is plain that a Palestinian state, tolerated for the vulnerability of its borders and the subservience of its economy, must be the source not of a settlement but of continuing strife. Power abhors a vacuum. And certainly it should not be beyond the capacities of political intelligence to rearrange territorial frontiers so that each state in the area contributes overall to establishing a Palestinian entity of credible independence; with the conquests of the Six Day War as the major material for inclusion or exchange. Nor given a Palestinian component of compatible importance in size and population, would some confederal scheme, with Jerusalem as the capital, and including perhaps the Lebanon as a counterweight to Israel's economic superiority, be out of reasonable reach.

But to pose this possibility is to feed rather than appease the rival rages of nationalism in the Middle East. For the settlement would essentially have to be reached by the various regimes; and each sees only what might be lost by the sort of society that it represents. And clearly, in the absence of a mass revolutionary movement committed to create a new, common social identity, freed of elites and the nationalist preoccupations which these promote, any such settlement must dangerously demand an accommodation of societies differently organized and divided; a synchronization of economic and political clocks that tell different times; a merging of nationalisms so much of whose dynamic lies in their very incompatibility.

The truth is that the Middle East is caught in a struggle which belongs to the variations in the social circumstances of mankind. Here, where the conflict of different identities has so momentously taken place before, as manifestations of a conflict between societies in different stages of development, the conflict is again far deeper than merely one between a Jewish state and its enemies. It is a conflict between the society of advanced industrial technology under liberal-capitalist management, and societies seeking to build their own structures with the material of their own particular past.

Indeed, it is yet more complex. The conflict is not only between one sort of society and another, but within each. Arab society has liberal-capitalist elements and impulses: as it has feudal traces still; influences of colonial dependence; and the posturings of a state capitalism in uniform. And within Israel itself, a Jewish nationalism compounded of so many factors, from its tribal genesis, through an imperial experience and the long degradations of the Diaspora, to the revolutionary vision of pioneering and the present engagements of statehood, is involved in economic processes that mock its pretensions. The third temple is being raised not to Jehovah, or even to Marx, but to the golden calf: whose laws are the laws of material self-devotion, and whose priests are the prophets of the gross national product.

It is deceptively easy to see disaster imminent in Israel. It seems impossible that the society should escape being overwhelmed by its problems. One eminent journalist has predicted collapse so often, and been proved so wrong, that he has now taken refuge in a ritual cynicism. 'There is, let's face it, such a thing as luck. And Israel has been above all lucky. Heaven knows, it has been lucky in its enemies. The Arabs could not have been more useful if they had tried. But they are only part of the puzzle. Who would have said that despite the troubles of the dollar, more money would have poured in from the United States, as contributions and loans, in the last two years than at any time before? And this, while the borders have been quiet, and our government has clearly been resisting American pressures for a settlement? Who would have predicted the presentation of a new rallying call, to the Diaspora and at home, in the release of so many Soviet Jews for immigration? Who would have supposed three-quarters of a million tourists this year to feed the balance of payments?

'The leadership is not rigid. It is practised in the recognition and exercise of power. It knows its strengths, as it knows the weaknesses opposed to it, and it exploits both. It may not believe in luck, but it knows how to take advantage of occasion. The country has muddled through for so long. Why should it not go on muddling through for as long as matters?'

To see the future as a mere repetition of the past is as absurd and dangerous as to project a future that belongs to nothing but itself. Any future is conditional. And given the conditions, the corresponding consequences can scarcely be escaped. It is necessary to remark what should be unremarkable, because so many Israelis, especially in the leadership, speak and act as though the present were sufficient to itself or to the past, and not a process out of which the future takes shape.

At an after-lunch question-and-answer meeting with the governors of the Hebrew University on 21 March 1972, Moshe Dayan gave his reaction to the proposals, made a few days before by King Hussein, for a federation of the West Bank, the Gaza Strip and the East Bank in a new entity under Hashemite rule. Dayan agreed with Hussein on one point only: that there was room for a Palestinian state 'neither east of the Jordan river, nor to the west of it'. Israeli forces should remain along the Jordan. Jews should be able to live in Jericho and Hebron. 'This is our homeland. It is not a matter of rights. It is a matter of feeling.' The Arabs should not be made to leave. But continued Jewish immigration to Israel was imperative, for a large enough Jewish majority to secure the Jewishness of the Jewish state.

All but a few in the audience applauded the answer, as they applauded all the other answers. They stood applauding when Dayan arrived, and they stood applauding when Dayan left. It was like those meetings in India where the multitude assembles not to hear, let alone assess, what the leader says, but merely to be there, in a mood of mystic communication. I found myself wondering, a visitor in their midst, whether these governors were responding to what Dayan was saying or to what he was; whether what he was simply what they wanted, what they needed him to be; whether they would go on applauding his answers, wherever the 'matter of feeling', however outrageously, took him.

Yet what were the implications of Dayan's remarks? For the Jews, a homeland beyond the windows of early 1967, let alone those of twenty years before; for the Palestinian Arabs, some interminable diaspora beyond the Jordan or across the vastnesses of the Arab world, or as the new Jews among the old ones. Naboth's vineyard began as one fact and became another. And a Jewish people that will neither allow a nationalism to the Palestinian Arabs nor abandon its own is creating the facts of an Israel in bondage to battle.

Perhaps the leadership sees so far. But if it does, it sees also an Israel bonded by battle and sustained by a vast investment from a proud and fearful Jewish Diaspora. Yet, again, what are the implications? The leadership itself can do no wrong when it represents the survival of the state. If there are erratic cries of discontent at home, they are drowned in the applause from the Diaspora. And the discontent at home must be inhibited by the dangers of division to an imperilled state. Is the leadership already arrogant and remote? It would be less than human if the ascendancy that crisis gives it at home, and the facile appreciation with which it is lapped by the Diaspora, did not make it still more so.

And what of the society over which such a leadership will preside? In a recent copy of *Lillit*, an English-language periodical that had its beginnings on the campus of the Hebrew University and tends to reflect troubled young Anglo-Saxon Israeli attitudes, there appears an essay by Paul Drake, written in early 1970, but scarcely less valid now.

> A few days ago, a small group of schoolboys wrote to the Prime Minister; a letter gently questioning the direction of our political and military policies ... Here is her reply: *'There will always be a few boys who are afraid to go into the army; but do they have to make an ideology of it?'*
>
> No alternative. We say it in answer to everything and it does not admit challenge. Our official political line has hardened into a doctrine of national faith, a moral value in itself. We are a nation of the totally convinced, proud beyond pride of our uniformity of thought ...
>
> Are we looking at sites for new Israeli embassies? Buy the most expensive real estate in town. Get in there with the Americans and Russians, the British and French. The Big Five must stick together. Never mind that the Treasury is empty, the American Jews will pay. There is nothing we cannot arrogate to ourselves, haven't we got the greatest air force in the world? Isn't ours a special destiny among nations? Ah, but instead of lighting the gentiles, we are becoming just another pale reflection of their darkness. *Well, what did they expect, anyway?**

The greatest air force in the world? Dayan was more circumspect in talking to the governors of the Hebrew University. Israel had the fifth largest air force in Europe! He was replying to a question on the immigration of Soviet Jews. His welcome for the immigrants was warm: and not only because Israel had been established as a home for all Jews. The air force needed pilots of quality, and these needed to be backed by a sufficiency of scientists, technicians and other skilled personnel. A population of five

* *Lillit,* No. 9, Pesach 1972.

million Jews would be needed in Israel, and Soviet Jewry promised to be the major source of the required immigrant flow. Of course there were economic problems involved. But 'we can do it'. And he made clear that 'we' were the Jews not just of Israel, but of the resourceful Diaspora.

However the Israeli air force may be competitively listed, Tel Aviv must be among the ugliest cities on earth. It cannot, to be sure, help having no mountain or hillside to climb, or central wide river along which to glide: though it does have the sea, and instead of washing itself there, seems to turn impatiently from it. It is confused, agitated, distraught. The very buildings look like cars in a traffic jam: squat; hostilely pressed together; ready to move off in different directions at some sudden extricating command. There are no great parks and squares to wander in and find quiet with a sense of space. The few old buildings with something of the poor but magnanimous striving and devotion and pleasure, the triumphant personality of the pioneering period, rot with neglect or fall to the developer. And the new ones seem agelessly shabby almost as soon as they have been built.

Yes, the past and its pressures are in part responsible. But the present and its pressures are the occasion for yet more near-sighted haste rather than repentance. The bulldozers are busy: to make not parks and squares and apartment blocks of inviting design for a city populous with graceful surprises, but an ever faster supply of housing and commercial units to sell, for a city without kindness or dignity.

It is a frantic activity that at once disguises and promotes the degradation of the poor. Of the 383,000 inhabitants,* some 120,000 are living near or below the poverty line; and some 28,000 families, or an estimated 110,000 people, reside in slums. On the basis of these facts, the municipality presented to the government a five-year plan to solve the housing problems of 12,000 slum families, whose situation it described as critical, at the rate of at least 2,000 families a year. The plan was approved in principle; but the Housing Minister announced that his department would be able to help rehabilitate at the most 1,600 families in 1972/3. *Ha'aretz*, the country's leading independent newspaper, in a sharp editorial called this statement 'tantamount to ignoring the grave

* In the city as officially defined.

proportions and potential danger of Tel Aviv's impoverished population'.*

And as Tel Aviv goes, so goes the nation. This is not only because the Tel Aviv urban sprawl attracts more than its due share of any increase in the country's numbers. But a nation whose priorities accept and promote the Tel Aviv there is, will recklessly reflect Tel Aviv in the overall quality of its life.

There are no available resources for creative urban development. But there are apparently resources available for the abundant private profits of building contractors and real estate speculators. Dr Haim Gunner, adviser to the National Council of Research and Development, and a visiting professor at Tel Aviv University, could hardly be harsher.

> The whole notion of development that we should build up the nation as speedily as possible, sacrificing our beaches to high-rise apartment buildings, sacrificing the Jerusalem skyline, is in direct conflict with the notion of total land use. We have a National Master Plan of 1965 but it is largely disregarded. In Netanya and Tel Aviv they are avoiding having local master plans because they feel this would curb the capacity of the cities to develop. What's happening there is really fearsome. It's a wholesale grab bag open to the investor with most money.†

The master plan for Jerusalem, presented early in 1969, seemed rather more concerned to get as many Jews settled there as quickly as possible, in the cause of creating political 'facts', than to develop the city as its historical significance, its natural setting, and the comfort, cohesion and contentment of its inhabitants demanded. It projected a population increase within the city proper from 267,000 (198,000 Jews), to 400,000 (295,000 Jews) in 1985, and 600,000 (440,000 Jews) in the year 2010; with an increase in the number of motor vehicles from 15,000 at present, to 110,000 in 1985, and around 400,000 by the year 2010 (when the metropolitan area would contain some 900,000 people).

The planners certainly exercised themselves to protect the Old City from outrage. But for the rest, they 'seem to have more

* 21 February 1972.

† Quoted in *Lillit*, No. 9, Pesach 1972.

compliantly deferred to the "unavoidable" urban processes and their conventional resolutions, neither of which has been especially kind to historic cities elsewhere: demolition of old neighbourhoods rather than renovation, letting real estate values determine land functions instead of vice versa; widening and rerouting streets to accommodate traffic rather than restricting traffic to accommodate streets.'*

A conference of architects and town planners, called the Jerusalem Committee and containing many participants of much renown, was convoked by Mayor Teddy Kollek to discuss and, it was clearly hoped, approve the plan. Instead, the Committee passionately assailed it as a prescription for urban disaster. 'Collective hara-kiri,' one participant raged. The plan has since been remitted for 'further study'. But, meanwhile the government seems bent on increasing the Jewish inflow more rapidly than even the plan itself envisaged. Land values and housing costs soar, as assisted immigrants pour in, and rich Diaspora Jews buy a place, for occasional residence, in Jerusalem the Golden.

The high and ever-rising rate of accident and death on the roads is remarked and shrugged aside. There are far more graves filled with victims of traffic than of war.† Yet national expressions of grief and of the value that Judaism attaches to a single human life accompany only the ceremonies of the second. The Minister of Transport is reported to have sought a few million pounds for the adequate lighting of roads at night, but was told that the country's finances could not afford it.

The stock market booms, while social workers demonstrate against the inadequacy of welfare allowances. Slums are less conspicuous than such 'luxurious residential quarters ... for gracious living in Jerusalem' as the Kiryat Isaac Wolfson, whose tower blocks symbolically rise above both the Knesset and the Israel Museum: but they contain rather more people. At the Dan Hotel in Tel Aviv, the touts lie in wait for the tourists.

Israeli journalism gives a view of the real Judenstaat very different from the version Herzl so hopefully envisaged.

* Hillel Halkin, 'Building Jerusalem', *Commentary*, Vol. 52, No. 3, September 1971, p. 62.

† There have been some 20,000 people killed on the roads in 20 years, according to a letter in the *Jerusalem Post*, 28 March 1972.

Jerusalem Post, 20 March 1972

TV MEN BEATEN AT FUNERAL OF UNDERWORLD FIGURE

A TV news team, attempting to film the funeral of Ilan Asherov – a Tel Aviv underworld figure whose bullet-ridden body was found on the Carmel Coast last week – was yesterday set upon and beaten by irate friends and relatives of the dead man ... The police believe Asherov was killed by his underworld associates 'squaring accounts'.

Jerusalem Post, 17 March 1972

PRISONS CAN'T CURE DRUG ADDICTS

The Prisons Service cannot cure drug addicts or provide certain kinds of psychiatric treatment, the Commissioner of Prisons, Mr. Arye Nir, told the Tel Aviv District Court yesterday.

Mr. Nir was replying to a recommendation made by the court in a sentence passed on a drug addict who was convicted of attempted robbery. In its judgement, the court instructed the Prisons Service to treat the prisoner for his addiction.

Replying that the Health Ministry had not included prison clinics among those institutions permitted to deal with drug cures, Mr. Nir pointed out that the courts often made stipulations which the prisons simply could not carry out.

Jerusalem Post, 13 March 1972

WHERE HAVE ALL THE MISSING UZZIS GONE?

The Israel-made Uzzi sub-machine gun has not only won acceptance in numerous foreign armies, it has also become the chief weapon of violent crime at home ...

Very few soldiers have used their arms for crime and almost no known criminals have served in the army ... Cases of the first type have, indeed, occurred recently – like the soldier on furlough who shot his father with his Uzzi, or another who tossed a grenade into a Holon steakhouse 'for kicks' ...

Cases of guns stolen from soldiers' homes or left in strange automobiles after an abrupt awakening at the end of a hitch-hike are frequently reported to the police, and the weapons are not all recovered ...

Still, this would hardly seem to explain the flow of several dozen guns a year, most of them Uzzis, to the underworld. Police estimate that there are at least several hundred illegal firearms in the Tel Aviv district alone ...

Jerusalem Post, 19 March 1972

YOUTHS SET FIRE TO 'PEACE PLANE' IN PARK

Two Ramat Gan youths were remanded in Tel Aviv Magistrate's Court Friday on suspicion of burning Abie Nathan's 'Peace Plane', which was on exhibit in Ramat Gan National Park ...

The plane is the famous Piper Cub in which Abie Nathan flew to Cairo in March, 1966, to talk with President Nasser.

According to Dr David Shichor, in the Department of Criminology at Tel Aviv University: 'A large proportion of the population flagrantly violates most of the minor regulations connected with sanitation, traffic and business, but on the other hand is utterly conformist when it comes to political or public issues.'* He finds an explanation in the *galut* (exile, or Diaspora) attitude of many immigrants from authoritarian societies in Asia, North Africa and Eastern Europe, who have brought with them the practice of 'getting away with things'. As Israelis, they express this feeling of minor defiance in disorderly social conduct, from littering the beaches and highways to cooking the books. But in their political attitudes, faced as they are moreover by the Arab challenge to the very survival of the state, they revert to the submissiveness of a Diaspora minority.

There is certainly some substance in this. Yet there is no remarkable propensity among Sabras to show greater respect for regulations, or regard for the comfort, convenience and welfare of the community at large, than do immigrants. Nor is it plain that Sabras, and at least the older among immigrants from democratic Western societies, are significantly less given to political compliance before the external threat. Organized crime and juvenile delinquency may owe something to some particular Diaspora experience; though democratic Western societies are

* *Lillit,* No. 9, Pesach 1972.

scarcely to be counted here as propitious backgrounds. But they probably owe much more to the conditions in Israel itself which promote their rising incidence.

Speaking to the 18th National Conference of the Association of Americans and Canadians in Israel (A.A.C.I.), Dr Eugene Wiener, head of Haifa University's Sociology Department, reported on the sense of *déjà-vu* among newcomers from North America. 'They are astonished to find here the beginnings of many of the ills of a modern technological society which many of them thought they had left behind. These include pollution, juvenile delinquency, overcrowding, slums and social discrimination.'*

Indeed, the character of social indiscipline in Israel today, from the warfare on the roads to the increase in crimes of violence, finds its closest parallel not in 'Asia, North Africa and Eastern Europe', but in contemporary America. And it does so not because so many Israelis come from the United States, but rather because Israeii society is in so many crucial respects American.

For what is more American than Israel's frontier mentality, with its implicit assumption of infinite resources to be exploited for the triumph of man over nature? What is more American than Israel's concentration on the present, in the faith that the future should be left to look after itself? What is more American than the prevalent Israeli confusion of material with moral advantage? The obsession with growth, one way or the other; the ascendancy of commodities over people; the commercialization of sex; the feverish search for entertainment: all are a mark of Tel Aviv and New York alike. Is New York rather more advanced in the process? But it is the process that counts.

Is there a high and rapidly rising crime rate? As in the United States, there is a large, distinctive community within the nation some of whose members, especially among the young, feel themselves disparaged and deprived because of their membership. For them, crime is often a manifestation of social revolt. As in the United States, there are those among the young of prosperity and privilege for whom mere material consumption is not enough, and who drive too fast, or take other risks with the law, 'for kicks'. As in the United States, there are those who might, surely, make

* Report in the *Jerusalem Post*, 13 March 1972.

money enough within the law but for whom, in a society so ordered by money, there is never money enough; and who resort to crime as a form of private enterprise because the prospects of profit involved sufficiently outweigh the risks.

The countries are far apart, but a steady flow of influence from the one washes the other. Cinema and canned television films, with their diet of greed and snobbery and violence, come from American studios, or their pale British and European counterparts, to dominate Israeli screens. The American tourists bring their travellers' cheques, but also their preoccupations and their manners. The government of Israel encourages the building of hotels and restaurants and shops to cater for their tastes. But at the same time helplessly it must encourage the rapid growth of a service class in Israel whose own living standards are manifestly lower, and whose covetousness and resentment are accordingly nursed. The government looks forward eagerly to one million tourists in a single year soon. But what will this mean to a population barely three times as large? Lotteries and football pools already feed and sharpen the 'get rich quick' appetite that the essential direction of Israeli society excites. How long before there are casinos, mainly for tourists of course?

The United States has peculiar destructive impulses, to be sure. But then, Israel has them also. Perhaps the co-existence of so much social indiscipline with so much political compliance may be largely explained by itself: perhaps the strains set up by the political compliance promote the social indiscipline. And perhaps living on the edge of war and destruction all the time is cumulatively conducive to hysteria rather than heroism; violence rather than vitality; a hatred that must spill over to corrode personal and collective relationships.

The changing of the pioneer Zionist dream into the nightmare of the merchandising, merchandised society has identifiable material causes. The conflict with the Arabs has promoted and excused the idolatry of the gross national product; the forced feeding of industrial investment and skills by the bribes of competitive consumption; the enticement, with little or no regard to the ultimate social cost, of resources sufficient to make the military machine as formidable as it is. But there is an emotional basis, too. For so many Israelis, the culture of commodities is an escape; a refuge from the ravages of the personality that a seemingly endless future of conflict demands.

Yet what does America demonstrate but that such a refuge is in its own way no less a ravaging of the personality; that the cure is at least as destructive as the disease? Is there anywhere on earth a people more resolute for personal happiness and fulfilment, and more desperately, self-destructively unhappy and unfulfilled, than are the Americans?

But then an already significant, and increasing, number of Americans, primarily among the young, are in revolt at a social functioning that equates people with their possessions; individual freedom with corporate profit; fear and greed with the creative human impulse. In Israel, it is said, university students are so docile that when the lecturer begins with 'Good morning', they write the phrase in their notebooks.

Alexis de Tocqueville wrote eloquently in 1835 of the despotism exercised by democracy in the United States:

> where the authority of the majority is so absolute and so irresistible, that a man must give up his rights as a citizen, and almost abjure his quality as a human being, if he intends to stray from the track which it lays down ... It seems, at first sight, as if all the minds of the Americans were formed upon one model, so accurately do they correspond in their manner of judging. A stranger does, indeed, sometimes meet with Americans who dissent from these rigorous formularies; with men who deplore the defects of the laws, the mutability and the ignorance of democracy; who even go so far as to observe the evil tendencies which impair the national character, and to point out such remedies as it might be possible to apply; but no one is there to hear these things besides yourself, and you, to whom these secret reflections are confided, are a stranger and a bird of passage. They are very ready to communicate truths which are useless to you, but they continue to hold a different language in public.

It is seldom, however, the majority from whom the despotism directly comes. Theirs is, rather, a mood which a vociferous few

* *Democracy in America*, trs. Henry Reeve (London: Longman, Green, Longman and Roberts, 1862), Vol. 1, Chapter XV, pp. 314–15.

employ to promote their own ascendancy and the intimidation of all threatening divergencies. And these few are able to enjoy the initiative only in part because they are confident of popular acquiescence. They depend as well on the ease with which those of a contrary opinion can be made to feel desperately isolated and seek safety in silence. And the consequence, of course, is steadily to make the popular mood more intimidating still, under pressure from only one vigorous opinion.

It is when those of the contrary opinion, few though they may be, refuse to be intimidated and sufficiently project their own commitment as essential to the overall good, that the mood of the majority itself may be made to shift. Such is what happened, for instance, in the rise of the American abolitionist movement against popular antagonism and often violent reproach. Such has begun to happen with the campaign for homosexual law reform in the United States.

There can be few societies of professing liberal sensibilities where the homosexual is made to feel so lonely an outcast as in Israel. This is not because there are so few of his number. It would be surprising if, despite the dominant cult of conspicuous virility and the thunderings of Biblical law, the ratio were significantly smaller than in other societies of the great Western cultural compass. It may even be that cult and law together have results for the psyche quite different from their intentions. But homosexuals themselves, confronted by a vociferous hostility from the few claiming to represent general opinion, succumb to a more or less furtive acquiescence in their own indecency.

They are rather like their American counterparts of the 'fifties. And, indeed, a comparison between the United States of the 'fifties and Israel today is useful. There are no Israeli congressional committees of inquiry under the command of a deceitful demagogue hunting down dissent as subversion. But dissent is none the less intimidated: mainly by the furious condemnation from the few who seem to represent the weight of public sentiment; occasionally by the surreptitious enterprise of slogan-painting* and telephoned threats. It is the fear of strident rebuke and social isolation that keeps disquiet from confronting the despotism of

* As against Myron Benvenisti, of the Jerusalem municipal authority, attacked as a traitor for his defence of Arab interests in the incorporated city.

'national security'. And the absence of any vigorous offensive from dissent in turn promotes the self-confident offensive of the more extreme loyalists on the mood of public opinion.

In the climate of a nationalism effectively so repressive, political argument is closely confined to the irrelevant. It is not only that the security issue seems increasingly restricted to speculation over how many kilometres of sand are worth abandoning for a settlement with Sadat. While specific aspects of its functioning may provoke sudden storms of complaint, the nature of the society is regarded as self-evidently inescapable. And how is this or that functioning to be changed, when such is no more than the manifestation of a nature sacrosanct, inevitable?

But as developments in the United States since the 'fifties have demonstrated, the inhibition of criticism and dissent only ensures that in their emergence they will be the more searching and turbulent. The entire nature of American society has come under increasing assault as its functioning, found fundamentally impervious to amendment, has excited an essential disaffection.

How in Israel is the high rate of inflation to be seriously reduced when the state cannot otherwise even pretend to satisfy all the demands on its resources? The hard line on the borders would scarcely be credible without a military expenditure that continued to consume more than a quarter of the national product. Without the allurements offered to new immigrants, from Soviet persecution and Western prosperity alike, how is the demographic vigour of the national home to be promoted, and the society prevented from a slide into Levantine culture? How may satisfactory living standards be denied to the more skilled and talented of the Jewish population without augmenting the already considerable numbers of Israelis now resident abroad? How may a satisfactory rate of profit be denied to private investment without driving foreign money away and discouraging indigenous enterprise? And if private investment is to be guaranteed a satisfactory rate of profit, how is industrial labour to be denied its equivalent reward without strikes that would cripple the economy?

But if inflation may not be avoided, neither may its consequences. As house prices soar, more and more young Israelis, native and of the dominant Western strain, find themselves able to obtain decent new accommodation, if at all, only by taking on debts that loom over their lives for as far as they can see.* Taught by their cultural values to be assertive, they are unlikely to prove a tractable social element. Indeed, it may well be that the most formidable thrust of social discontent will come from within the relatively advanced Western community.

Students at Bar-Ilan University hold a two and a half week strike, and even sit in at the administration building, to demand changes, including an end to B.A. comprehensive examinations. Students at the Technion in Haifa insist that the administration take their opinions into account when promoting academic staff. At Haifa University, the 'Yesh' list scores a 'runaway victory' in elections to the Students' Council.

> The list, made up of new immigrant, Arab and *kibbutznik* students known for their leftist leanings, won 32 of the 40 seats on the Council. The remaining three lists—'Student Reform', 'For the Students' and 'Central Block' which are affiliated with various political parties—won only eight seats between them. Of the 3,550 eligible voters, only 1,500 cast ballots. [The report failed to mention that the poll in previous elections, which had resulted in safe Student Councils, had been rather lower.]
>
> The victors have promised to agitate for greater student participation in political affairs, such as their sympathy strike with the Autocar workers some months ago ... †

But then, as the Black Panther protest movement indicates, the supposedly quiescent traditions of the Oriental community may also be wearing very thin. History provides ample evidence of how rapidly such quiescence evaporates when economic advance is

* Housing Minister Zeev Sharef, addressing a Labour Party meeting on 27 March 1972, revealed that housing prices had risen by 28·9% in 1971, alongside an 11·8% rise in the general price index.

Hillel Halkin has written of Jerusalem: 'It is now almost impossible to buy a new, two-bedroom apartment anywhere in the city for less than 100,000 Israeli pounds (some £10,000 sterling), and when one reflects that this is close to ten times the annual income before taxes of the average Israeli worker, who cannot even look forward to receiving the 50,000-pound government mortgage that is avaliable to every new immigrant, it is clear that most local residents are completely priced out of the building boom that they see all around them.' ('Building Jerusalem', *Commentary*, Vol. 52, No. 3, September 1971, p. 65.)

† Report in the *Jerusalem Post*, 10 March 1972.

arrested or reversed. Revolt is far more often the response to a blind being raised and then lowered over the window, than to a wall without a window at all. To be sure, the Israeli leadership has cause to claim that the Orientals are now far better off, in the main, than they were before coming to Israel. Yet this is very much to the point. For so many of them, theirs has been an enormous stride, material and psychical. But suddenly the ground seems to be flashing past from under their feet, and they see themselves falling behind as others forge further ahead.

Perhaps this would not matter so much were submissiveness a cultivated social virtue within Israel itself. Instead, however, there is the cultivated aggressiveness not only of competitive materialism in a market economy, but of a state that must always be ready for war. In those emplacements on the Suez Canal, there are telephones available for soldiers to call up their families at home. It does not need an exceptional imagination to envisage the gathering shame and rage of those whose homes do not have telephones at all.

Yet this is not an exclusively young Sabra or Oriental problem. With the cost of credit reaching beyond 16% a year and seldom, even for loans from pension funds, falling to single figures, it is easy enough to understand why the Bank Hapo'alim, supposedly committed to the interests of the workers, and the Mizrachi Bank, supposedly committed to the interests of God, should be able to declare soaring profits.* Is it any less easy to understand why industrial labour, equipped with sufficient economic muscle, should demand immediate wage rises of 25% or 50%, to compensate for the price rises that have already occurred and are yet to come? Or why those who do not have the economic muscle, must fear that the flood of rising prices will suck them under?

And meanwhile the phrase 'secure borders' is endlessly mouthed: without asking 'security for what?' Possession of the Golan Heights and Sharm-el-Sheikh may look good on the map. But what protection do they offer a society whose conflict is increasingly within? It may well be that if the society continues to func-

* In 1971, bank profits increased by 50%, according to Dr Meir Het, the Bank Supervisor. Part of the increase, he said, was due to regular business transactions, and part to one-time transactions such as devaluation; *Yom-Yom*, 16 February 1972.

tion as it does, because its nature continues to be what it is, the soldiers of Israel will be required to guard not only the borders of the state, but more and more the borders within it, between authority and revolt.

There is a stirring of disgust and despair over the conventional parties and politicians. In a *moshav* (co-operative village) near Tel Mond, the aged Yemenite immigrants were volubly grateful for all that the government had done to resettle them. Their Yemenite son-in-law, an agricultural labourer, said that he voted for whichever party paid him the most. The Moroccan immigrant neighbours were loyal supporters of the Labour Party. Their married daughter, a teacher, denounced all the parties as 'dirty'; attracting the voters 'by underhand means'. There was corruption everywhere, and she did not vote.

Dayan himself, addressing the Lashiluv younger leadership circle of the Labour Party, was harsh enough. 'The Labour Party is far from being united; worse still, it is hardly a party at all – no internal discussions are held on the real policy-making. A man is not elected to public office because he is the right man, in keeping with his views.'

His own solution was 'to do away with the former party divisions once and for all ... I have no difficulty in forgoing my old party label, and I do not need internal consultations.'*

There is in this the cry of a de Gaulle against the party faction and spirited double dealing of the professionals. And it is a cry to which many Israelis, like the young Moroccan teacher and even the Yemenite labourer, might respond. Certainly, within the headlong Americanization of society, down to the development of Tammany Hall machines at the local political level, there is a flavour of the French Fourth Republic: not least in the strength which a nationalist mysticism gives to radicals on the Right.

There are few engagements as rich in risk as political prophecy. And it would be a bold endeavour indeed to make political prophecies about a people that has defied so many reasonable assumptions. But whatever temporary cohesiveness may be secured by a flare-up in the conflict with the Arabs, the essential polarization of Israeli society overall seems, on present trends, sufficiently probable. And whether or not peculiarly Gaullist remedies will be

* Report in the *Jerusalem Post*, 15 March 1972.

tried for a time, the underlying drift must be to an increasingly repressive authoritarianism.

For clearly, a culture of competitive consumption is so socially divisive; the despotism of property is so personally thwarting and destructive; that only the corporate state seems able to secure them from the processes of disintegration and revolt. And how much more powerful must be the movement to such a solution when it is reinforced by a pride in national military strength; a record of conquest; an aggressive religious revival; and a continuing, seemingly interminable, threat to the very survival of the state from a clamorous enemy.

But, of course, this is only half of the story. For the other half is of a revolt against the repressions that such a culture entails; and against the yet more searching denials that the securing of such a culture demands. And how much more powerful must be the movement of this revolt among a people for whom the horror of history has been so much a record of repression; for so many of whom the endeavour to manifest their identity was founded on a faith in the free and equal brotherhood of man.

Neither Jew nor Arab can safely afford to ignore that the present climate of conflict serves to encourage the development of an insensate authoritarian nationalism in Israel. Neither Jew nor Arab should be blind to the idealism that was so much a part, and still is, of the Jewish historical experience and the experiment that is the state. To suppose that out of the very engagement to a Jewish nationalism there might emerge an engagement to humanity itself is not to defy reason, but to explore it; not to discard faith, but to find it.

There is, too, surely no less edifying a spectacle than that of an Arab nationalism calling on the Jews to abandon their own and execrating the militant disciples of Jehovah with cries to the dominion of Allah. The danger of a religious totalitarianism in the Arab world is scarcely less than that of a theocracy in Israel. The social mutilations of military or para-military regimes are not so remote in Cairo or Damascus as to allow a comfortable repugnance at the prospect of such in Jerusalem.

Socialism strutting in a braided uniform or sedate in a Savile Row suit is as serviceable to a solution of the conflict with Israel, not to speak of a solution to the problems of ignorance and poverty within the Arab states themselves, as is the blood-letting within the Ba'ath movement. The cry to justice raised against Israel would be more eloquent if it did not disguise the determination of elites to maintain themselves on a structure of popular misery.

But the disguise is wearing thin. Increasingly the failure of Arab regimes to defeat Jewish nationalism must stir a searching discontent with the social systems that they represent. And if this discontent is itself largely nationalist in departure, it may well, in the course of travelling, come to see the ultimate deception of the nationalist commitment.

For, paradoxically, Arab nationalism is both an impulse to revolution and a denial of it. It illuminates and sharpens the social conflict between the prerogatives of power and the corresponding deprivations; but then, as Nasserism or the Ba'ath movement has shown, what change ensues is merely a new variation on the theme of the divided society. And how should it be otherwise? The frontiers between state and state, and the frontiers between class and class, are mutually promoting. The divisions without and the divisions within have a common source and sustenance in inequality.

And this is fundamentally no less true of Israel itself. The more powerful that Jewish nationalism proves to be, under challenge from its Arab counterpart, the more divided, by prerogative and deprivation, the society of Israel becomes. Inseparable in their separate commitments, Jew and Arab move from one false dawn to another, within the nationalist night.

And yet, paradoxically again, it is the Palestinians, perhaps the most fervently nationalist of the Arab peoples in their very homelessness, who may first sufficiently discover and declare the futility of the engagement. The concern of the younger radicals with conventional revolutionary prescriptions may have so far been largely a search for the consolations of rhetoric. But there is in it, too, the stirring of an awareness that the mere confrontation of nationalisms is a closed circle, and one from which they are themselves excluded. For it is not their own nationalism that the repeated triumphs of Israel on the battlefield fortify with an all-Arab involvement, but the particular nationalism of an Egypt, a Lebanon, a Jordan, that discards them as strangers.

The Jews, in the tribulations of their Diaspora, became disproportionately a force of faith in the revolutionary possibilities for a united mankind. It would be one of history's most notable ironies if the Palestinians, similarly dispersed by a Jewish nationalism, should adopt the same faith that the Jews, in achieving their own nation-state, seem so overwhelmingly to have abandoned. And yet: who may explore Israeli society today without sensing that this faith has been not so much abandoned as suppressed? that it needs only a sign of significant adherence in the Arab world beyond to rise and challenge those who would deny it?

The Egyptian professor was a man of painful shyness; steeped in European as well as in Arabic culture; delicate of manner and perception. On the conflict between Arab and Jew, he became suddenly passionate. 'There is no hope of peace, as things are. In the end, I more and more think, only a revolutionary fire that sweeps across Jew and Arab alike and burns away with it all the old ideas, all the old stupidities, will bring peace.'

Peace? There will never be peace, if by peace is meant the end of human conflict. There will, and should be, conflict about ideas: a conflict that opens and creates. But the conflict that exists, within the idea of the nation-state, precludes this. It is a conflict that closes and destroys. And perhaps it is here, in the Middle East, where its cruel absurdities become ever more manifest, that it will meet, therefore, a crucial defeat.

APPENDICES

APPENDIX I

The structure of the National Congress of Popular Forces

Eight categories were established, with the number of delegates in each set to reflect its respective 'social value'. This measure was to be the mean between 'demographic weight' ('the number of members enrolled in organizations' as a percentage of the total population enrolled), and 'the contribution to the national income' made by those so organized.

Thus: 3,200,000 *peasants*, of whom 1,154,332 were enrolled in organizations, had a 'demographic weight' of 44·3%; an estimated £E 173 million contribution to the national income of £E 650 million (26·6%); and 35·4% of the total social value. But this value was then reduced to 25%, and the number of delegates fixed at 375; with 265 of these, members of agricultural co-operatives.

1,600,000 *workers*, of whom 466,328 were organized, had a demographic weight of 17·9%; an estimated £E 200 million contribution, or 30·8%; and a social value of 24·4%. This was reduced to 20%, or 300 delegates: 120 to represent 518,000 workers in the industrial sector; 26 to represent 125,000 salaried employees in the commercial sector; 64 to represent 325,000 salaried employees in the services sector; and 90 to represent 329,000 government workers.

The sector of *national capitalism* was assessed at 600,000 persons, of whom 276,824 were organized. It had a demographic weight of 10·6%; a contribution of £E 56·2 million (8·7%); and its social value, of 9·7%, was raised to 10%, or 150 delegates, with half drawn from industry and half from commerce.

Members of professional associations came to 172,957, all organized: with a demographic weight of 6·6%; an assessed contribution to the national income of £E 143·2 million (22%); and a social value of 14·3%, rounded upwards to 15%.

Of 700,000 *non-unionized functionaries*, 194,000 belonged to various trades unions. With a demographic weight of 7·5%, and a contribution of £E 71·3 million (10·9%), their social value was assessed at 9·2%, adjusted downwards to 9%.

University teaching staffs contained 7,500 members, all organized, with a demographic weight of 0·4%; and an assessed contribution to national income that was £E 6·3 million (1%). But its social value, of 0·7%, was increased ten times, to 7%.

Students, at 305,000, all organized, with a demographic weight of 11·7% but no contribution to national income, were given a social value of 7%.

And 6,500,000 *women*, of whom only 25,457 were organized, representing a demographic weight of 1%, received no assessed specific contribution to national income, but an eventual representation of 7%, or 105 delegates. Among these delegates, a decisive majority, or 63, came from the professions (34 from teaching), while 5 were artists.

APPENDIX 2

Nasser's resignation broadcast, 9 June 1967

'In the morning of last Monday, 5 June, the enemy struck. If we say now it was a stronger blow than we had expected, we must say at the same time, and with complete certainty, that it was bigger than the potential at his disposal. It became very clear from the first moment that there were other powers behind the enemy – they came to settle their accounts with the Arab national movement ... Indeed it can be said without emotion or exaggeration that the enemy was operating with an air force three times stronger than his normal force.

' ... All the peoples of the Arab nation, without exception, adopted a stand of manhood and dignity all along the Arab homeland; a stand of resolution and determination that Arab right shall not be lost, shall not be humiliated, and that the war in its defence is advancing, regardless of sacrifice and setbacks, on the road of the sure and inevitable victory.

' ... I tell you truthfully and despite any factors on which I might have based my attitude during the crisis, that I am ready to bear the whole responsibility. I have taken a decision in which I want you all to help me. I have decided to give up completely and finally every official post and every political role ...

'The forces of imperialism imagine that Gamal Abdel Nasser is their enemy. I want it to be clear to them that their enemy is the entire Arab nation, not just Gamal Abdel Nasser. The forces hostile to the Arab national movement try to portray this movement as an empire of Abdel Nasser. This is not true, because the aspiration for Arab unity began before Abdel Nasser and will remain after Abdel Nasser ...

'In doing this I am not liquidating the revolution – indeed the revolution is not the monopoly of any one generation of revolutionaries. I take pride in the brothers of this generation of revolutionaries. It has brought to pass the evacuation of British imperialism, has won the independence of Egypt and defined its Arab personality, and has combated the policy of spheres of influence in the Arab world; it has led the social revolution and created a deep transformation in the Egyptian reality by establishing the people's control over the sources of their wealth and the result of Arab action; it recovered the Suez Canal and laid down the foundation of industrial upsurge in Egypt; it built the High Dam to bring fertile greenness to the barren desert; it laid down a power network over the whole of the north of the Nile Valley; it made oil resources gush out after a long wait. More important still, it gave the leadership of political action to the alliance of the people's working forces, the constant source of renewed leaderships carrying the banners of Egyptian and Arab struggle through its successive stages, building socialism, succeeding and triumphing.'

APPENDIX 3

AVERAGE GROSS ANNUAL MONEY INCOME PER URBAN JEWISH EMPLOYEE'S FAMILY—BY CONTINENT OF BIRTH AND PERIOD OF IMMIGRATION OF HEAD OF FAMILY AND SIZE OF FAMILY (1965–1969)

Continent of birth and period of immigration of family head	*Average no. of persons, 1969*	*Families (percentages) 1969*	*1969 income in IL*	*1968 income in IL*	*1967 income in IL*	*1966 income in IL*	*1965 income in IL*
All families	3·9	100·0	10,500	9,600	9,400	8,700	7,800
Continent of birth and period of immigration							
Asia–Africa	4·9	41·6	8,300	7,700	6,700	6,800	6,200
Immigrated: up to 1947	4·8	5·2	9,100	9,400	9,200	8,500	7,800
1948–1954	4·8	23·4	8,700	7,900	7,000	7,100	6,200
1955–1960	4·9	7·0	7,900	7,000	6,100	{ 5,700	{ 5,500
1961–	5·2	6·0	6,900	6,300	5,400		
Europe–America	3·1	46·7	12,000	10,900	11,100	9,900	8,600
Immigrated: up to 1947	3·1	17·1	13,100	12,800	13,500	12,500	10,400
1948–1954	3·3	18·9	11,100	10,400	10,300	8,900	7,900
1955–1960	3·0	5·3	12,200	9,700	9,700	{ 7,400	{ 6,900
1961–	2·9	5·4	9,500	8,700	6,900		
Israel-born	3·6	11·7	11,900	11,400	11,000	10,600	9,400

A family whose head immigrated from 'Asia-Africa' up to the end of 1947, had in 1965 the same income as the average. But by 1969, while its income had increased to IL 9,100, the average had risen to IL 10,500. The prevalent Israeli belief that economic backwardness is a consequence of recent immigration from backward cultural areas is not borne out by such figures. If the intake previous to the establishment of the state is still having to find its feet, the ground that the state has provided is not as firm as it is advertised to be.

It is also necessary to stress that the table deals with the families of urban Jewish employees. There are no such figures available for the urban self-employed, who constitute a substantial sector of relative prosperity, and who are overwhelmingly not of Oriental origin.

Yet even from this table, taking the family income together with the number of persons dependent on it, the economic discrepancy between the average citizen from an Oriental and the average citizen from a Western background is considerable: with the first enjoying the equivalent of just over IL 1,700 a year; and the second, one of IL 3,870, or well over twice as much.

APPENDIX 4

Tables

I. Israeli Experts Abroad, 1958–69

	1958–67	*1968*	*1969*	*Total*
Africa	1,719	265	250	2,234
Asia	255	53	66	374
Latin America	258	91	103	452
Mediterranean Area	350	44	46	440
	2,582	453	465	3,500

II. Foreign Trainees in Israel, 1958–69

	1958–67	*1968*	*1969*	*Total*
Africa	5,328	469	475	6,272
Asia	1,589	300	420	2,309
Latin America	1,572	225	206	2,003
Mediterranean Area	1,818	157	129	2,104
Others	262	12	63	337
Total	10,569	1,163	1,293	13,025

SOURCE: *Facts About Israel* 1971, p. 78 (both tables).

APPENDIX 5

I. Distribution of Disposable (after-tax) Family Income; Urban Wage and Salary Earners' Families: 1950 and 1956/7

Income Group (by decile)	*August 1950*	*1956/7*
Bottom 10th	5·8%	3·7%
2nd	7·0%	6·6%
3rd	7·8%	7·1%
4th	8·4%	8·9%
5th	9·1%	8·9%
6th	9·6%	9·2%
7th	10·4%	10·8%
8th	11·4%	11·6%
9th	13·3%	14·0%
Top 10th	17·2%	19·2%

II. Distribution of Disposable Income; Urban Wage and Salary Earners' Units: 1954 and 1957/8

Income Group (by decile)	*1954* (% share	*1957–8* (% share)
Bottom 10th	3·5	2·7
2nd	5·5	4·9
3rd	7·5	6·7
4th	8·6	7·7
5th	9·3	9·4
6th	9·3	9·6
7th	11·2	11·1
8th	11·4	12·4
9th	14·3	15·2
Top 10th	19·4	20·3

III. Contribution % to the Net Domestic Product by the Three Sectors of the Israeli Economy

	Total	*Public*	*Histadrut*	*Private*
Net Domestic Product	100	21·5	20·3	58·2
Agriculture, forestry and fishing	100	0·8	32·0	67·2
Mining, quarrying and manufacturing	100	4·3	22·2	73·5
Construction	100	10·6	31·9	57·5
Public utilities (water and electricity)	100	100·0	–	–
Transportation and communications	100	40·3	37·0	22·7
Banking, finance and real estate	100	1·1	9·1	89·8
Trade and other services	100	1·7	15·8	82·5
Non-profit institutions	100	–	37·6	62·4
Government services	100	97·0	3·0	–

IV. Gross National Product, at Factor Cost, 1965–9
(categories by percentage at current prices)

	1965	*1966*	*1967*	*1968*	*1969*
Agriculture, forestry, fishing	7·9	7·7	8·4	7·8	7·3
Industry, mining and quarrying	23·7	21·8	22·5	24·3	25·3
Construction	9·7	7·4	5·8	6·7	8·1
Public utilities (water and electricity)	2·0	2·2	2·2	2·0	1·9
Transportation and communications	8·4	9·0	8·9	9·1	8·7
Finance, insurance and real estate	5·1	5·5	5·6	6·0	5·9
Ownership of dwellings	7·1	6·9	6·8	6·4	6·3
Public sector and non-profit institutions	18·5	21·2	22·0	20·3	19·2
Commerce	9·6	9·8	9·6	9·3	9·5
Other services	8·0	8·5	8·2	8·1	7·8
Net domestic product at factor cost	100·0	100·0	100·0	100·0	100·0

SOURCE: *Bank of Israel Report* 1969, May 1970, p. 15.

INDEX